HER FATHER'S
DAUGHTER

HER FATHER'S DAUGHTER

THE BONNIE HENDERSON STORY

DEBI MARSHALL

RANDOM HOUSE AUSTRALIA

Random House Australia Pty Ltd
20 Alfred Street, Milsons Point, NSW 2061
http://www.randomhouse.com.au

Sydney New York Toronto
London Auckland Johannesburg
and agencies throughout the world

First published 1997
This edition published 1998
Copyright © Debi Marshall

National Library of Australia
Cataloguing-in-Publication Data

Marshall, Debi.
Her father's daughter: the Bonnie Henderson story.

ISBN 0 09 183723 5 (pbk.)

1. Henderson, Bonnie. 2. Henderson, Sara. 1936-. 3. Ranchers –
Australia – Northern Territory – Biography. 4. Women ranchers –
Northern Territory – Biography. I. Title.

636.01092

The author and publishers would like to thank Janette Wilson,
Alan Howard and Charlie Barron for permission to use their
photographs.

Typeset by Asset Typesetting Pty Ltd, Sydney
Printed by The SOS Printing Group Pty Ltd

10 9 8 7 6 5 4 3

To my late father, Dennis, who loved
the outback and was with me in spirit
through every word, and to his "Half-pint",
my lovely daughter Louise.

ACKNOWLEDGMENTS

Debi Marshall

'Self-doubt, dark despair, fear of consequence, fear of language, empty brain, empty heart, no imagination, nothing to say, you name it: I know every reason in the world not to write.' I read these words in a newspaper article many years ago, but at various times during the writing of this book, each of them applied to me. For those who helped get me to the end of a very tight deadline ... many, many thanks.

In Darwin, for their recollections, photos and last-minute faxes during research: Ross and Lynette Ainsworth, Bonnie's sister Danielle and Susan Seppelt. For accommodation and encourage-ment: Kev O'Brien and Paula Compton. And Bonnie, for her guts in telling it, warts and all, her willingness to continue through some bad times, and for believing me when I told her we could do this.

In America, for their hospitality and invaluable help: Fraser and Becky Henderson, Gus and Nancy Trippe, Margaret de la Mater and John Volatile.

In Sydney, for her literary knowledge and support: Jo Thyer.

In Hobart, for his unending patience and brilliant computer skills in retrieving lost copy: Steve Marskell. For support and excitement at every increasing word count: Traceelea and David Peberdy and my brother, Wayne Marshall. For their help with my daughter when I was busy or away: my sister Barbara Morgan, Heather Hocking, Nirelle Barnes, and Jenny Robinson. For her unconditional love and friendship when I was wrung out, strung out and washed out and thought I'd never finish: my mother, Monica.

And last, but not least, my beautiful daughter, Louise, for whom this book is dedicated.

Bonnie Henderson

I would like to thank all the people who have crossed my path and made my life so rewarding. Most, but not all, appear in these recollections of my life, so far.

Special thanks to the professional photographers—Charlie, Allan and Wills—who allowed the use of their photos with only a verbal promise that I won't forget them if I'm ever better off! These photos bring my story to life.

Thanks also to Selwa for her help, encouragement and understanding over the past four years.

This is a record of my memories (as best I can recall) seen through someone else's eyes. I never meant to, and hope I don't, offend or hurt anyone. A lot of research material gained from other sources has even helped me make some better sense of my life. Some I disagree with; however, these are other people's memories, and I have no right to edit or change them to suit myself.

I have been to a few places and done more than a few things. I've done pretty well in fields that interest and excite me, but above all, I think that kids are the real meaning of life. One can get so enthused looking at life through their eyes and with their energy. We want so much and often expect too much.

I remember my dad saying, 'Bonnie, I just want you to be happy.' Well, old mate, I am.

PREFACE

I first met Bonnie in 1994 whilst researching and writing a series of articles on extraordinary bush women for a national magazine. Some months later Bonnie's husband, Arthur Palmer, called me. He was outraged that Sara Henderson, Bonnie's mother, in her book *The Strength in Us All*, had claimed she had spent time with Bonnie and Arthur's children. The reality, he said, was a far cry from that.

'The truth is,' he told me, 'Sara has no relationship or association at all with our children. She has never sent them a birthday or Christmas card, has never cuddled them, played with them or talked to them. She knew so little of Georgina's illness, when she almost died, that she got the dates wrong in her book. It is a fantasy she made up to redeem herself in the reading public's eyes.'

He continued that Bonnie and her father, Charles, were the real driving force behind the success of Bullo River Station, and he discussed the celebrated court cases between Bonnie and her mother, and between Gus Trippe, Charles' business partner and friend, and Sara. Would I be interested in going back to the Territory to talk to Bonnie about an article to set the record straight?

I initially approached the story with some degree of trepidation. Sara Henderson was, after all, a national icon, and Bonnie had made it clear she had no interest in any further airing of dirty linen. What she did want to do, however, was tell the story from her perspective as the estranged daughter of a high-profile woman, who was suddenly thrust, through little choice and no consultation of her own, into the public eye.

The article duly appeared, but there was much more to this family than could be covered in such a short piece. I found myself being asked questions by the reading public. What was the real story behind the feud between mother and daughter which Sara had glossed over in her books? Was Charles really the bastard Sara made him out to be? What made Bonnie tick?

When I began research for a possible biography of Bonnie Henderson, I was confronted with a multifaceted woman who was, initially, reluctant to talk about anything beyond her own adventures. It took time—and trust—for her to open up about the complexities of the family feud and the role her father played in her life. Once that hurdle was jumped, she spoke candidly. At times it was harrowing and emotional for her to dig into the past, but she was always honest.

'I want you,' she told me, 'to write the truth—be it good, bad or ugly.'

There are unique difficulties in writing a biography of a living person, not least of which is the fact that life, literally, goes on during the writing process. In Bonnie's case, that seemed doubly so. With three children, a business to run and a farm to keep up, she also had emotional pressures to deal with, including the breakdown of her marriage.

The geographics of living on different sides of the continent—Bonnie in Darwin, myself in Hobart—proved a logistical nightmare. In three months we got together on five separate occasions—in the

Northern Territory, America and Sydney—to continue our research. With the deadline looming, Bonnie talked, and I wrote—in planes, restaurants, cafes, wine bars, and at her farm. When we were apart, we communicated by phone and fax. Many times, I had to wait for information from Bonnie while she boned out meat for dinner or finished making a saddle.

From the beginning, Bonnie gave me a list of people with whom she thought I should speak. And not just people who could offer glowing praise of her; to her credit, she was always prepared to accept the bad with the good. She agreed not to editorialise nor to change anything in the book on the basis that she simply didn't like it. What she did do was meticulously check the factual content of the manuscript, ensuring that the anecdotes, people, places and times were correct.

The majority of the information I received came from Bonnie: from her memories, old papers and court documents (where these have been quoted they have been edited down to avoid pages and pages of legal documentation). There were no flights of fancy on her part, no colouring of the story to make it either more dramatic or to show her in a better light. In this respect, her innate sense of honesty and fairness shone through.

The Territory sources used were invaluable, not least because the players involved had worked at or visited Bullo River, had seen the family first-hand and known Bonnie for years. In Cloncurry, Bonnie's sister, Danielle, shared her unique perspectives on the family. Like Bonnie, she was insistent that the balance be fair. As the youngest daughter who has maintained a relationship with everyone in her family, she was at times in an unenviable position, but her contribution was invaluable.

Bonnie and I travelled to America together to continue the research. In telling the American part of the story, particularly with regard to Charles' and Bonnie's early life, I needed to see the places and to meet the people involved. Bonnie's half-brother, Fraser, who lived and worked at Bullo for years and now lives outside Washington, DC, was generous with both his time and his memories of the family. From Fraser, and his mother Barbara's own writings, which she allowed me to use, I gained an insight into the formative years which shaped Bonnie's character. Charles' sister, Margaret, who is now living in their mother's home at Lloyds Landing, painted a picture of the colourful life they led and of her brother's personality. In knowing both Barbara, Sara and all the children, she gave balance to the story and offered hitherto unknown facets of Charles' life prior to his meeting Sara.

In Los Angeles, Gus Trippe—a pivotal part of the manuscript—pored over old documents and shared his reminiscences of a lifetime spent with Charles both in America and in Australia's wild Northern Territory. He presented his side of the story about his bitter rift with Sara. His wife, Nancy, also offered some telling comment.

Some of the stories I was told would have made sensational reading, but at all times I checked both my conscience and the facts before committing them to the page. Where stories could not be substantiated through fact or had the potential to mortally wound the person involved, I left them out. There were only a few exceptions to this, and they were the stories Bonnie told me about herself. I was often surprised at her courage in laying bare her soul.

Over the years, Arthur Palmer, Bonnie's estranged husband, and I worked together on various magazine articles in the Northern Territory. During those times, I came to know him on a personal level. Arthur offered me the story about Bonnie's feud with her mother, which was subsequently published, and many other insights into the Henderson family. At first, he enthusiastically supported this project, but when his marriage collapsed, he withdrew all support. His last words to me—'If you are looking for the truth about that family, you will never find it.'—rang in my ears during research and writing. It spurred me to dig deeper, look harder.

No licence has been used with regard to interpretation of people's thoughts. These are drawn from Bonnie's understanding of the individual personalities within her family and from both Charles' and Sara's own writings.

In opening up to me in the way she did, I came to know Bonnie well. At times my questions to her bordered on cross-examination: how did she remember events with such clarity; why did she act on occasions in the way she did; how did she perceive herself? What I found was a woman who appeared, on the surface, to confront life with a devil-may-care attitude; but underneath was a person of great depth. I expected a toughness born from her life in the bush and from mixing with men; what I discovered was a warm woman who laughs a lot, cries easily, who loves to sing, dance, drink and entertain; a woman who adores her children and embraces life.

Bonnie is far from tough, but she has great inner strength. People are drawn to her like moths to a flame, for her honesty, her intelligence and her spirit. Her joie de vivre is infectious. This book was never intended to be a vilification of Sara's life, but a celebration of Bonnie's. She is, as one Territorian put it, 'the genuine bush article'. And fascinating at that!

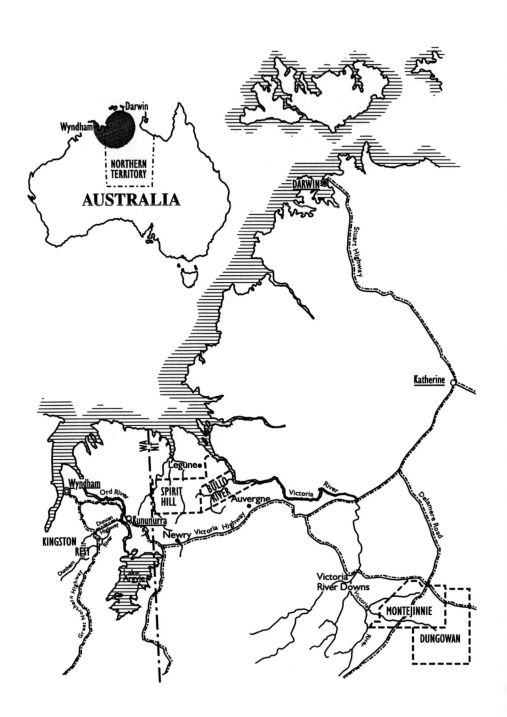

Wyndham
Darwin
NORTHERN
TERRITORY
AUSTRALIA

DARWIN

Stuart Highway

Katherine

WA
NT

Legune

SPIRIT
HILL

BULLO
RIVER

Auvergne

Victoria   River

Delamere Road

Wyndham

Ord River

Duncan Highway

Kununurra

KINGSTON
REST

Duncan Highway

Newry

Victoria Highway

Great Northern Highway

Lake
Argyle

Victoria
River Downs

Victoria

River

MONTEJINNIE

DUNGOWAN

PROLOGUE

The coffin, sleek and shiny, is incongruous against this bleak, grey day. Bonnie walks behind it, behind her family, shivers in the trail of dispassion and coldness they leave in their wake.

Her father's ashes will be scattered out there at Bullo River, out there, outback, on the edge of madness, but she will not be welcome. She thinks of a line from his favourite poem—'If you can keep your head when all about you are losing theirs, and blaming it on you'—watches as the hearse slowly inches away down the street. Alienated, alone, she huddles against the rain as it skates down her face and mixes with her tears.

CHAPTER ONE

It was a year when the world was immersed in bloodshed and hope.

The year that the thirty-fifth president of the United States, John F Kennedy, was assassinated. The year that Martin Luther King had a dream. The year that boys were used as cannon fodder and sent to Vietnam.

And the year that a terrified Sara Henderson gives birth to a baby girl, her second daughter.

'Baby is not moving into the birth canal and the mother is greatly distressed. We cannot risk a natural delivery.'

Sara's anguished wails resound through the labour ward as the Catholic doctor prepares for a caesarean. He is unused to such unholy commotion; in this country, birth, like death, is an un-remarkable part of life. Calm and fervent, he fingers the gold cross around his neck and speaks in measured, precise tones.

'Whatever else happens, we must save the child.'

Trussed into a surgical gown and bundled onto the bed, Sara's fear is palpable. Suddenly, searing pain wracks her body in sweat, driving through her with ferocious force, and a sea of red stains the sheets. She is swimming in and out of the light, in and out of the anaesthetic, and somewhere a far-off voice is screaming: 'The labour has started! Baby is coming now!'

The minute hand of the clock glares and grins, moving round through night and day, as the contractions threaten to tear her body apart. The stench of the streets two storeys below doesn't reach this labour ward where the atmosphere is sterile, geared for genteel birthing, but the noise filters through. Outside, traffic moves at a snail's pace; and infants, suckling at their impoverished mothers' breasts, cry with hunger on the Manilan sidewalks. Inside, the world could have stopped, may have stopped for all Sara knows, and the midwife is yelling: 'Push, Mrs Henderson! Push, push now!' Forceps yank and pull as a tide of contractions reach their crescendo. Around dawn, silence creeps through the hospital wards, broken only by the occasional car horn and the mother's tormented cries.

The pain is worse than dying and they are asking her to push, one last time, but all Sara's energy is gone. Her mother is here with her, fearful and tense, watching for the slap of life, listening for the infant's feeble cry. When it comes, her mother's gentle, concerned face floats into vision.

'Everything's okay, Sara,' she says with obvious relief. 'You have a beautiful little girl. She weighs four and a half kilos and they nearly killed you to save her. Charles is coming in now.'

Sara's husband, Charles, has been pacing the hospital corridor all night. He has vivid memories of other hospitals, other hallways, other children; has heard his wife's distress through the thin walls.

Grabbing staff as they walk past, he demands to know what is happening inside the labour ward. He finds this women's business exhausting, alarming; two years ago, with their firstborn, Murray-Lee, he had waited out the labour with a few stiff bourbons that mellowed his jagged nerves. He grins broadly when he hears the news that he is a father again, his words spilling out in a rush and tripping over each other.

'Well, bugger me! That sure took a long time,' he bellows. 'Are they both okay? Another daughter, eh? Well, bugger me! She will have her mother's name—Sara—and the name of my mother's Maryland estate—Lloyd. Yes, suh! Sara Lloyd Henderson. That's my girl!'

Too sore to move, Sara huddles in a foetal position and tastes the salty tears as they trickle down her face. The world might seem far away, but her pain certainly isn't. She takes a cursory glance at the baby swaddled tight in a pink bunny-rug, notices her tiny head is battered black from the forceps.

'Never again, Charles,' she tells her husband. 'Never again.'

On a steamy late-April morning in 1963, the child is christened. From the outset, Sara bestows the small girl with the nickname of a pet she owned in childhood.

The dog's name was Bonnie, and the name sticks.

Charles is worried. The Philippines is becoming a political maelstrom, and the glittering veil that has for so long hidden the covert corruptness is fraying at the seams. Charles wages a remorseless battle to buoy up his sinking financial ship, but reality kicks in hard. The Hendersons' cosy world is about to end. Spoilt and protected, it is a world that neither Charles nor his wife will surrender happily.

The years in the bustling capital are heady times: amahs look after the children as he and Sara swan through a colourful social calendar, eating canapés here, drinking French wine there, fixing business deals over languid dinners. They are, as a smiling Filipino shrewdly remarks, a formidable combination: he with his southern charm, she with her Australian graciousness. Charles English Henderson III has chosen his partner well, and he knows it.

His lifelong friend, business partner and cousin, Gus Trippe, who moved out to Manila with Charles in 1946, watches the turn of events with growing concern. In the burgeoning postwar years, they had cast their eyes to the East where opportunity beckoned. Money was their goal, and they aimed to make a lot of it. They started with a small freighter, a part cargo of war surplus and three boats to tow. The initial operation was a disaster: after eighteen days at sea, buffeted by raging storms and tornadoes, the freighter was towed in by the British Navy. But if the exercise was a portent of things to come, the partners ignored it. Brash, young and opportunistic, they were determined their dreams would come to fruition. They were in the right place at the right time, and nothing would stop them. Forming a shipping and trading company running between Hong Kong, Manila and Sydney, they moved in illustrious circles, stitching up huge financial deals through chartering and agency work. Operating multiple ships at one time, loading logs, copra, and chrome ore, they quickly expanded, opening offices in Taiwan, Japan and, later, Korea and Thailand. They dealt only with the men at the top.

With their ears close to the Australian Embassy in Manila, they learned by chance of the Northern Territory's need to find new markets for its cattle. The Philippines was perfect: the country desperately needed cattle to meet growing local demand. Over cocktails, the Minister for the Territories offered the young men an opportunity. Would they be interested in combining a shipping and trading operation? Their answer was a definitive yes, and over the course of the next few years, Charles handled the receiving end in Manila and Hong Kong, while Gus travelled the length and breadth of Australia buying cattle.

Tired of the boom and bust routine, Gus had long ago accepted that he and Charles operated differently in business. Charles was flamboyant, a big spender: Gus took a steadier approach. His boyhood friend, Gus says, was a brilliant strategist, with the vision and charm to put together concepts and organisations which could win the world. But as far as making them work on a day to day basis, he really had no interest. They reached agreement to split any liabilities and assets from their previous business dealings in the Philippines and to go their separate ways. It was, Gus believes, one of the best decisions he ever made, but he is saddened as he watches Charles' financial demise in the Philippines.

'Charles had taken over our old shipping company and within a year had turned it into a major tramping operation. He was single-minded and most effective. Charles' trading company had become a major force in the world charter market, and I was very proud of his achievements, even though I knew he was stretched to the absolute limit. Charles was completely unaware that his largest and most important charterer, who was running coconut oil, was also running a massive scam. He had borrowed huge sums from the banks against warehouse or tank receipts. This was a perfectly normal borrowing and lending practice, but tragically the certified warehouse receipts were not backed up by the actual contents of the coconut oil tanks. Of course the banks immediately doublechecked receipts versus tank levels and found them substantially wanting. Within hours all of Charles' vessels, which were carrying coconut oil in their double bottoms, were arrested as soon as they hit port. All charter hire monies due were frozen. The news spread like wildfire.'

Without this major source of charter monies, Charles could not meet his time payments for the purchase of his vessels. Shipowners panicked and withdrew their ships. Cargo owners also took measures to cover their bases.

'Charles was devastated and had nowhere to move. He lost everything, including his house, yacht and personal belongings. It was a sad ending to what could have been a brilliant shipping career. I shared his grief and his miserable bad luck. In a way, though, this was Charles as he was during the war. Full steam ahead, all guns blazing and damn the consequences! He fought this way, played this way and did business this way.'

The world is in turmoil. Martin Luther King's vision for a free and equal nation has ended in a hail of bullets. Race riots, bitter and bloody, are threatening civil war in America. The voice of the people is rising up in anti-Vietnam protests, and peace seems further away than ever. Closer to home, Bonnie knows nothing of her father's financial crisis. By day, she and her four-year-old sister, Murray-Lee, whom the family call Marlee, see the world from their high-back prams, wheeling through lush parklands with their amahs. At night, their nannies sing them Filipino nursery rhymes and wipe the bright lipstick from the girls' cheeks left by Sara before she goes out.

Charles accepts the invitations to high-society functions and accepts, too, the phone numbers shyly, surreptitiously slipped into his pocket from the brown-eyed girls who have left their innocence behind in the villages where they grew up. Sara isn't happy; one of the girls has been audaciously indiscreet and has told her she is expecting Charles' baby. Bonnie's amah holds her tight and covers her ears as her parents' fight over this reaches its climax. Frightened, Bonnie snuggles against her nanny's warm breasts, is rocked back and forth until the screaming abates. Only when silence finally creeps through the house does she close her eyes for sleep.

During his boom years Charles looked to Australia's vast, wild Northern Territory to expand his entrepreneurial dreams. Bullo River Station—an almost one-million-acre property which bordered the mighty Victoria River and the much smaller Bullo River— caught his fancy. A small station by northern standards, this harsh, isolated and unforgiving land lies in the northwest corner of Australia near the Timor Sea. It is three hundred and nine kilometres south of Darwin, as the crow flies, and almost eighteen kilometres from the West Australian border. From the Victoria Highway there is a gruelling seventy-nine kilometre access road which cuts across the southern ranges before the station proper looms like an oasis in the desert.

In 1959, a lease was granted by the land court to open Bullo for development. Bullo was formerly a hunting ground for the Aborigines who had roamed the top end of Australia for thousands of years. Separated into distinct tribal groups, these nomads followed the seasons and lived by their own rules and codes. The young men had to pass stringent requirements to enter into warriorhood, and one of these was to spear an enemy.

White managers of nearby stations were deemed to be the enemy. In 1928, prompted by another in a line of spearings, a group of angry graziers, looking for retribution, made into the upper Bullo country and massacred more than five hundred Aborigines. The managers' revenge was quick, bloody and severe: now, only the caves, bones and ghosts of the slaughtered tribe live on.

'Old John' Nicholson, then thirty-four, was hired by Gus Trippe to manage Bullo in 1963 when Charles purchased the property. There was nothing there but a few kilometres of rickety fences and rough paddocks; not a building in sight. John, one of the best cattlemen Gus says he has ever known, started from scratch: he built solid yards, good fences and an effective plant. He brought in strong horses from Queensland, and good ringers. Then he went out and—literally—caught cattle. Starting from nothing, in two years he had turned off close to eight hundred head.

It is to Bullo River Station that Charles decides to go when things fall apart in the Philippines.

'Charles was obsessed with coming down to Bullo and starting again,' says Gus. 'He had absolutely no money. He would have to borrow the plane fare to get there. I virtually begged him to stay in Manila and fight; surely the banks would not blame him for the fiasco. But he would not hear of it: once Charles has made up his mind, nothing will change it. I could feel a disaster in the making and crossed my fingers.'

CHAPTER TWO

To get to paradise by road, you have to go through hell. Bullo River. Isolated from the outside world by its geography and terrain, getting to this natural fortress of sandstone escarpments, treacherous river, rugged tracks and impassable creek crossings is, in the wet or dry, a punishing ordeal for even the most experienced bush driver. The only safe and sure means of getting there is by air. The 'Mickey Mouse' airline, McRobinson, made the regular mail run in the mid-sixties. Nuggetty stockmen, hitching a ride to the station after a spell in the big smoke of a township not much larger than a wayside inn, nurse their hangovers on the long flight back; chaplains, making an outback pilgrimage to save souls, pray the Lord will offer guidance on the journey; and slick cattle buyers with keen eyes and glib tongues tally lengthy livestock reports. This is man's country.

But today the Mickey Mouse is flying to Bullo with unusual cargo: an elegant, well-spoken woman dressed in a white designer outfit complete with hat and gloves from a swanky Manila boutique, and two little girls wearing pristine frocks. The pilot shrugs; you never know what you are going to get on this mail run. He has been flying around the Northern Territory for years and has grown increasingly tired of the drunks who throw up as soon as the plane is airborne. Before he started with McRobinson Airlines, he'd taken to refusing passengers transport if they were three sheets to the wind. Looking them up and down, from their Akubra hats to their RM Williams boots, he'd shake his head and say in affected, mournful tones, 'Sorry, Ocker, the Fokka's chokka.'

The plane has been flying over Bullo's vast expanse for what to Bonnie seems an eternity. This, then, is the enchanting place she has heard Daddy talk about, where she and Murray-Lee can run feral and free, unfettered by ribbons and shiny shoes.

On the ground the red dust, stirred by the turbulence of the propeller blade, rises, dances to form a billowing cloud behind the aircraft as it comes to a halt. In the silence, the middle distance, blurred by the shimmering heat, reveals an ochre earth, reflecting the harsh dryness of the season's end. The river—rich, deep and brown—snakes down from the high country, sweeping haughty and majestic through the flood plains; and the grassy flats rise up to the sandstone ridges and escarpments to form the natural boundary of the Bullo River valley. Pockets of natural springs feed a forest of massive paperbark trees. All around is a vastness, a stillness. Time has etched its markings on the landscape and then left Bullo behind.

Bonnie's eager face is pressed against the aircraft window. Mummy has told them they are moving to their new country home in the Northern Territory and that they will have wide, open spaces as their playground. The idea excites her. Only two years old, she is already easily enthused. She quickly accepts that their amah will not be moving with them. From now on, Mummy says, the girls will have to try very hard to do things for themselves. Bonnie doesn't mind; she has never much liked anyone fussing over her, anyway.

Clambering out of the plane after it lands on the dirt runway, she runs to explore the surroundings. A new tin shed, already ageing from the weather's harsh temperament, rises out of the earth, grey and stark and austere. The heat is blistering and the canopy of iron does little to assuage the forty-degree temperature. A caravan is parked in the middle of the shed, covering the grease pit; to her horror Sara realises this has been used as someone's bedroom. Some swags are rolled up nearby and a mountain of empty rum and beer bottles are strewn on the cement floor. This forlorn, man-made monstrosity has quite obviously hosted countless sessions in its day. She shudders and waits outside until Charles arrives to take them to the homestead.

The old Aboriginal woman, Mary, greets the new arrivals with a sheepish, toothy smile. She knows this country like the back of her hand; her ancestors have gone walkabout over every square mile, moving around as the seasons dictate. Her skin, almost purple, bears the hallmarks of a tough life; wiry, lank hair hangs to her shoulders, and her hands are cracked and calloused.

Sara scans the landscape with an ominous sense of foreboding. She has railed wildly against moving out here, but not even her vivid imagination could have prepared her for the reality. This is hell on earth. It's also deserted and the nearest neighbour is over two hundred kilometres away by road—if it can be called a road, for the track leading out of Bullo is impassable for much of the year. Where the hell is Charles? He said he would meet them here. Mary may have some idea where he is. God knows, there is no-one else to ask.

'Is Mr Henderson here yet?' Sara asks in a querulous voice, unable to disguise her anger. 'Is he at the homestead?'

13

Mary looks puzzled at the question, runs her hands over a grubby blouse that fails to hide her sagging breasts. She ponders the dust before replying, looking up from underneath hooded, heavy eyelids. 'Him big boss not here, no, missus, nudding. Day must be somewhere.' Pleased she can be of help, Mary suddenly decides she will repeat her answer. This time, she steals a shy, sideways glance at the children. 'Day must be somewhere, but not here, missus. Nudding.'

Mary is intrigued with the white children, a feeling which is reciprocated. They watch her curiously out of the corners of their eyes, and Bonnie makes a snappy decision. She'll follow Mary; that's got to be better than hanging around here waiting for Daddy to arrive. Sara is in a thunderous mood; covered in dust and despair, she sags to the ground.

'Where the hell is your father?' she screams.

After dusk, as the bush animals begin foraging for food and darkness quickly settles over the lonely landscape, the distant rattle and roar of a motor minus its muffler precedes the sight of a single headlight in the distance. The vehicle shudders to a halt. Amidst the mushrooming dust, the creak of doors on rusty hinges and the unmistakable odour of diesel oil, Charles steps out from the truck. He wishes he hasn't: his reception is icy and bleak. Hardly surprising really.

'It's about time you arrived!' Sara greets him. 'Where on earth have you been? We are tired and hungry and we want to go to the homestead. Where is it?'

There is a moment's silence before Charles responds. Bonnie, her face and dress now covered in dust and dirt, peers up into his face. She is glad Daddy has arrived; maybe now her mother's mood will improve. With a flourish of his hand, Charles points in the direction of the tin shed.

14

'That is our homestead,' he says with authority. 'You are looking at it, my dear.'

All eyes turn to the shed, its grey panels now silhouetted against a darkening sky. Sara looks as if she has been slapped, wheels back to face her husband. Her chest is heaving with rage, her eyes cold with fury.

'No, Charles, no!' she cries. 'You can't expect me to live here! It's only a tin shed, in the middle of nowhere! Is this your idea of a joke?'

Charles draws a deep breath, scratches the top of his head. 'Trust me, Sara,' he says. 'Everything will be fine. This is not Manila, ah know, but we will make it home. Have some faith in me.' His voice, warm and smooth like a blended whisky, betrays no hint that trusting him is the last thing she should do.

Charles, despite his rampant belief that adversity builds character, has spared Sara the details of Bullo's shortcomings; but he is under no illusions. He knows it is no place for a woman and in a letter to his mother he pulls no punches.

There wasn't a single building on the place until late 1964 when an equipment shed was constructed. This became the 'homestead', a tin roof on a broad plain, no trees, no water and surrounded by a wide circle of deep bulldust. The bulldust was cultivated by vehicles and a mob of horses which passed that way several times daily. The water problem was overcome by a thirty-two foot surface well dug by the manager, John, and the boys. The water was so salty that only the hardiest could drink it without getting diarrhoea; it was good only for filling the nearest water trough and having a tub, curing constipation, and a good excuse for drinking rum. No-one would dare poison a good drop with that rank water. The drinking water was hauled from the nearest billabong, a distance of one to four miles, depending on how late in the dry season it was.

When we arrived in August 65 there was no running water, no toilet facilities, no electricity, one bed, three chairs and a pressure light which didn't work. There was a wood stove, a small kerosene refrigerator and an old temperamental radio. To these romantic surroundings I brought three ladies, aged twenty-nine, four and two respectively. All were from air-conditioned, ever-servanted, suburban Manila. They arrived just in time for the end of the cool season.

'Hey missus, me takin' children walkabout longa billabong,' Mary informs Sara a few days after their unauspicious arrival. 'Dem like dat water.'

Mary's extended family are huddled in a group, talking and laughing. Bonnie is fascinated with their mercurial hand movements and gentle ease with each other. Back at the homestead they move cautiously around white people, taking instructions with downcast eyes. Here, they rollick and sing, blending with their country. Through their eyes, Bonnie is to learn the 'blackfella' way; in her they plant the seed, the spirit of their land.

It becomes a daily excursion, setting off with old Mary to find and pick waterlilies, walking by the river and trying to catch the beautiful butterflies that fly past lazily, showing off their burgundy and yellow wings. She watches Aborigines track geckos, turtles, freshwater crocodiles and kangaroos, and listens to their Dreamtime stories told in the traditional way. Bonnie loves these stories more than fairytales; told with gusto and feeling, the animals, trees, sky and earth come to life.

Some places are sacred; and the days drag when Mary goes

walkabout to deal with women's business. Then, Bonnie sits on the brown earth outside the shed, drawing childish pictures in the dust, and waits for her return.

The days and nights are getting steamier; a wet heat descends like a blanket and hangs heavy in the windless air. This is the build-up, the worst three months of the tropical year when tempers fray and physical strength is sapped. Up here they call it the suicide season. No-one escapes the testing liquid heat, not even those who have lived in the north all their life. It is a temperamental mistress. Territorians have an expression for the build-up's intensity: 'Nine months of the year you're on honeymoon, but for the next three months you wonder why you married the bitch.' But complaints about the weather from southerners—that's anyone who has been in the north less than twenty years—are met with no sympathy and a wry reply. 'If you can't handle the heat, you ain't drinkin' enough beer!'

The start of the rainy season is dramatic. Lightning skips across the heavens in a breathtaking visual display. The thunder is a guttural drumbeat, echoing around the escarpment; and the clouds, moody and threatening, dance to its rhythm. When the rains come—rains that fall from heaven in floods that can last for weeks—Bonnie lies in the caravan, lulled to sleep at night by its incessant beating on the roof and old Mary's stories from the Kimberley region.

Sometimes, on a very still night, she can hear the strains of singing from the Aborigines' camp by the creek a kilometre from the homestead. The Port Keats mob, as they are known, are young, happy-go-lucky blokes who work as stockmen at Bullo. Slim Dusty songs are a favourite; when they run out, they start on American stand-bys, always including 'Home on the Range'. Bonnie loves to listen to their singalongs. As the words and music float through the small window, she wishes that one night she would be allowed to wander down to their camp fire and sit with them.

The sight of the old blitz truck rumbling past with its load of wild scrub bulls; the jangling hobble chains around the stock horses' necks; the mule packs rattling; and the men, dusty, rugged, smelling of tobacco and rum, stir Bonnie's reckless spirit. She longs to join the adventure as the truck clatters through the scrub down to the cattle yard.

Mummy is in tears again, fearful and despairing at being stuck in this Godforsaken wilderness. Bonnie is confused by her mother's desolation, her terror of the country: this place is magic, if she would only leave the shed to find out.

Murray-Lee, always sympathetic and supportive of her mother, never moves far from her side when another black depression hits, and she scoffs at her sister's suggestions that they go outside and play. Bonnie shrugs, bewildered, wanders away to find old Mary.

Some odd characters come through Bullo, but few as eccentric as John Nicholson's mother, Noel, who visits him every year. Bonnie is fascinated with her: donning bathing suit and a huge straw hat, she swims daily in the Bullo River, unperturbed by the threat of crocodiles and swordfish. Noel, in turn, is fascinated with the radio. She can be heard miles from the house bellowing the Bullo River call sign into the unplugged microphone.

'SOV ... SOV ... SOV ...' Bonnie copies her, running around with a stick which she pretends is a mike, yelling 'SOV ... SOV ... SOV ...'

There's a famous family story about Noel, and Bonnie sits wide-eyed at the dinner table as her father recounts it for visitors. He is highly amused; in between a slug of rum and loud laughter, he splutters out the story.

'Noel sends an SOS from SOV—"Come quickly, Dan from Port Keats mob is dying!" John, laconic as ever, says, "He'll be right, someone's probably read the thermometer wrong," but he sends Noel in to check on him anyway. Well, poor old Dan, fine fella that he is, has got a temperature of one hundred and five and rising. There is, indeed, a good chance that he will shuffle off this mortal coil any tick of the clock.

'Anyway,' Charles continues after taking a drag from his pipe, 'he'd been delirious most of the day, ranting and raving, and the lubras are hysterical. Despite no evidence to back it up, one of the old blackfellas offers some sanguine advice: "Him got dat measles, and my missus she died of dat measles", which sends everyone into a jig. Another blackfella then decides to give Dan some tribal medicine—the simple cure of spitting into his eyes. By this stage John has had enough, and so has Noel, who keeps getting drenched with the misdirected spittle! Dan is moaning, utterly convinced that with so much attention he is about to cross over to the other side, and Noel jumps on the radio again, screaming for the flying doctor.'

'Well, what happened then?' a guest asks.

'Oh, then,' Charles says, with his usual habit of keeping people in suspense. 'Then he died.'

'He died! What's so bloody funny about that?'

'There would be nothing funny about it, ah suppose, if it were true,' he laughs. 'Dan lived. That tribal medicine must have fixed him after all!'

* * *

Marlee is being bossy again. She has organised a game in which she and Bonnie must jump from a pile of cement bags stacked against the wall onto a forty-four-gallon drum. The solo jumps are tricky enough, but Marlee has directed that this time they hold hands and jump together. Bonnie isn't keen: small, weedy and clumsy, she eyes the mission with extreme reluctance. But she knows better than to cross Murray-Lee; she is the ringmaster, and she cracks the whip.

In the next room Mummy is talking on the daily schedule via the outback two-way radio known as 'VJY'. The radio is their only means of communication with the outside world and the daily schedules are vital. Any racket during this time is a punishable offence; and in this house rules are rules and there is no room for debate. A quiet disagreement with Murray-Lee will turn into a full-scale screaming match. It is easier to close her eyes and jump.

Pulled through the air, Bonnie feels an excruciating crack in her forearm as it hits the rim of the drum. Howling with pain, she begs Murray-Lee to let go of her arm. Her sister examines the injury, and knows immediately she is in strife.

'Keep quiet! Don't tell Mummy!' she says in a fierce whisper. 'You'll be all right!'

Bonnie straightens up, wipes away a tear with a defiant swipe of her good hand. Sara has heard the commotion and, dropping the radio, runs outside with a withering look to demand the girls quieten down. Bonnie stiffens, tries unsuccessfully to hide her arm hanging like a coat hanger twisted out of shape. She peers up into her mother's eyes.

'Can I cry yet, Mummy?'

Tearing back inside, Sara screams in panic into the radio microphone. 'VJY, this is Sierra Oscar Victor. Do you read? Over.

'This is an emergency. Get the flying doctor. My daughter has broken her arm.'

It is the first time Bonnie is carted to hospital by air ambulance, but certainly not the last.

Almost a full cycle of seasons has passed and Charles is restless again. Leaning against the tin shed and stretching out his long, lanky frame, he stuffs his short brown pipe with Henry Winterman tobacco and stares reflectively out to the bush. In the nine months they have been here, Sara has nagged him mercilessly to leave Bullo and her pleas are becoming increasingly desperate. She feels let down, she says, thrown into the middle of nowhere and expected to cope. Her suburban Sydney upbringing hasn't prepared her for this; this lonely, parched land is way beyond her control. Charles has tried to placate her, sharing his wild dreams and visions of what Bullo could be, talking silky smooth when her despondency is at its worst. But he is tiring of her sulking and pouting, tiring of her inability to rise to the challenge without whining. And the isolation is getting to him too. The only other females around here are the black women and, besides, he needs some intellectual stimulation as well.

'The brain is a powerful machine!' he exhorts to the lumbering tradesmen who occasionally come through the station with a quick-fix plan and no lateral thinking.

'If you don't use it, you lose it!'

Charles looks back at their time at Bullo as successful. When he first arrived he didn't know one end of a cow from the other, but he has learned fast. John Nicholson, a fine cattleman, has agreed to take a half share in the station in return for management, care and attention. The kids have settled in well here, more at home in the scrub than the city, but a dose of civilisation won't hurt them either.

He uncoils from his dusty seat and saunters in to talk to Sara.

'You had better pack,' he announces. 'We're going to America.'

21

CHAPTER THREE

It has been a long time since Charles has been home. For years he has kept a polite but bitter distance from his conservative, Victorian father, Charles English Henderson Jr. Tall, stiff-backed and eloquent, the Princeton graduate and investment banker is not a believer in forgiveness. His son, he says, has disgraced the family's good name by not honouring his debts, and there can be no redeeming himself from that.

Charles' mother, Margaret, known as Bomma to her family, is now in her seventies but neither time nor age has dimmed the matriarch's indomitable spirit. Still elegant and attractive in her dotage, she despises the modern fashions, preferring to wear the long silk dresses so popular before the war and her hair swept up in a French bun. Her house dress is always impeccable: a lace shawl on cool afternoons and gloves during cocktail hour. A lady, she says, can be distinguished by her straight back and always boasts a handkerchief in the sleeve of her frock. The servants, too, are prim and austere; aprons and caps must be worn at all times.

A hearty drinker despite her attendance at church every Sunday, Bomma shocks Maryland society by swearing in the presence of an archbishop. But she refuses to apologise for the indiscretion. The Hendersons are among the top echelons of society and have connections. They maintain a stiff upper lip, and will kow-tow to no-one.

Bomma's family is proud of the fact that its ancestors were among the earliest residents of Maryland's exclusive eastern shore, settling in pockets around the fertile river country of the Chesapeake Bay in 1666, forty-six years after the *Mayflower* landed. Bomma's grandmother raised orphan, Francis Scott Key, who later wrote the American national anthem, The Star-Spangled Banner. Her father graduated from the elite West Point Military Academy in 1844 and rode with Robert E Lee in the Mexican War of 1846–48. He was known as a gentleman farmer and banker, and Bomma was the youngest of his eight children. Her marriage to Charles English Henderson Jnr was regarded as an excellent match; the young man had pedigree and boasted membership to exclusive clubs. Pillars of society, the couple wanted for nothing, helped by Bomma's sub-stantial family inheritance.

Cossetted from birth, Charles, Bomma's first born son, recognised early that to get what he wanted, he merely had to ask. But the concept concerned him: better a challenge, better to earn the right to respect. He learned to speak early, rattling off sentences with intelligent comprehension, questioning everything and ruffling the stiff correctness of his father who believed children should be seen and not heard. Suggestions that Charles was bordering on the savant were met by Charles Jr with quiet pride, but Bomma would have none of it.

'Rubbish, Charles,' she contradicted. 'He is a normal child; he simply has boundless energy and a vivid imagination.'

Bomma straightened her curly, golden hair in front of her Victorian dresser, counting the strokes as she went. It was a nightly ritual, and a sacred one. Charles Jr once strenuously beat a maid who dared glance in the open door as she passed while Bomma was brushing. The children were not exempt from punishment either: at two, Charles' brother, Edmond, was mercilessly thrashed when he wandered into his mother's room whilst she was wearing only a petticoat.

When his younger sister, Margaret, was born, Charles talked even more, but whether it was to drown out the sudden attention lavished on the new arrival, no-one ever knew.

Throughout Charles' childhood—and in fact for the rest of his life—his closest friend was Gus Trippe. The two grew up on adjacent waterfront farms on the Tred Avon River, which in turn runs into the Choptank to meet the mighty Chesapeake Bay. They shared a special bond: Charles' grandfather and Gus' great-grandfather were brothers. But it was a bond that ran deeper than familial ties. Born only four months apart in 1919, they proved to be inseparable, spending endless days fishing, crabbing, sailing, hunting rabbits and riding horses. Their childhood freedom, unhindered by financial concerns, stamped their early sense of independence and marked the foundation of their friendship which would endure through even the toughest times ahead.

'Our first joint venture at the age of eight was capturing some ducks which were swimming in the river off our neighbour Jim Bartlett's farm,' Gus recalls. 'Our transport was an old rowing boat; our weapon, a crab net which was to go over their heads. The ducks registered our efforts with considerable noise and commotion which alerted Farmer Bartlett. He ran down to the water's edge and fired a shotgun blast across our bow. We abandoned the chase and rowed home. There are some who say we have been poddy-dodging ever since.'

At ten, Charles was sent to a fashionable boys boarding school to rein in his increasingly wild streak. A nonconformist, he proved popular with his classmates, amusing and alarming them with his antics. A precocious, bright student, he also excelled in athletics, notably football and track and field. A good loser, he was interested in the sport and could handle defeat—if it was to a better opponent. By thirteen, his love of sailing and his native daring earned him the honour of being invited to crew on a 1500 nautical mile race to Bermuda. His yacht won. At seventeen he was the skipper of a yacht which raced on the magnificent Chesapeake Bay where some of the world's greatest sailors have cut their teeth. On the bay, removed from the restrictive hand of his father, Charles had the liberty he craved. He thrived on the challenge of this personal battle with the elements and the opportunity to prove his natural sailing skills.

Handsome, tall, with intense blue eyes and a fatal, practised charm, Charles was invited to debutante balls and once dated the homecoming queen. Later, displaying the acerbic wit and acid tongue which could crush even the most confident person, he was heard to remark that it was a shame the girl was such a crashing bore. He had already decided that his life's mission was to be devastatingly attractive to women. They were his playthings, his addiction, and, like everything else he tackled, he hated any challenge to elude him. The southern belles, with their tinkling tea cups and delicate handling of jelly cakes, bored him rigid; Charles wanted excitement, and required discretion. Even at so young an age, he instinctively understood women's emotions and frailties, but failed to forgive their lack of tolerance for his wandering eye.

25

'Rudyard Kipling got it right,' he would often say. 'The female of the species is far more deadly than the male.'

Charles' dream to study at Princeton, the prestigious University of Virginia, was dashed when his father insisted he attend the northern university, LeeHaigh, instead. Champing at this enforced restraint, Charles enlisted in the navy as soon as the opportunity presented itself. After a stint as a submariner, which he undoubtedly found suffocating and confined, he was accepted into flight school. It was here that the dichotomy in his character became so evident: socially reckless, he also earned a reputation as a man dedicated to detail. Near enough was not good enough; when he took command, he drove his crew to perfection.

At this time Charles was a frequent visitor to his parents' new home, Lloyds Landing, in tobacco farming country in Maryland. The original farmhouse reeked of old money and old-world charm. It was not as palatial as the nearby Georgian mansions with their sandstone columns and silk window dressings, but it was a mansion nevertheless. Geared for leisure and comfort, the Victorian furnishings—chiffoniers, chaises longues, a mahogany davenport—were framed against heavy velvet drapes and American oil paintings. In the long, glorious summer months the family sailed the endless waterways and reclined on the Chesapeake beach, known to their circle as the 'pleasure shore', before retiring for ice-cool drinks on their porch. Looking down the avenue of trees to an estuary of the glittering Choptank River, they were summoned at sunset for sumptuous dinners of chilled asparagus soup and soft-shell crab in the elegant dining room. During winter, when the woods were shrouded in a white blanket and the marshlands iced over, they rose before dawn to hunt ducks and geese, returning precisely at ten for a full cooked breakfast and hot-buttered rum. Bomma was adamant no food be served outside the dining room: every meal, however humble, was served with aplomb on fine English china with shining silver cutlery. These winter days were short; at night, the men retired to the drawing room after supper to boast about the day's kill in front of a roaring log fire.

God surely lived in Maryland, south of the Mason-Dixon line.

Happily accepting the born-to-lead mantle from his father, Charles knew there were great inequities in the racial system of America's south. He knew, too, that if change was to come, it would come slowly. He was kind and respectful to the Negroes, but some lessons were ingrained: when they came to the house, they came by the back door.

In 1941, Charles' itch for challenge found dramatic expression. The war in Europe was a long way from home, but he watched its direction carefully. When it exploded over the Pacific following the bombing of Pearl Harbor, he joined the action. Resigning his commission as a naval engineer, he enlisted at Pensacola Flying School in Florida. He passed officers' school with flying colours and, bored with the routine and regimentation of the navy, flipped a coin to go over or under the sea. Heads.

He would see this war from the air, in the naval air force.

Flying Avenger torpedo bombers from the USS *Enterprise*—sluggish and underpowered aircraft compared with other machines of war—Charles determinedly set to the task of annihilating the Japanese enemy. The air force had its rules, but Charles English Henderson III was hellbent on not following them. Lazily drifting the skies in search of enemy aircraft, he often flew with his shoes off, feet resting on top of the instrument panel, and smoking his favourite cigar. It was a modus operandi that would later become his trademark—and his daughter's—when he cruised the 'Henderson Highway' out of Bullo. Flying with deliberate disregard to the calls from exasperated air-traffic controllers demanding his position and flight plan, he became known as 'that eccentric bastard Yank'. During the war, he was simply labelled an eccentric hero, one of the most successful Avenger pilots of his time.

'Flying, cigars, whisky and wild, wild women are the real joys of life,' he winked to his colleagues. 'Yes, suh! There ain't nothin' better!'

His reputation as a pilot who stared death in the face without showing fear quickly spread amongst his unit.

But his inner circle, with whom he entrusted the truth, understood the reality behind this image. It was not that he was unafraid, but that he considered every move with cool logic before he made it, forcing himself to build up his courage prior to every attack. He was a leader, he made bold moves, but as the skipper of his squadron he never lost a single man. Demanding perfection, he made many people nervous and most people angry. Given the choice of carrying a payload of either one 2000-pound torpedo, two 1000-pound bombs or four five-hundred-pound bombs, Charles elected to carry the latter.

'Why would ah go for one target,' he drawled, 'when ah could go for four.'

His crew wanted to drop their bombs and dash back to friendly territory, but that wasn't Charles' style. He preferred to stay near the action until he was forced to come in, and, increasingly, he found it difficult to muster colleagues to work with him.

During one bloody attack, Charles sunk two ships and left an aircraft smoking, returning to his carrier only after he ran out of ammunition and was almost out of fuel. His delay in returning to the *Enterprise*, and so slowing the ship's departure, earned him a severe reprimand from the admiral. Charles was unrepentant, insisting the admiral view the films taken on the exercise. Acknowledging the incredible success of Charles' mission, the reprimand was quickly revoked.

Charles loved a dogfight, and the dirtier, more dangerous, the better. And he loved to regale other airmen with intricate details of these chases.

'One hundred yards, a black void. Fifty yards, nothing. My fingers caressed the trigger. I could feel the sweat running down my back, yet it was very cold. Then a blur, darker than the dark, and the tail of a large aircraft appeared like a phantom. I eased forward in tight formation, my port gun behind his starboard engine, manoeuvring into position to fire. Then suddenly I saw the blur of his wings—an inverted V!'

He would pause here for dramatic effect, take a long, slow drag on his cigar.

'So intense was my frustration that I very nearly squeezed the trigger. How dare he not be Japanese! What was an American aircraft doing at this time in this place? Clearly he was friendly. Equally clearly, I was not. In truth, I had never in my life felt less friendly. Finally I located his frequency on my data sheet. He was from that miserable squadron operating near Okinawa. I called over the radio with a distinct Japanese accent: "All same looksee starboard side, Mellican boy." He pleasured me with a violent diving turn to port as he peeled off for the deck. And thus ended another unfriendly encounter.'

Charles was a legend before the war ended; after it, he earned the distinction of being awarded the US Silver Star with bar for gallantry, four Flying Crosses and six air medals for meritorious combat service.

His success lay in his ability to understand the Kamikaze spirit. Death was the price you paid for ignominious failure. He had another secret, too, which he later passes on to Bonnie. Never expect a man to do something you are not prepared to do yourself.

All the same, he could never understand how he survived those war years, and he regarded all that followed as a bonus. Agnostic until his last breath, his adventures livened every dinner party. No-one was sacred and God was his ultimate stooge. After saying grace in exaggerated, pious tones, he would boast to his guests that he had met God in the war, and had no fear of meeting him again.

'There we were, at 14 000 feet and He appeared in front of me and told me it was wrong to shoot enemy aircraft out of the sky. Well, I told Him, "Don't you sass me, boy, just don't you sass me!"'

Whilst he was on R & R leave in Vancouver in 1942, Charles, cutting a dashing figure in his uniform, stepped into a hotel elevator with his colleagues. The girl operating the lift was a vision: a tall brunette with laughing eyes, long, slim legs, and an open, intelligent face. She immediately caught Charles' eye. The girl, Barbara, now in her seventies and suffering the early stages of Parkinson's disease, has lost none of her beauty, and that long-ago time when she first fell in love is still vivid in her memory.

'I opened the door to three young naval air force officers and during the time it took that rather slow elevator to reach their floor, there was much chitchat and hilarity which, to some degree, involved myself. I thought what a charming bunch they were as I discharged them.

'A few minutes later there was a buzz from the same floor. I answered the call and in stepped one of the young pilots. He was cocksure and it was obvious that he thought the world was his oyster, but his warm, infectious grin induced an immediate response. When we reached the ground floor he informed me that he would like to go to the top floor, and when we arrived at that floor he expressed a desire to go to the ground floor again. By this time, he had asked if he could see me again.

'It was, of course, Charles.

'The very next evening he arrived at my father's apartment and, after introductions were made, the three of us went out to dinner at the officers' club. I saw him twice after that and gave him my home address when he asked for it. I didn't really think I would see him again. I was flabbergasted when just one week later I answered the phone in my mother's house to discover it was Charles. He had gone to no end of trouble to find me as the address I had given him was incorrect—not by design, but through carelessness. My mother was charmed with him and a few months later she gave her consent to our engagement. We married in 1944.'

If Barbara's mother was charmed by Charles, his own father was not. Maryland social mores decreed that a man pay his debts. Charles had proudly endorsed his son and heir to membership of the prestigious Maryland Club. It was for gentlemen only: conservative, dignified, stuffy; the club badge was indeed a badge of honour. Membership also entitled a warm welcome at affiliated clubs overseas, and Charles used the privilege at every opportunity. However, word had filtered back to the banker that his son had failed to meet his financial obligations to these clubs. Charles Jr was appalled and ashamed at his son's behaviour: to renege on a gentleman's debt was a disgrace. He would not pay the bills for him; nor would he forgive him either.

'You are,' he admonished Charles with undisguised disdain, 'nothing less than an utter animal.'

It was a bitter rift, only healed just before his father's death in 1961. But even then the resentment extends beyond the grave: to Charles' chagrin, his young brother, Edmond, is made executor of the will.

With his young bride in tow, Charles took up a position as a senior officer with the United Nations, assigned to the task of delivering supplies and food up the Yangtze River to the war-ravaged

Chinese. Gus was in New York, and both he and Charles were eager to conquer new challenges. They hatched a plan.

'Just after the war in China there was a dearth of automobiles and many big-moneyed Chinese wanted cars,' Gus recalls. 'We put together a package and despatched a number of late-model cars to China. The write-up was astounding! We made our first bank.'

Flushed with their success and motivated by a spirit of optimism, Charles and Gus moved to Manila in 1948 to establish their shipping enterprise. If the old walled city, levelled by war, was a grim backdrop for their youthful dreams, they didn't appear to notice. Here Charles could also indulge his lifetime passion for sailing. In deference to his beautiful wife, he named their yacht, on which they lived, the *Lady Barbara*.

By now Charles and Barbara's son, Charles English Henderson IV—nicknamed Toddy—was almost seven. A lively, charming child with a mass of blond hair and an impish smile, he was the apple of his father's eye. They spent many days sailing the Manila harbour, sharing manly secrets, and Charles was determined their relationship would be happier than the one he shared with his father.

'You, mah boy,' Charles grinned, 'can be anything you want to be!'

On a warm March day in 1953, Barbara returned with Toddy and her two younger sons, Jack and baby Murray, to the yacht club with the promise they could go sailing on their dinghy which was tied up to the *Lady B*. Toddy and Jack went on ahead with a boat boy whilst Barbara waited on the wharf with Murray. Their Filipino friend, Sato-son, was busy painting the yacht and told Toddy he couldn't come aboard. The order confused the little boy; Mummy told him he was allowed. He climbed impatiently over the railing, buffeted by strong winds as he ran toward Sato-son on the bow.

The wind propeller, which Charles had installed for air-conditioning on the yacht, was in full momentum, swinging wildly on the deck. Sato-son watched, horrified, as the propeller hit the child with violent force, knocking him to the deck. Picking up Toddy's crumpled, bloodied body, Sato-son jumped into the dinghy and rowed frantically to shore, praying out loud with every dip of the oar. Sobbing, he placed the unconscious boy in his mother's arms.

Distraught, Barbara stood on the boulevard, clutching Toddy to her and desperately trying to flag down a passing motorist. The minutes flew past and her desperate cries for help went unheeded. An antiquated jeepney, loaded with passengers, eventually stopped. Careering through the heavy late afternoon traffic, it seemed an eternity before they arrived at the hospital.

Charles had been notified and, ashen faced, paced the emergency ward corridors with Barbara as they waited for news of their son. When the doctor finally emerged, his haunted face confirmed their worst fears. Toddy was dead.

In a final salute to his little sailor, Charles, alone and hearbroken, sailed the *Lady Barbara* out to sea and dropped the wind propeller into the water's murky depths. He had not only lost a son; he had lost an heir.

More than six months after Toddy's death the family had grown closer in its shared grief. Rocking Murray in her arms after giving him a drink of juice, Barbara put him down for his afternoon nap, then left the room for five minutes. When she returned she noticed he looked uncomfortable, lying face down with one arm underneath him.

'Turn over, darling,' she told him, picking him up and laying him gently on his back. The child was motionless, his face pale blue.

Screaming for the amah to phone the doctor, Barbara massaged him but still got no response. A cold sense of deja vu enveloped her; in despair, she wrapped him in a blanket and drove at breakneck speed to the hospital. Passing Charles on the road, they made the long journey together, Barbara nursing the limp child in her arms. His lungs full of liquid, they arrived too late. They had lost their little man.

Once again the family made the desolate trip to Maryland with the ashes of their dead son, whom they buried in a grave next to Toddy.

By 1959 Charles and Barbara's marriage was in its final throes. Toddy's and Murray's deaths haunted them both, and their grief was a pain that neither could escape. With a mixture of reluctance and relief they agreed divorce was their only option. Charles had proved monogamy did not suit him; he hated the loneliness of a single bed on his frequent business trips and took his chances where he could. Barbara, too, was tiring of their chaotic lifestyle and sought support and love in other quarters. With their four delightful boys—Jack, Hugh, Fraser and David—of whom they agreed to share custody after their separation, Barbara moved to Sydney to live.

Employing the same seduction techniques he used on Barbara fifteen years before—charm, determination and the southern courtesy of first winning the mother's confidence—Charles sets about wooing Sara when they meet in Sydney.

Sunbaking on a boat with her boyfriend, Neville, Sara is immediately smitten with the tall American who unceremoniously climbs aboard without being invited. Seeing the writing on the wall, Neville bows out of his relationship with Sara who immediately embarks on a heady, fast romance with Charles. Filled with flowers, fancy dinners and champagne, their love is passionate and stormy from the start.

Charles' divorce from Barbara had not yet been finalised and he omitted to tell Sara that he was still legally married until long after he had swept her off her feet.

At twenty-three—tall, attractive and athletic—Sara offered Charles the partnership he needed. Beautifully spoken, she was gracious and intelligent in company and had the inner fire necessary to keep up with his dreams. Intoxicated with his infectious joie de vivre, Sara was fascinated with Charles' lifestyle and drive to succeed. If his sudden, unexplained disappearances and glib tongue concerned her, she ignored the niggling doubts. After a whirlwind courtship, Sara became Mrs Charles Henderson III in a civil and church ceremony in Hong Kong, sporting her wedding ring with happy pride. It was 1960, life was good, and they were to live in the Philippines where Charles had his business base.

CHAPTER FOUR

Relieved to be back in civilisation once more, away from the crocodiles, redback spiders and snakes, all of which terrify her, Sara nonetheless feels intimidated at Lloyds Landing, constantly deferring to Bomma. When Charles had telegrammed that he was to marry again—this time to a 'native Australian' girl—Bomma took the news with characteristic calm. Inwardly, however, she had battled with the unsavoury image of having to receive a black daughter-in-law home for cocktails. Only after she had viewed the wedding photos could she bring herself to mention the marriage to her friends.

'Our son Charles,' she would say, swirling her sherry and staring whimsically into the glass, 'has married a charming, acceptable Ostraalian girl. May the good Lord bless their union.' To herself she would add, 'And may he honour his vows this time.'

The matriarch, strong and firm, often hints that while Sara spoils Murray-Lee, she is too tough on her youngest daughter. Others notice it, too.

'A great deal of attention was showered on Murray-Lee,' says Margaret, Charles' sister. 'She had everything she wanted. But Bonnie was usually left out. She was stoic, reserved, within herself. In many ways, I don't think Bonnie was a happy child. I don't ever recall her mother cuddling her, and there were many, many times that child needed a cuddle. She and Sara never saw eye to eye, even when Bonnie was small. There was a distance between them, which grew wider as the years went on.'

Sara, usually the soul of tact, lets Bomma know what she thinks of her interference.

'She told Mother one day that she was an old lady and had lived long enough,' Margaret says. 'That comment broke Mother's heart.'

Charles decides he and Sara need some space and the small farmhouse on the estate offers the perfect solution: close enough to enjoy the social soirees, far enough away for privacy. However, the peace of their rural existence is often shattered with heated fights between the couple. Bonnie pulls the feather eiderdown over her head, seeking comfort and refuge in its warm oblivion. When they lived with Bomma, she talked to her when she was troubled, and they were good friends. But in the dark of night, down in this house, Grandma seems a long way away, and the bedcovers provide little shelter from her parents' angry voices.

'For God sake, Sara, be sensible,' Charles implores. Bonnie knows the tone, knows that at this moment her father's jaw has moved almost imperceptibly sideways, that this is a fight he is determined to win.

'But it's only a part-time coaching job, Charles!' Sara retorts angrily. 'What can possibly be wrong with that?'

A car accident years before cut short Sara's dreams of a brilliant tennis career; seeded for Wimbledon, it was a blow that took her years to get over. She is tired of rambling around this rural estate, waiting for Charles to return from his 'business trips'. Instead of sitting home with the children, she could be out there training champions. Close to tears now, she is frustrated and furious at the real reason her husband doesn't want her to coach tennis: there are young, fit men at the club, and she is very attractive. Charles will have to try another tack.

'Please, darling, think about it. We don't need you to work and, frankly, I'd prefer you didn't. I have some business trips coming up and I'd like you to join me on them.'

Bonnie knows her father will be moving closer now, wrapping his arms around her mother's shoulders. A glowering silence will continue for days, but it has ended as Bonnie knew it would. Daddy has won. Again.

She drifts off to sleep, wriggling her injured arm to get comfortable. Tomorrow she will be free of the plaster straightjacket she has worn since her accident with Marlee at Bullo. It has been hard to climb trees with this strapped from her elbow to her wrist, but she has tried anyway.

In the surgery the next day the doctor hurts her, sawing through the mould with savage indifference to her pain. She tries to be brave; Mummy is making enough racket for the both of them, abusing the doctor for his carelessness and insisting she will not pay the bill. Bonnie straightens her arm, now scratched and bleeding from the ordeal, stares at it in triumph and makes an astounding discovery. Anything that is broken can be healed.

Charles doesn't speak much to the children on the occasions he is home. He smiles gently at their small overtures for affection, but is preoccupied with his entrepreneurial dreams. His self-absorption and arrogance astonish even those who know him well, but no-one dares question his detachment. Child-raising, according to Charles, is a woman's domain. He is interested only in his children's abilities—if they have any. He is mostly indifferent to Murray-Lee, who appears to spend an inordinate amount of time near her mother, but he notices Bonnie.

'What for heaven's sake is wrong with that child, Sara?' he asks. 'She falls over every time she crosses a room; she has had more broken bones than I've had hot dinners, and she's a deathly shade of pale. You should build her up, feed her more.'

Sara accepts the rebukes with a resigned air. Bad enough that Charles is rarely home, she has to worry about keeping the children in line when he is. Long ago she learned her role was to be disciplinarian, that the small tantrums and occasional outbursts— never in front of Bomma or their father—are to be dealt with as quickly and quietly as possible.

Someone has left a half-drunk glass of chocolate milk in the fridge while Sara is out, and the milk is curdling on top.

'Marlee, Bonnie, whose drink is this?' Sara asks the girls because the housekeeper has gone home. Bonnie doesn't know, and Marlee doesn't want to get into strife.

'Tell Mummy it's yours, Bonnie,' she says. Her tone is definite; she will brook no disagreement.

'But it isn't mine, Marlee. I didn't put it there!'

'Yes, but say you did anyway. Then we can go outside and play.'

Bonnie faces her mother, owns up to her monstrous sin. 'It was my milk, Mummy,' she says. It's easier like this, better to take the punishment and get it over and done with.

Sara's face darkens. Waste is not to be tolerated, and Bonnie will drink the milk and stay indoors for the rest of the day.

Bonnie stares at the unpalatable crust floating on the surface, takes a deep breath and downs the milk in one gulp. That part of the medicine is easy enough, but staying inside all day is tough. She'd planned to climb the old tree down near the river; still, if she goes to bed early, morning will come faster.

The next day the housekeeper is humming, tidying the kitchen. She goes to the fridge, looks for the milk she left there yesterday.

'What are you looking for?' Sara snaps. Her temper hasn't improved much during the night, and Charles is in New York on another 'business trip'.

'I gave the girls a drink yesterday, Miz Sara, and had one myself. But I didn't drink it all. I was jest wonderin' where it got to.'

Sara hauls Bonnie into the kitchen, eyes blazing with rage. 'You lied to me!' she shouts. Bonnie watches as she pulls out the switch, knows she is for it. She throws a helpless glance at Murray-Lee, tightens her jaw and grinds her teeth to prepare for the painful punishment. She will not cry.

Later, when Bomma hears of the incident, she shakes her head sadly. 'That poor child just can't get it right. It's a case of damned if you do, and damned if you don't.'

The strap has mixed results with the girls. Murray-Lee, when she is beaten, feels it an affront to her childish sensibilities and afterwards sulks for days. Bonnie, on the other hand, accepts it as her lot, appearing to shrug it off. Angered by her seeming indifference, Sara demands that next time Charles gives her the strap. Bonnie knows she can be naughty: she doesn't always blow her nose when told to, and forgets to keep her knees together like a lady should. Mummy says she is incorrigible, and it isn't long before she is due for another hiding.

'Go upstairs with your father!' Sara demands. 'You don't take any notice of me!'

Charles closes the bedroom door and, in a stage whisper, tells Bonnie to scream loudly when he gives her the nod. He raises the strap above his shoulder, tells her to scream now, and thumps the switch across the bedding. Satisfied that punishment has been seen to be done, he leaves the room, advising her to wait a few minutes before she follows him downstairs.

Sara has brought chocolate for the girls, which she invites them to share.

'Murray-Lee, you break the chocolate in half,' she says. Roughly divided, it is deliberately uneven. Sara knows exactly what her eldest daughter is up to and decides to teach her a lesson.

'It's Bonnie's turn to have first pick,' she says. 'Bonnie, choose the one you want.'

Bonnie sizes up the situation. Mummy obviously wants her to take the largest chunk, but if she does, she will have Murray-Lee's wrath to contend with when they are out of adult earshot. Best to cut her losses early.

She reaches for the smaller piece and puts it in her mouth before there is any more argument on the subject.

Sara looks at her angrily, speaks through gritted teeth. 'You are so frustrating! When are you going to learn?'

A few days later, Charles, obsessed with his work and oblivious to the problems at home, finally agrees to spend a day with the family. They will go swimming down in the bay. Bonnie knows Mummy will tell her to wear her one-piece costume because it is more suitable but her bikini is brighter, more comfortable. This time she decides to circumvent a negative

41

response and go straight to her father.

'Daddy, should I wear the one piece or the bikini?' she asks.

He eyes both suits with slow deliberation, as if he has been asked to choose a pope.

'Wear the bikini, Sara-Lloyd,' he finally answers. 'A lady always looks nice in a bikini.'

Sara is resentful that Bonnie has bypassed her to get what she wants from her father. Somewhere in this small child is a core of strength, a wild spirit Sara doesn't understand. She has seen it in only one other person, and that frightens her too. Bonnie is surely her father's daughter.

It is the late sixties, and the social fabric is breaking down. In the cities flower power is the hallmark of a generation calling for peace and love, and African-Americans are demanding real equality. Racial tensions that have simmered for years are now boiling over, and the violent unrest is extending into schools and classrooms. Sara feels uneasy. It is better, she feels, to teach the children at home.

Bonnie, now five years old, squirms under the relentless tutelage of her mother. At kindergarten she could dream the day away seated at her wooden bench, staring out at the playing fields which invited her to run and skip and jump. School work is easy, and that's a drag.

Murray-Lee wants to have riding lessons, but the idea terrifies Bonnie. Still tiny and weak, horses tower over her, suicidal mountains of bone and hoof. It's a dead cert she'll never get on one—not willingly anyway. She tries every trick in the book to avoid the lessons but she also has Maryland social conventions against her. Young ladies should know how to ride.

Bonnie eyes her tormentor—a small, black, vicious pony named Lucky—and knows she'll be lucky to be alive at the end of the day. 'Please, Murray-Lee,' she sobs. 'I don't want to get up on that horse.'

Her fear is unmistakable; beads of sweat run down her forehead and her lips tremble. This beast will kill her, for sure.

'You'll be okay, Bonnie,' Murray-Lee shrugs impatiently. 'You have to learn to ride one day, so you may as well start now.'

The next few weeks are an excruciating ordeal, hauling her bruised body from the blackberry bushes that rim the country lane and extracting the barbs that hook on her legs. If this is fun, Bonnie thinks, they can keep it.

Charles watches them ride when he is home. Murray-Lee is a natural horsewoman; there is little challenge in that, and nothing to aim for. He watches Bonnie more closely; she still looks weak and undernourished, but she obviously tries to conquer her dread of horses. He admires her courage.

Bonnie is sick of playing Cowboys and Indians with her older sister. The contest is never even: Murray-Lee insists on taking the lead role in the game and no amount of persuasion can induce her to change characters. Bonnie makes a good squaw, sneaking up behind the tree and ambushing the enemy in her imaginary teepee, but that has a predictable ending. Murray-Lee doesn't like to lose, and she stomps off in disgust.

Sara is in the last stages of pregnancy and their little brother or sister is due any day now. Bonnie is thrilled; soon things will be different.

Danielle's birth, in 1969, is greeted with unsuppressed excitement. A porcelain doll, she is Sara's little treasure, the first child whose nappy she has to change, whose crying she has to attend to. In the Philippines the girls each had their own amah who looked after their every need. Bonnie adores her little sister and looks on her as a mate. Six years older, it never occurs to her to boss Danielle around as Murray-Lee bosses her. It is good to have another Indian on her side.

Charles has started murmuring again about his property in the Northern Territory. It is a means for him to make an impact on the world, he says, an opportunity to shape the future. The future, Charles feels, has his name all over it. There are also other, more pressing reasons to return. Financially the family is in dire straits. There was a nasty incident a few months ago when Charles looked at his bank balance and realised something must be done, and quickly. He asked Bomma for some money but when she politely refused to bail him out again, he lost his temper. The small-town rumour mill went into overdrive, with shocked whispers suggesting, when his mother capitulates to his request, that the money has been lent under coercion. Margaret recalls their mother paid for the family's ticket back to Australia and that the substantial loan was never repaid.

John Nicholson, holding the fort back at Bullo River, is threatening to leave, and Gus Trippe is worried—the Territory operation needs a steady hand. On the home front, Sara has caught Charles out on yet another infidelity, blasting him with that icy gaze and a hollow silence that lasts for weeks. She has taken to sleeping in the children's room during these monumental no-speaks but, increasingly, neither she nor Charles cares. The shine, Charles realises, has long ago left this marriage. He tries to smooth over the latest affair with a nonchalant wave of his hand, but that fails to work. He will have to make a better peace offering.

'Come back to Bullo,' he says to Sara, 'and the station is yours—lock, stock and barrel.' Their stormy relationship is already marked by separations, and Charles knows that in many respects their relationship is over. But he wants to keep his family together, and offering his wife general directorship of the cattle station is one way of doing this.

To his surprise, Sara accepts. She loathed the place when they were there five years ago but Charles understands human nature only too well. Money is a tempting seductress.

Bonnie adores Bomma and the Maryland lifestyle—the endless round of parties and sailing on the Chesapeake Bay with her father—but she is thrilled to be going back to Australia. She still remembers old Mary and the walks they used to go on across her country. Bonnie grins as she helps pack up the house. Her daddy's enthusiasm is infectious.

CHAPTER FIVE

Sara is stressed to breaking point. Charles is dragging her back to Bullo with his wild promises, and this time it threatens to be a long stay. In this bizarre and isolated world, it appears nothing has changed. The mail plane still comes in only once a week; urgent communication is by telegram only; there is no telephone, electricity or running water, and the only inhabitants appear to be throwbacks from civilisation.

Charles flies the family from Sydney, west through Charters Towers, across the Barkly Tableland, to Katherine and on to Bullo. As the urban centres disappear and they go deeper into the heart of Australia's wild country, Sara's mood disintegrates. Charles, in a buoyant frame of mind, has no time for long faces.

'Oh, cheer up, it's not the end of the world,' he tells Sara. Over the noise of the aircraft, he doesn't hear her reply.

'Oh yes, it is,' she mutters.

At Katherine, their aircraft refueller, a conservative family man with a sharp edge, wonders how the hell this quartet of white girls will cope out here. He notes wryly that this time they are travelling with a governess, but doubts that will make one iota of difference. The last time they were here it was a nightmare, and they only lasted nine months. It's typical of Charlie Henderson, he thinks, to assume it would work now.

'The only people that live at stations like Bullo are deadbeats, piss-wrecks, divorcees, blackfellas and jailbirds,' he tells his mate over a cold beer. 'Most of them are running away from something or someone.'

Charles is unfazed by the criticisms which reach his ears. 'Ah've never cared what people think of me, fortunately. Ah couldn't care less. They think ah'm bad news and ah would have to agree with them. Ah'm the biggest disaster, ah offend mahself at all times and ah don't know why ah go on livin'!'

Sara has insisted the governess, Marianne, travel with them to maintain the social graces and education the girls have acquired at Maryland. Down to earth, warm but strict, Marianne stays with them for a year and earns a reputation as the best governess they ever have. When she leaves, a succession of tutors follows, but all find the same problem. Increasingly feral, the children are almost impossible to control.

Bonnie has readapted immediately to the environment and the solitude, roaming about with a fearlessness that her mother finds daunting. The wild country with its myriad dangers—pythons, scorpions, crocodiles and wild cattle known as scrubbers—don't faze Bonnie. Sara doesn't share her daughter's enthusiasm. As well as a multitude of other problems, the old generator that has to be kick-started into action now continually gives up the ghost. The family is still living in that bloody tin shed, which dominates the landscape with its enduring promise of discomfort and heat. John, their manager,

47

hasn't given up the disconcerting habit of having a snort from a Worcestershire sauce bottle followed by a swig of rum to wake him up.

Sara remembers her own childhood in Sydney, filled with cheerful normality and suburban convention. Out here she doesn't know what is normal any more; the lack of rules terrifies her.

Charles has dragged something else out here too: his rigid Maryland social conventions and lascivious eye. In this outback empire, his word is law. Ruler of his isolated kingdom, he commands and directs operations like a captain giving orders from the bridge, stomping around, bellowing at anyone in earshot and revelling in conflicts.

He is determined to shape his family's destiny, free from other influences save his own.

The station carpenter, Raymond, has prewedding jitters. He's been stuck out at Bullo for weeks on end and his girl, waiting for him in Adelaide, is getting testy. The road, still drying out from the monsoon, won't take him through: even in good conditions it's a nightmare six-hour drive into Katherine. But get out he must; this place is starting to feel like a prison.

He nervously approaches Charles to ask when the next plane is coming through. His boss is known to be a tough man, but fair; if he explains the circumstances, he's sure to get a good hearing.

'I'm, ah, gettin' hitched this weekend,' he stutters. 'Not much of a do, a pretty small weddin', but if you'd like to come with your missus, you're welcome.' That's a good opening, he feels; invite the Yank bastard to his shindig and then tell him he needs two days off.

Charles hitches up his pants, cocks a curious eye in the ringer's direction. He has planned to take a trip into Darwin anyway, and it's easy enough to divert to Katherine en route.

'Ah haven't bin to a weddin' since ah got into double harness mahself, boy,' he answers in his southern drawl which always sounds so strange to these young fellas out here in the outback. 'But if you'd be wantin' a lift to town, ah'd be happy to oblige. No time like the present—no, suh! Ah'll go get the girls, you throw your swag in the plane.'

Bonnie clambers in the back seat with Marlee. She hates flying, but not as much as her mother does. Sara makes no bones about the fact that she loathes it, gripping the seats on takeoff and landing, and almost passing out when the aircraft hits turbulence. Getting off the ground, she thinks, isn't the tricky bit; staying in the air is. Still, she isn't about to miss this trip into the relative civilisation of Darwin, so she clambers on board.

The Cherokee 6 rattles along the airstrip, takes off and turns in an easterly direction. John Nicholson is in the front with Charles, going over muster plans. A film of oil is slowly but steadily seeping over the windscreen and Charles checks his oil pressure gauge. It's a bit low, but no real problem yet.

The sludge continues to creep upwards, slowly obscuring vision. John rechecks the oil pressure, looks aghast at the distance between the plane and the ground, and the rapidly diminishing pressure gauge.

'What the hell is happenin' here,' he yells to Charles over the hum of the engine. 'The oil pressure is dropping!'

Charles does another check, realises his reluctant copilot is right. Bloody hell. Bad enough to be carrying such a motley crew, without the aircraft packing it in as well.

'If you're that worried about mah flyin', why don't you get out and clean the windscreen?' he yells back.

The oil is reaching dangerously low levels; any minute, the engine will seize and they're only just within cooee of Katherine airport. Charles looks again at the instrument panel, feels the engine wheeze as the propeller stops midair.

'Mayday, mayday,' he booms to traffic control. 'Ah have engine failure, present position twenty-five miles from Tindal on descent from 7000 feet for a dead-stick landing!'

The traffic controllers cringe. Dead-stick means no power, and they recognise that voice, would recognise it anywhere. 'That mad Yank is up there again,' they say. 'Put emergency services on alert. He's making a forced landing!'

Sara's face is ashen, and Marlee's natural body functions have taken over. 'Mummy, I need to go to the toilet.'

'You can't go now, Marlee,' Sara grimaces. 'You'll have to wait.'

The plane appears to be hanging in thin air by an invisible wire; at any moment, Sara is sure, it will plunge to the ground.

'But I need to go to the toilet, Mummy, and I need to go now!'

'You're just going to have to hold on, Marlee,' Bonnie says. 'You can go to the toilet when we get on the ground.'

Bonnie is certain they will get on the ground safely; when Daddy is flying she always feels safe.

Raymond is hysterical, his nerves jangling and his eyes riveted to the oil oozing over the windscreen. 'Put this fuckin' thing down!' he screeches. 'I'm gittin' married tomorrow! I can't die now!'

He falls back in his seat, transfixed with horror. What a bastard of a way to go.

Charles lines up the airstrip, glides low to get it in his sights. 'We're goin' in!' he tells his passengers. 'Hold on!'

The stench of fear and excrement reeks through the cabin as the plane glides in for its final turn. Nicholson, not a praying man, closes his eyes and mutters to himself. 'God help us,' he says. 'God help us all.'

Suddenly Charles lets out a loud curse. 'Bugger me! When did they put up that bloody cyclone fence around the goddamn airfield?'

There it is—a three-metre chain mesh preventing any aircraft getting through. Quickly assessing the situation, Charles realises a nearby paddock only has a one-metre high fence around it. That's where he heads. He'll tackle the fence and worry about the consequences later. If those bastards don't like it, they can take the high fence down.

He banks the aircraft sharply to the left, clearing the paddock wire by metres. Bonnie looks out her side of the window, tugs at Sara's arm. 'Mummy, we're not on the airstrip!' she says.

Sara is in no mood for children; the end of this horror flight is in sight and that's good enough for her. 'Be quiet, Bonnie,' she hisses. 'It doesn't matter. Daddy knows what he's doing!'

The plane settles with a thump in the paddock next to the airport, coming to rest in the deep grass. They are greeted with full emergency honours: fire, police, and ambulance officers who have just ploughed down the new cyclone fence to get to them. A cacophony of noise—sirens and shouts—surrounds the aircraft as, slowly, the cabin door opens and out falls a ghostly-pale station manager.

John's legs can't carry him past the open door; sagging to the ground he shakily pulls out his packet of rollies, leans on the propeller which has stopped, and throws together a smoke.

'You can't light that!' a fireman screeches. 'Are you all mad?'

John glares at them, glassy-eyed, starts to tell them what he thinks of their rules, but changes his mind at the last moment. 'I was on that plane!' he retorts. 'You'd want a smoke, too, if you'd been!'

The ambulance officers look at each other, wonder what sort of mad rabble they've got here, and move the passengers inside to be treated for shock.

Raymond is gibbering, asking for a rum.

'Jesus Christ! Jesus Christ! That Charlie Henderson is a nut! He's not afraid of anything!'

He looks around at the ambulance men, his eyes wild and haunted like the devil himself is on his tail. 'I'm gittin' married tomorrow! I thought we'd all be killed!'

A week later his new bride, overwhelmed by the heat and dust and flies, sizes up their Bullo honeymoon quarters. 'You've got to be joking!' she splutters. 'This place is a hellhole!'

She spends a restless night under her tin canopy, eaten alive by mosquitoes and filled with dismay. Her nightmares are vivid: crocodiles stealing with sly stealth up from the riverbank, redback spiders marching across her wedding veil. When Raymond finishes his shift, she has them packed.

'It's either Bullo or me,' she demands. 'Get me out of here!'

This time Raymond takes his chances on the track. Better to face that, he figures, than the wrath of that mad bastard Charlie Henderson.

Bonnie is becoming more difficult. At eight she has perfectly adapted to the land, like a wild flower: bright and colourful in the sunshine, closing her petals whenever she senses trouble. She is also growing increasingly silent. People should only speak, she thinks, when they have something to say. Outdoors, Bonnie doesn't have to watch her p's and q's as she does indoors with her mother, and animals don't talk back.

But as she sizes up the fifteen-hand horse in front of her, she almost wishes they did. Perhaps then he'd solve her dilemma—how to climb onto his back when her head doesn't even reach the top of his leg. Charles, in his inimitable fashion, has taught his children that perseverance and focus are a person's best yardstick to success.

Bonnie doesn't understand what that means; lacking confidence, all she knows is that if she doesn't get up on this huge horse today, she may never get up again. She looks around the yard, finds nothing to help her elevation. There's only one thing for it—she'll have to get on the hard way.

Grabbing hold of the horse's mane, she hauls herself up until she reaches his back. Out of breath, she hangs motionless for a moment before dragging one leg over the other side. It's a good view from up here, and she is well pleased with herself. But the ground seems a long way off, and the horse has no saddle. That old fear returns; there is no-one around to get her down, and she can't just sit here all day.

She remembers the riding lessons she had in Maryland, on that awful pony with a vicious streak, and hopes this horse is gentler with her. Gingerly, she hits her bare feet on the side of his flanks and the animal moves underneath her. When they finally reach the fence, she clutches onto the railing and climbs off.

It is a few months later and here she goes again. The horse is rearing wildly, trying to throw her off his back, and Bonnie is going to hit the ground any tick of the clock. She grips her hands tighter around the reins, tightens her bum in readiness for the fall. He takes a leap and a plunge, trying to throw his rider, and just as Bonnie expects to be sitting on her bum in the dust, she realises she is still on his back. She jumps off, elated that this time she has sat the buck, realises that, finally, she can do this.

The mare is in a reckless mood. She rears wildly, desperate to follow Marlee's horse which has already galloped away, determined Bonnie will not throw a saddle on her.

'Stand, please stand still for a second,' Bonnie pleads.

53

It's a long climb up for a tiny ten year old, and the mare will not be placated. She rears again, striking her front hooves on Bonnie's head with violent force.

The world is spinning, and her cries sound a long way off. She touches her head, feels the blood gushing from her scalp, knows no-one can hear her. Slumping to the ground, she screams for help until blackness blurs her vision, broken occasionally by shafts of light filtering across the plains. Shortly, the moon will edge out the sun and Fraser, her half-brother, is calling to her down a long tunnel. Gathering her in his arms, he stumbles toward the homestead.

He looks at Bonnie, her head oozing blood. Please, God, don't let her die. He adores this child, recognises their daddy's irrepressible spirit in her, her inner strength. He suspects that she is their father's favourite because Charles recognises it too.

'Hold on, Bon,' Fraser says, as rough hands pile her into the Toyota. 'Hold on.'

Charles has looked at the encroaching darkness, made a tough decision. 'It's too late to take off in the plane, we'll never make Kununurra airport in daylight,' he has decided. 'They don't have any aids to bring us in.' His voice is tremulous, but in control. They could fly to the hospital in thirty minutes, but it will take hours by road. 'We'll have to use the fencing contractor's vehicle; none of ours will make it over that goat track.'

Bonnie stirs for a moment, wonders what Daddy is doing and why she is in this battered old vehicle when she should be riding the mare. The Toyota slips over the potholed track, greasy from recent rains, as Bonnie slips in and out of darkness.

'Mummy, I need a tissue,' she whimpers. Blood is pouring into her mouth, a steady stream gushing from her nose. It tastes foul, bitter and acid. The Toyota is in second gear, crawling, bumping and grinding over the sandstone and rock.

'Can't you go faster!' Sara urges, voice rising in panic, hysteria catching in her throat as she nurses her dying daughter.

Charles takes control. 'For Godsakes, stop panicking! Try to keep calm.' She always reacts like this in a crisis, and it only serves to make things worse.

The fencing contractor's knuckles are white as he grips the steering wheel. 'Sara, we've got another four hours ahead of us before we hit the highway and another two on the bitumen before we get to Kununurra. I can't push over this country any faster!'

They have been travelling for two hours, and Bonnie is tired of fighting to stay awake. Sara's tears wash her cheeks, wash away the blood and pain as she slips into welcome oblivion.

The Toyota has stopped and there is a strange, ethereal light shining in front of her. Stockmen and jackeroos, cradling pannikins of tea, are framed by the light of a camp fire. One of them has a guitar and is strumming bush songs; a didgeridoo wails and echoes in the night. They are calling to her in faraway voices, 'Come over here, Bon. It's warm. It's warm here.'

She slips one foot out of the truck, desperate to join them, to move toward the warmth of that fire. But she is stuck, a firm hand holding her down, and her mother's pitiful, haunting cry—'Bonnie, Bonnie, come back, come back, Bonnie *don't* you get out of the truck'—is drowning out the ringer's songs.

At the hospital a few days later the doctor examines Bonnie's head, removing the bandage with care and skill. 'You are a very lucky girl to be alive,' he says. 'Keep the bandages on for another few weeks, and try not to have any more accidents.'

Bonnie looks at her mother, sitting on a chair by the hospital bed. 'Mummy, if I was so ill, why did we stop the Toyota and sit beside the fire on the way?'

The question puzzles Sara; the child must have been delirious.

'We didn't stop, Bon,' she says. 'We pushed on until we reached Kununurra.'

For years, Bonnie flashes back to this near-death experience, recognises the fragile love between her mother and herself.

The girls have decided to go fishing down at Bullo Crossing. Careful of crocodiles, they know it is still relatively safe, but only a few short years later, when they are protected, this area becomes heavily infested with them. The Aborigines on the station have taught them that if they go near water that might have crocs in it, they must throw a dog in first. It is a crude means of finding if the water is safe, little better than the old days. Then, croc hunters used a live goat for bait, tying the poor animal to a riverbank and waiting for the prehistoric creature to slither out of its muddy hiding hole and stalk it. The croc was then caught by the nose with a snare so it didn't drown, but the goat didn't fare so well.

A five-foot croc eyes the girls with a cold stare, waiting silently in the water until they make a wrong move. The girls don't hang around long once they spot it, scarpering up the bank and dashing back to the homestead to get help. Armed with a branding iron, Sara marches back down with them.

Marlee's dog, Shad, has run ahead and jumped in the river, and the croc moves stealthily toward it, edging up at a right angle. Marlee is on the bank, screaming for Shad to come back; the croc is edging closer and both girls are halfway up to their hocks in mud, trying to pull the dog from the water. Sara, panicking, hollers for them to move back, flailing around with the branding iron to protect them. The croc is obviously not hungry. If he had been, he would have torn them apart. A boner from the meatworks goes down to the crossing the next day and puts a bullet clean between the croc's eyes.

Whilst Shad survives the ordeal, it teaches Bonnie a crude lesson: don't mess in crocodile territory unless you absolutely have to.

It's late afternoon as the last cow clatters through the gate, signalling the end of another day's work. Tired but cheerful, Bonnie, Marlee and young Danielle climb the yard rail and head down toward the camp. Bonnie picks up a pandanus palm fruit, hurls it down the flat at a tree stump, and hits the mark amidst cheers and yells.

'Let's have a game of cricket,' she suggests.

The idea is taken up with enthusiasm and bush ingenuity. A lump of wood is found for the bat, and a small, dead tree for the stump.

'Righto!' Bonnie yells. 'Let 'em fly!'

Pandanus nuts hurl through the air at alarming speed toward the batter, an Aboriginal boy with a keen eye and deadly wrist. He doesn't miss one.

'Fluke, fluke!' they cry as they send another pandanus missile in his direction and he whacks it out into the scrub.

Bonnie looks up at the dark clouds overhead, knows that pretty soon rain will interrupt play. She goes into a scrum with her sisters and they make an executive decision.

'Righto, you're for it!' she warns the batter as they pelt pandanus nuts at him, bombarding him with a ruthless assault. 'If we can't get you out, we'll knock you out!'

Bonnie never wears dresses, not out here. Dresses are for city girls. Preening and playing at dress-ups is not for her; a female equivalent of Huck Finn, she wears shorts, or jeans rolled up to the knee and

57

a T-shirt, and her feet are bare. Her hair, tousled and knotty, hangs around her face; she hates the routine of washing it in the stagnant water that smells like old laundry. When it gets dirty, she ties it in untidy pigtails, hoping to put off a wash for another day. On the occasions they go to town, she has to scrub her face until it shines like an apple and squeeze into a frock that feels like a straightjacket.

'Can't I stay home, Mummy?' She knows what the answer will be—it is always the same—but she asks anyway.

'No, Bonnie, you cannot stay home. Now, could you hurry and get dressed, please.'

She curls her toes in the shoes, thinks how silly it is to wear white socks around this red bulldust. Oh well, Mummy knows best.

It is such a full-time job trying to keep Charles happy, Sara finds there is little time left for the children and no time at all left for herself. Worn ragged with the heat, the dust storms and Charles' continual demands, she has taught the girls at a young age that when their school work is completed, chores have to be shared. Their homestead, constructed around the old tin shed, is coming together bit by bit, worked on when the weather permits building materials to be brought in and finances allow. At least they finally have a semblance of a kitchen, but they still rely on that damn generator.

Murray-Lee has the task of vacuuming and mopping the tiled floor. Bonnie's job is to sweep a larger sandstone area. It is boring, repetitive work, but a daily necessity: in the dry season, the super-fine bulldust chokes the air, settling in a red film over the floor. In the wet, it turns to a muddy slush, slippery and dangerous under-foot. Bonnie is fed up with her job. Housework is for girls, and she would much prefer to be outdoors. She makes a snappy decision to ask Marlee if they can swap jobs for a change.

'Can we, Marlee?' It seems a fair deal, taking turns a week about, but she is not confident of her sister's response. The generator has stopped again, spluttering out a dying breath and shuddering to a halt. Charles is out at stock camp with the mechanic, and the workmen at the meatworks don't understand the machine's idiosyncrasies, so for the umpteenth time this week, there is no electricity.

This will inevitably cause trouble down at the meatworks, which have only recently been established. Cattle prices have plummeted and Bullo had been turning off cattle to other meatworks. But the cost of road freight was prohibitive, and they had to work out another plan before bankruptcy knocked on their door. Charles decided to build his own meatworks on the station, initially supplying beef to Aboriginal missions. As the operation improves, boners and packers turn out smallgoods and sausages. The meatworks has other advantages: after years without decent power or water, living on corned beef and tinned foods, and with poor communications with the outside world, a bigger generator is purchased to operate the meat chillers. Overnight, their limited power extends to fifteen hours of electricity a day, and meat deliveries to town ensure fresh supplies of milk and vegetables can be brought back to the station.

No electricity also means no water pump, and no vacuuming chores. Marlee is well content. She sidles up to Sara, whose eyes have clouded over in that hollow way the girls are familiar with whenever anything goes wrong.

'Mummy, Bonnie wants to do my job. Do I have to let her?'

Sara's hands clench. Bonnie surely knows the generator has broken down again and is trying to get out of work. 'Bon-nie!' she screams. 'Come here now!'

The tone startles Bonnie: Mummy sounds very angry, but she doesn't know why. Marlee had taken so long to answer her question, she had decided to get on with her old job.

'You lazy, manipulative, spoilt little girl!' Sara storms. 'You know the generator has broken down, there is no water and you can't use the vacuum cleaner. For the next week you can do your own jobs and Marlee's too. Get the water from the horses' trough for the floors.'

Bonnie looks at Marlee for confirmation that Mummy has made a mistake, but her sister is looking the other way. She sets her jaw, feels the pain screaming through her nerve endings again, that awful pain which always comes lately whenever there is a confrontation. But there is no point in arguing, no point in defence. Rules are rules; it is easier to just give in.

'Yes, Mummy,' she says, turning away.

CHAPTER SIX

David, Bonnie's half-brother, is visiting the station. She looks at him with a critical eye, half expecting some smartarse city slicker who spends two days in the scrub and boasts about it for a lifetime. At fifteen, David is five years older than Bonnie; tall, like their father, but still gangly with adolescence. Quieter than Charles, he has the same dry wit and tireless energy. Instinctively she knows they will be friends.

And she's glad, for she and Marlee are drifting further apart.

Bonnie is sick of her sister's dominating manner, the way she demands respect without earning it. Yesterday, down at the back paddock, Marlee asserted her authority over Bonnie and booted her up the bum when she demurred. It was a moment of truth: standing straight, Bonnie suddenly realised she was a few centimetres taller than her sister.

'That is the last time, Marlee,' she said. 'That is the last time you'll ever do that to me!'

At the age of twelve, Marlee has already discovered there are other things in the world beside horses and cattle. Short at only a hundred and fifty-three centimetres, she walks with a sensuous sway, which does not go unnoticed.

'Must she prance about like some gushing fifties sweater girl,' Charles thundered to Sara over dinner last night. 'Speak to her, Sara. Bugger me, these are wild boys out here.'

Bonnie glanced down at her plate, sensing another fight was looming. She noticed Daddy's swag down by the riverbank again today, rolled up after a tumble with one of the packing girls from the meatworks and she wondered if Mummy has noticed too.

David is saddling his horse, preparing to ride out to fix the fences on the eastern boundary line. Better to head out with him than hang around the homestead peeling spuds. There is to be another dinner party tonight, the kind that Daddy loves most; a new blonde governess has arrived at Bullo, and he will be at his charming, swashbuckling best. The colour of her hair doesn't interest him, however; the fact that she is female is good enough. The stockmen have noticed this stunner, too, but know there is little chance of getting near her while Charlie is around.

'A blonde,' one chuckles in consolation as he throws a saddle on his horse, 'is just a redhead with all the fire fucked out of her.'

David ties the wire around the posts, hitching it into a loop with studied concentration. Everything in the bush is fixed with a wire, known in the bush as Cobb and Co. It is stinking hot, and his battered Akubra offers the only shade. Bonnie is ramming in the post, joking easily with him about their rudimentary fencing.

'This place runs on Cobb and Co and Araldite,' she grins.

David stays only a few weeks at the station. On the day he leaves, Bonnie watches his plane fly low over the escarpment until it's out of sight. She wishes he didn't have to go; they have become good friends during his brief stay and she will miss his easy company. Maybe he'll come back again one day. She writes a poem which she means to send to him but, too shy, decides to keep to herself.

'The children are not receiving the education they need here, Charles,' Sara declares one day. 'I would like them to go to boarding school in Adelaide.'

Bonnie wonders how long they'll be away this time. The idea of a conservative boarding school for young ladies doesn't greatly appeal.

Fraser, who is now living at Bullo River, and Charles elect to fly the girls to Darwin to meet their domestic flight to Adelaide. They are flying over wild, heavily timbered country, and the plains are under metres of water after the Top End's worst flood in years. The Cherokee 6 bumps through the clouds, the cartons of meat on board rattling and jumping with the turbulence and the noisy engines drowning out normal conversation. This plane is geared for work, not comfort. Suddenly an eerie silence fills the aircraft; devoid of noise, she seems to glide in a vacuum.

'Bugger me!' Charles yells. 'We've lost the goddamned engine!' Calling on his flying experience from the war, he tries to restart the dead engine midair, but this is one battle he knows he will lose.

'I'm goin' to put the plane down,' he commands. 'Lean forward and brace yourselves!'

He makes a quick mayday call, but is uncertain he is heard. The HF call signal is damaged.

Marlee, protective and terrified, throws herself over Bonnie, shielding them both from certain disaster. Bonnie isn't frightened.

Daddy says he'll land this thing, and she has no reason to doubt him. A carton of meat has fallen on her, and she tries to move it as the plane makes a sickening descent toward the ground.

With seconds to spare, Charles makes a fast decision to put the plane down, undercarriage retracted, in front of a towering ant bed in a tiny clearing between two huge gum trees. The nose of the aircraft digs into the high grass and flood water. Charles leans back and surveys their position, with one foot out the door and resting on the wing. He lights a cigar.

'Ah don't like the look of this,' he tells Fraser. 'We could be stuck here for a very long time. There's little damage to the fuselage and though flight service have our position, it will be forty-five minutes before they are in VHF range. We'll save our battery until we hope they're near.'

Bonnie and Marlee head off into the scrub to make camp. This is a great adventure; slipping and sliding over the swamp, they eventually find a sheltered area and build a fire.

'Bloody great!' Bonnie splutters when it is finished. 'We haven't got any matches!'

Fraser is preparing to walk into the nearest community at Port Keats, a hundred and fifty kilometre trudge through crocodile-infested swamps. It is, he decides, their only chance of survival. He remembers another occasion, when he was six years old and visiting Bullo with his parents and his brothers, when a family picnic at a waterhole almost turned to tragedy. Hopelessly lost, a bushman on their excursion offered to head back to get help, but Charles didn't agree. He wasn't about to place his faith in someone else's hands, particularly in this country. He walked ahead of the party with a shotgun, Barbara and the kids following. They eventually found water and made it back to the station, dehydrated and exhausted, but alive.

Charles, now using the VHF radio, makes an executive decision: they will all stay put and wait for help. Bonnie retrieves some av-gas from the plane to light the fire, and five hours later a thin pencil of smoke guides the rescue helicopter to their landing site. So dense is the scrub, the chopper hovers over them for many minutes before it recognises their position.

Interviewed in Darwin after the crash, Charles tells reporters that he has an easy explanation for the near tragic accident. 'Most probably, my girls sabotaged the aircraft. They were on their way to boarding school!'

The first term flies quickly, despite the discipline and confinement which Bonnie finds claustrophobic. The dormitories are cramped and she misses her younger sister and the freedom of the country. Danielle misses her, too.

'Bonnie was always the nurturing one,' she says. 'She gave me solace when Mummy wasn't around. Both she and Marlee were my teachers, and by the time I was four I could count to ten in three different languages. Bon taught me how to swim, ride and fence. She was always there for me, and I missed her when she was away.'

The lessons are easy and Bonnie spends little time studying; Sara has been a good teacher and has demanded a high standard. Bonnie enjoys her new friends, hooting around the dormitories at the end of the school day, playing reckless games of hockey and basketball. Her best mate is an unruly Irish girl, Susan O'Grady. Both bright and energetic, they ignite each other's wilful flame, raiding plum trees after dusk and climbing on the roof of the school house. The teachers shake their heads—these bush kids are wild and hard to tame. But there is something special about this girl from

Bullo. Tough and strong, she obviously adores her father, and is determined to rise to the challenges he presents.

In her introduction to the class, Bonnie states: 'My father does not influence my life, he simply directs it. He sets the truth before you to accept or disregard, but more often than not you are forced to muster the determination to face it, to take the good and make it better, take the bad and make it good. You are positioned like a pawn on a chessboard, and one day the pawn might become a queen.'

Her teachers also notice that Bonnie has an extremely high IQ, and is sensitive, too, which is reflected in the poem she writes for an English class.

I wish I were a bird
That flies before a storm.
I wish I were a flower,
Just fresh and newly born.
Or maybe be the wind,
Invisible to all,
And blow the leaves up high,
Then watch them slowly fall.

Oh how I'd love to be the sea,
So mysterious and deep.
Never never will you know
The treasures that I keep.
But though I long so much
For these things I'd love to be,
When I really think about it
I'm quite happy being me.

She counts down to the holidays with increasing impatience; boarding school might be fun, but it's not a patch on station life.

* * *

Charles has picked his daughters up at the airport, flying the Beaver aircraft.

'You didn't write, Sara Lloyd,' he chastises. 'You could have made more of an effort. Your mother wrote to you every week.'

Bonnie looks down at her hands, decides to speak in her own defence. 'There wasn't anything interesting to write about, Daddy.'

Marlee always collected the mail first, and Bonnie is surprised to learn there was weekly news from home. The only message she ever got was a stern lecture from her older sister to write to their parents. The food parcels, sent religiously, haven't reached her either.

Charles is adamant: Bonnie will spend her time on the two-hour flight back to Bullo writing a carefully presented, dated and signed letter, one for every week of the school term. Her tears and frustration at the task fail to move him; she will do this, and finish before they land.

Sara greets them at the airstrip, looking less refined than Bonnie remembers. Her face is ruddier, browned by the sun and dust, and her clothes have a yellow tinge from being washed in stagnant water. Charles quietly hands his wife the folded letters.

'Read these, Sara,' he says. 'Sara Lloyd did not let us down after all.'

Marlee opens her mouth to protest, is frozen by a caustic look from her father. He calls to a workman to unpack the suitcases from the aircraft, sallies ahead of the women. Not then, nor ever, does he tell Sara when the letters were written.

The second term is over and Sara is reading the girls' report cards. Bonnie has hightailed it up a tree to hide. She has made little effort this term and that will surely show in her marks.

Marlee's academic achievements look bleak on the page, and Sara is in an ill temper. Best to stay clear.

'Bonnie, Bonnie … Where are you, Bon?' Sara calls.

'Bon' is her mother's affectionate name for her, and raises hopes that, perhaps, all is not lost. Even if she has failed, she can't ignore the call: the penalty for being in earshot and not answering is the strap.

Clambering down the tree with reckless speed, Bonnie comes face to face with her mother waving the report card in front of her eyes.

'You have done so well, Bon. Straight As in every subject, except sewing. We are very proud of you!'

Bonnie is amazed. She grins, digs her hands deep into the pockets of her jeans, her face lit up with pride. She has rarely before been given credit for any achievements; her talents and abilities have gone largely unnoticed.

Charles silently puts a hand on Bonnie's shoulder; surprised, she notices his eyes are wet. Tearing into the living room, she jumps the rattan lounge chairs, whooping with delight and bucking like a wild horse. She vows to repeat her success again, in whatever field she tackles. Everyone loves a winner.

Charles has overstepped the mark this time and Sara has had enough. His dalliances with other women are common knowledge, and his escapades are often the talk of the bush telegraph. While the men shrug their shoulders and accept it is part and parcel of Charlie's philandering nature, the women find it harder to accept. They question why Sara always appears to turn a blind eye to her husband's affairs, question her self-respect. Tough and resilient, bush women don't put up with this sort of nonsense. They get out.

This time Sara has found Charles in bed with the French governess, and all hell breaks loose. More intent on man-hunting than teaching the children, the governess is a wildcat with a flirtatious manner. She is seriously beautiful and a great threat to Sara. A coldness creeps into their relationship; Charles is impossible to tame and Sara has given up trying. Charles Henderson can go to buggery, but not before she talks to her lawyers. Let him run bloody Bullo on his own; she is sick of being buried in a mountain of paperwork, always the one the workers whinge to and harass. She resents the sacrifices, giving up her own emotional balance to keep Charles happy.

'Sara,' Gus Trippe says, 'not only hated Bullo, she grew to hate Charles as well.'

At the start of the girls' final term at boarding school, Sara moves to Adelaide with Danielle. In the comfort of their rented suburban house, with all its suburban amenities, Sara reflects on the madness of Bullo. The day before they left there had been yet another motor vehicle accident. Dick, who has been with them at Bullo for years, tinkers with the poor excuses for vehicles to try and keep them in working order. Fraser had found Dick in town, when he had wandered over to his truck. They had started yarning and Dick had made a proposition: if Fraser took him back to Bullo, he'd work for little money if he had board and keep. He'd proved to be a rough diamond, a loyal worker, but a demon on the grog. Sara rations the beer and rum supplies, but when potatoes or pumpkin mysteriously disappear from the kitchen, she knows it's an odds-on bet they will resurface in liquid form: a homebrew that spells death to a healthy liver.

Charles had been running around in a foul temper that day, exacerbated by a hacking dry cough that had plagued him for weeks. Dick was in town, undoubtedly on a bender, and had left

69

another mechanic in charge. This one was a good apprentice in more ways than one: up all night drinking a lethal brew, his eyes were bloodshot and raw, and his hands were shaking. Clearly there wouldn't be much work out of him today.

A workman jumped into the Toyota, stopping to tell Bonnie he was going to check a bore. She nodded okay. There was so much work to be done here, she wished she didn't have to go back to school. School was for girls.

The Toyota skidded and slipped in the dust, and the workman hit the brakes. Nothing. He pumped again, pressing down with a hard foot. Still nothing.

'Jesus bloody God!' he shrieked as the truck lurched onto its back.

Stepping gingerly out from the upturned door, he checked under the bonnet when the Toyota was finally righted. His voice reverberated around the valley.

'That filthy, mongrel bastard has drunk all the brake fluid!'

It is good to be back in civilisation, and Sara has no intention of returning to the Territory in a hurry. Bonnie hates it here in the city, hates their small backyard and the neighbours' small minds, but she knows there is no point complaining. At least Danielle is here; they share an easy rapport, something she lacks with Marlee, but not even that assuages her desperate homesickness.

Charles is despondent. The cough he couldn't shake has been diagnosed as double pneumonia and, too ill to organise his workers, the station is deteriorating. 'This place,' he grumbles to Dick, 'is goin' down the shit shoot!'

Sara is being stubborn. Charles has repeatedly asked her to come back, and he misses her and the girls' help. Although Sara hardly ever goes outdoors, she runs a tight ship indoors. At six Danielle is still too young to be of any great help on the station, and

70

Marlee vacillates between bouts of energy and laziness, but Bonnie is starting to really pitch in. Give him her help to two other workmen any day.

By now desperately ill, Charles travels to Adelaide to make one last pitch for their return. He promises Sara a surprise—an airconditioner for their bedroom—and she finally capitulates. Bonnie is totally confused. Her mother has repeated like a mantra that the girls should stay away from men, that they are manipulative and poisonous, but now she's going back to Charles. Bonnie makes a quiet decision: if she has to leave Bullo again, they will have to drag her out.

CHAPTER SEVEN

It is Bonnie's twelfth birthday and she is very excited. Until now all the presents she has received have been whacked up between the kids; nothing is ever exclusively hers for long. They share everything: clothes, toiletries and toys. They even share their knickers, which Bonnie particularly loathes. The only things that are sacred are her swag and her dogs; her sisters know better than to mess with them.

As far as Bonnie can see, the more possessions she has, the more trouble she has trying to look after them. It is easier to grab her swag and bolt. Sometimes she feels as if she spends her whole life running away from trouble and conflict; and because she doesn't make demands, her needs are ignored.

Marlee's birthday is twelve days earlier than Bonnie's and so her party is usually thrown in with her older sister's. But this birthday is different. Daddy has promised Bonnie a very special gift.

A week ago, she ran a big bullock back to the mob wielding a stockwhip she had plaited herself from greenhide. The effort earned high praise from her father.

'You're doing a very good job, Sara Lloyd,' he said. 'You're a great help to me.'

Glowing with pride, Bonnie seized the opportunity to tell him of another achievement. She has overcome her fear of horses and has broken in her horse, Titan, without any help. It has been a slow, excruciating process. Every time she felt a pang of terror, she pushed herself harder to ignore it. For the past two years she has made herself useful on a horse, staying with the coachers—the quiet cattle—and tailing along behind the mob.

She has been joining the stock camps for a few days at a time, sleeping out in swags with the Aboriginal stockmen, and helping look after the horse plant. The plant is a group of active horses used for work purposes. When one plant tires, another is used while the first is spelled. It is a job she hates. Slow and monotonous, it is away from the action and danger of working close to wild cattle. Bonnie longs to join the best men on the best horses up on the wings or scouring the outlying scrub for more feral mobs to run in. She is good enough to hold her own now, and is itching to prove herself. Working with the horse plant is also fraught with disaster. On one occasion when the plant was turned out of the yard, the horses took off in a cloud of dust and had to be found before Charles found them first. Old Rosie, the cook, jumped on a night horse to help Bonnie retrieve them. Picking up their tracks, they left the yard flat strap, the Aboriginal woman's bare breasts flapping and skirt flying. Rosie, as nervous as Bonnie of Charles' wrath, gave chase over a six-kilometre run. Drenched with mud and perspiration, they finally found the plant of horses grazing beside a billabong, and brought them back in just ahead of the men. Horse plants are a nightmare; Bonnie wants to work with the real McCoy.

Unwrapping her birthday present, Bonnie feels exceptionally proud. Daddy has brought her a rifle and is going to teach her how to use it. She has had some lessons over the years, but never a gun to call her own. She has seen Daddy sitting out on the verandah shooting buckshot at the stars while he drinks Bullo River Specials—rum and grapefruit juice. She figures if he can handle a gun when he's drunk, she can handle one when she's sober.

The care of guns and rifles, and an appreciation of their dangers, is an ingrained lesson, and one Bonnie never intends to forget. She slides a round into the breech, goes outside to practise. There's a lot to be said for wide open spaces.

Bonnie is well aware of Charles' legendary exchanges with authority figures. On one occasion Charles had taken off in *Snoopy*—a sixty horsepower machine with only three instruments, no brakes and a tail skid—from a bad clearing near a stock camp. Surrounded by trees and long grass, they have half a killer on board which is threatening to spoil. The heavy load and hot, windless conditions are a dangerous combination. The trees gently brush the aircraft wheels as they take off, and they are now in full stall, hanging only by the propeller. The plane slowly wheels left and flies square into a tall, dead tree. It butts the tree hard, then drops to the ground as if it is a helicopter. Thankfully no-one is hurt. A safety officer is sent out to Bullo to investigate the crash. This is not his first visit.

'What happened?' he asks. He resists the temptation to add 'this time', looks at the aircraft's broken fuselage, the dead tree, and back at Charles.

'I ran into that tree.'

'Why?' He is a reasonable man, who asks reasonable questions.

'Pilot error.' Bonnie shoots a look at her father, amazed that he has admitted guilt. Charles is acutely aware that this is a dreadful response, but what else can he say? People just don't go around butting trees, and this safety officer, an ex-RAAF pro, has heard all his excuses before. Reluctantly he acknowledges that this time, truth is the only recourse.

'Why did you tell that man what happened, Daddy?' Bonnie asks him later.

'Well, Sara Lloyd,' he answers, his eyes twinkling, 'if you can't baffle 'em with bullshit, baffle 'em with the truth. One way or another, you got to win.'

In the quiet time of the wet, Bonnie watches the ringers preparing their gear. It fascinates her the way these old boys hold the needle and sew the unrelenting leather so easily it seems like putty in their hands. She decides to have a go. One of the horses needs a set of rings—a running martingale which attaches to the girth and holds the reins down.

She rivets the straps, copying the way she has seen it done, working through the night with no help. Her hands are raw and blistered by the time she has finished. Standing back to appraise her work, she is sure she has got it right. The morning will tell.

'C'mon, boy,' she instructs her horse the next day. 'Have a go at this lot.'

The straps are inside out and back to front, but the concept is right.

'It doesn't look real pretty,' she tells the ringers when they come to inspect her handiwork. 'But it works.'

The more work Bonnie does lately, the more she seems to knock herself around. Somewhere between that hellish drive into Kununurra where she hovered between life and death, and Bonnie's less dramatic, almost weekly injuries, Sara has given up worrying

75

about her daughter. She can't be everywhere, all the time, and Bonnie will simply have to learn to look after herself.

New tiles are to be laid on the lounge room floor, and Bonnie is giving a hand. Barely able to lift the box, she struggles halfway across the room with it before unceremoniously admitting defeat. With a crashing thud, the box slams down on her feet, chopping off the joints between her middle and big toe. The pain is excruciating. In a contorted dance, Bonnie circles the floor before falling down.

'Not again!' Sara screams, grabbing the first-aid box and tearing into the bathroom. Her bush nursing skills are rudimentary but effective, and she sticks the toes back where they belong and wraps them in a bandage. It is an hour before last light, and her cries over the emergency radio mingle with Bonnie's screams. The ambulance staff moan.

'Here we go again. It's Sara Henderson and that bloody kid of hers. She's an accident waiting to happen.'

The homestead is taking shape. An open-plan affair that allows the cool night breeze to flow through, what walls there are are thin. Charles and Sara have their own bedroom but the latest extensions, put on while Bonnie is out in the scrub for a few days, seem to have absorbed the bedroom she had, which was really only a thorough-fare with a place to lay her head. The other girls have a bedroom, but Bonnie doesn't make a fuss about getting her own. Somehow, in the renovating plans, her needs have been overlooked.

With no dresser or wardrobe, Bonnie's clothes are piled where they fall on the floor. Designer linen is important for the guests, but the other luxuries will have to wait. Sara has gone into retreat, shut down in an isolated silence from Bonnie who no longer tries to get her attention. Increasingly independent, her daughter doesn't appear to notice the ceaseless annoyances around her. But Sara does. This place is a madhouse, a stark asylum, and she can't escape the inmates.

For a while Bonnie sleeps out on the couch, but that soon becomes too uncomfortable. The lounge room resembles a bus station, noisy and industrious, and uninterrupted sleep is impossible. She desperately needs some space. Rolling up her swag, she takes to the night with her dogs and a pannikin of tea. It is quiet out here, far from the mayhem, and no-one asks where she's been the next day. Lately she feels like a ghost at the homestead—present, but invisible. She prefers the stock camps where a man is measured by the work he does.

Lying in the blackness, she ponders the universe around her, a single star shining over the river, and the moon bright as a torch. Some nights are freezing cold, what the old stockmen call 'three-dog nights', when only a cosy swag shared with the dogs keeps the iciness from your veins. Her favourite dog, Fuzzy Bear, inches in close to her neck, sniffing the air when a lone dingo brays and when the heavy thwack of a crocodile's tail hits the muddy river's embankment far away in the distance.

Sometimes, if she's not too tired, Bonnie lights a fire, staring into its flames and writing poetry by its gentle light. She had started to write one a few days ago; unrolling it from her swag, she pencils in the last few lines.

There is something in this land I find enchanting,
Something in the winter's breeze that sends whirlwinds dancing.
And in the sun rays of the morning, that reflect from dewy grass
I find a beauty hidden there that cannot be surpassed.
And when I think of all those people in the cities far away,
Where only concrete buildings rise, to greet a newborn day,

Where the stench of petrol fumes hangs thick and heavy in the air,
I think of them, I sit and smile, without a care.
For they think that they are lucky, and dare to pity me.
I'd forgive them all their ignorance, if they'd only look and see
But they are dumb these people, and they are deaf and blind
To the beauty of this country. It isn't so hard to find.
So few will brush away the dust and find a waterhole
Or look beyond the bleaching bones to see a newborn foal.
Few are those who stand and listen to a bird's song from above
But fewer still I find are those who search their hearts for love.

Bonnie snuggles into the swag, feels a perfect peace. She has learned the lessons of swagging well: never camp under a tree near a river, the fruit bats will shit on you; never camp on a track, the snakes will bite; always roll up your swag so snakes and scorpions can't get in; and camp close to a fire, but not close enough to set the swag alight. She always carries a gun with her now she has learned how to use it. It is tough going at first; ambidextrous, Bonnie finds it hard to know which hand to use. Sara doesn't touch a gun, wouldn't know how to use one, and on many occasions, Bonnie and Marlee have had to aim straight and kill the deadly browns that slither into the homestead.

The camp fire is dying, and the night is getting colder. Bonnie looks up into the inky vastness overhead, picks out the Southern Cross—what the bushmen call 'the drover's watch'—shining like a lamppost in the sky. She thinks for a moment about the men who work the Barkly Tableland in the northeast of the Territory, where the nights are so bitter they spread hot ashes on the ground and cover them with dirt. It's a natural sleeping bag, but thank God it doesn't get quite that cold here. One of the stockmen from that region had spoken to her yesterday, telling her about a lonely bush grave he had chanced upon in the middle of nowhere. The old, simple headstone was crumbling at the edges, but the anonymous inscription was still clear.

Here lies a man who once was wild
Yet all he craved was the warmth and the nearness of a woman
And the sweet, warm kiss of a child.

She often thinks about the old bushmen; brooding men who formed friendships around the camp fire after a hard day in the saddle; men whose lives could be mapped by the lines on their faces. For them the dawn brought with it a promise of riches—an honest day's work with a good muster. Fortune and fame was for city people; the bushmen's happiness was measured by the heat of the day, the rustle of the herd and the quiet laughter of old mates.

Marlee is giving Bonnie the shits. They have been out all day at twenty-two-mile camp, and she has made a fuss about wanting to return to the homestead for the night.

'We've got to be up again at first light, Marlee,' Bonnie protests. 'What's so important that you need to go back?'

Marlee throws her little sister a filthy look. 'I want to have a shower, if that's all right with you!'

A bloody shower! What the hell does she do in there anyway, Bonnie wonders. It always takes her forever to emerge, stepping out like some queen of the outback. Bonnie shrugs, plunges her hands into the pockets of her jeans, wonders if one day she will also get an overwhelming urge to dash back from camp for a scrub, but she doubts it. She's just as happy having a wash from a jerry can of water and, if she could, she would do what the blokes do—just get down and get dirty.

Danielle notices the competition between her two sisters, whether silent or overt, increasing around this age. Marlee, dominant and forthright, likes to be in charge; Bonnie, candid and stubborn, listens to orders but ultimately makes her own decisions.

'Bon always had high and low mood swings,' Danielle remembers. 'She craved sweets, and would sit down and eat a pile of chocolate fudge at one sitting. It is very possible that she had a deficiency that made her crave such a large sugar intake. It's also possible that some of the conflict between Marlee and her was as much a result of this as it was their different personalities.'

Ross Ainsworth, the new vet, has flown out to Bullo with Gus Trippe. This man is different. Seriously handsome, with dark hair and brown eyes, he cuts a dash in the barren landscape. Witty and educated, he is a far cry from the ringer mentality the young, impressionable girls are used to. Raised on a dairy farm at Gippsland—spud and peas country—he finds Bullo a world beyond his experience. He realises immediately he turns off the Victoria Highway that he must leave the rule books behind. At twenty-six, he is about to embark on a boy's own adventure.

'You go to other places in the outback and they're dusty holes where mosquitoes bite you and the only thing people do is work,' Ross recalls. 'But not Bullo. I used to cap a hip to get out there. It was Disneyland in the outback and there was nothing else to do but indulge. From the word go, there was an ambience, an aura of excitement and danger about this place in the middle of nowhere run by this hedonistic, amoral bastard from Bible Belt old money. But you couldn't help liking him. The place was run on feudal values. Both Charles and Sara dished out favours where they wanted and treated other people with indifference bordering on contempt.

80

Charles ran the place like his kingdom and treated Sara and the girls like his serfs.

'Charles obviously didn't go much on his wife at times and was indifferent to Marlee and Danielle. You couldn't impress Charles unless you were extraordinary, but once he noticed you, it was like being blessed. He loved Bonnie. She was the inheriting daughter, the one Charles trusted. Of all his children, it was Bonnie who shone, who clearly had the most talent. There was nothing that girl couldn't do if she put her mind to it. But it was a heavy burden of responsibility for a young woman.'

The girls adore Ross. He teaches them how to castrate horses and how to take general care of the animals, and they teach him a lot too. He must pass their rites of passage, riding across swollen rivers, his horse thrashing and disappearing in the water, emerging wet and uncomfortable with prickly heat for the rest of the day. This is sport, and anyone is fair game. Before long, Bonnie realises the inevitable: Ross and Marlee are engaged in another, more horizontal form of sport.

Marlee has always had the reputation of being the looker in the family and Bonnie has never felt much need to compete before. Had she taken time to look in a mirror, however, she would have seen the beginnings of a beautiful young girl, taut and slim with an open and honest face.

To those outside the station, the Henderson girls have an air of mystique. Kept almost completely isolated from the rest of the world, apart from their 'holidays' down south, they become known as the untouchables. Charlie's daughters. His girls will change the world; the world will not change them. Despite his own womanising, Charles runs off any male above four years old who dares look sideways at 'his women', chasing the fellers out to bush camps or over to another station.

Ross, who visits Bullo regularly while working at another station, never fails to be amazed by its excesses. 'Charles purposefully cut the girls off from the outside world, and Sara was very often away. It was like living in Kenya in the 1930s; nothing was ruled out, there were no limits. It made Michael Jackson's household look normal.'

In his first week at Bullo, Ross attends one of the legendary family dinners. Charles, at the helm as ever, is discussing the option of sending Ross to neighbouring Montejinni Station, owned by Charles and Gus, to argue numbers and payment for boundary-mustered scrubbers on Victoria River Downs. Trevor Christianson is a notoriously tough and violent bushman, and the family is appalled at Charles' idea. Only Charles himself, full of booze and bravado, is in favour.

'Bonnie, get my gun!' he demands. He is obviously drunk—very rarely does he call her by her nickname.

She pretends not to hear the order, keeps swirling the food around on her plate.

'Bonnie, get my gun!' he repeats. His voice is louder now, with a more urgent tone.

Bonnie slips off her chair, goes into the storeroom and returns with the pistol. Charles walks to Ross' end of the table and slaps the gun down in front of him.

'Use this, young man,' he says, 'if that Trevor Christianson gives you any trouble!'

In the cool, sober light of day, Ross quietly returns the pistol to the storeroom. But from that time on, whenever there is a drama, the catchcry becomes, 'Bonnie, get your gun!'

Intrigued with the romance of Bullo, some tour operators think of making it part of their top end itinerary. Owners of a swanky Darwin hotel decide to go one step further: it would be wonderful

Charles in military uniform.

Charles aboard the *Lady Barbara*.

Barbara and Charles.

Barbara and the boys.

Bonnie on Gus Trippe's Beaver VH-WOG at an
aerobatics practice day.
Alan Howard

Years later, training for the 1994 world titles in the Extra 300S.

Bonnie, aged eleven, on Chablis.

Bonnie's love of horses was evident in the many sketches she made of them.

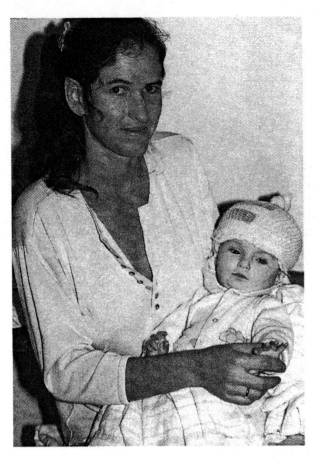

Bonnie and Georgina, who is wearing a turban after her shunt operation, recovering from meningitis and hydroencephalitis.
Charlie Barron

Georgie, aged five.
Janette 'Wills' Wilson

Georgie, Bon and Hattie.
Janette Wilson

Amelia practising her poddy riding on the bucking drum.
Janette Wilson

for their guests to spend a night in the wilderness, to really experience the outback. Bullo, they reason, would be just the ticket.

'They soon found out how wrong they were!' Ross laughs. 'They arrived to find the kitchen garbage bin overflowing with quivering fat from a fresh killer, and an hysterical woman trying to get away from Charles' advances. To her horror, the poor woman realises she is stuck until he flies her out. The homestead is infested with crawlies and Dick is marching around with his false teeth out, star gazing and high stepping, pissed as a newt on brake fluid. They soon realised that Bullo would hardly suit their spoiled, toney guests, used to five-star hotels and supreme luxury. The idea was quickly dropped!'

CHAPTER EIGHT

Bonnie wakes early, cosy in the predawn darkness. In an hour or so the moon will dip over the edge of the escarpment and a lazy sun will rise over the other side. She is going out on a muster and is itching to get there.

Her feet hit the floor and, groping in the blackness for her jeans, she tiptoes barefoot out of the room so she doesn't wake Marlee. She doesn't wear shoes, and doesn't own any boots; like the Aborigines, her soles are hardened to this country and she can move faster on bare feet.

Annie, one of a litter of nine pups she helped coax into the world four months ago, is waiting for her on the verandah. She snuggles into Bonnie's lap, keeping perfectly still as Bonnie drinks her coffee. It's good and strong, but not the heart-starter the stockmen talk about. Their coffee is liberally laced with rum.

'C'mon, girl,' Bonnie calls as she heads down to saddle her horse. From six weeks, tripping and stumbling, Annie has followed her everywhere. They are good mates and inseparable now. The pup's cattle-dog blood is starting to show, and she jumps as high as she can before Bonnie catches her and sets her in front of the saddle. Her horse, Titan, doesn't flinch; a good old boy, patient and quiet, Bonnie has raised and gentled him from a foal.

Charles is already at the stock camp, barking orders. In the glow of his pipe, Bonnie sees him eye her dog before he speaks to her.

'You can't bring that mongrel along, she'll get in the way and stir the cattle up. Take her back to the house and leave her there!'

Bonnie knows his grim temper, knows argument is pointless. Any defence that Annie is a good dog would fall on deaf ears this morning. Cantering back to the house in miserable spirits, she finds Nick, the chief butcher, messing about outside. He also has a pup from the same litter; he'll look after Annie until she gets home.

'I'm going out with the cattle, Nick,' she tells him. 'Could you keep an eye on my dog for me?'

Something in his look stops Bonnie in her tracks. Nick is always cheerful, going about his business whistling old drinking songs. But not today.

'Take your dog somewhere else, Bon; I haven't got time for this,' he says gruffly. He doesn't look at her as he speaks, turns back to busy himself tidying a workbench.

God, Bonnie thinks, what the hell is wrong with everyone this morning? She remains on her horse, hot tears now scalding her cheeks. 'Please, Nick. Daddy said I have to bring her back. I can't take her out on the muster with me.'

Nick looks up at Bonnie, sitting astride her horse and holding the pup at arm's length toward him. He pauses for a moment, eying her carefully. Then he shrugs. Orders are orders. He has known Bonnie for two years now, seen her toughen as she moves toward adolescence. But she really loves this dog—she must be tougher than he thought.

'Okay Bon, give her here,' Nick replies grimly. 'Now get goin'. You'll be late.'

Bonnie gallops back through the scrub to where the line of men are working through the trees, pushing the cattle ahead of them toward the far corner of the paddock. The line is only four kilometres away but a good two hours ride, constantly doubling back to pick up any escapees who have broken out on the plains. The cattle trot down the fence line and are boxed up in the corner. The dust rises above the herd as they wheel and mill. Five men and horses spend a tense thirty minutes as they block and hold them; finally, they start them on the slow walk back with some semblance of control and order.

The two best riders in the lead wings are always at the ready to block a troublemaker if it tries to make a break and take the mob with it. Titan is moving up the line to the lead wing. He tenses, easing up the side with a quickening in his step. His attention is on the herd as he watches and waits. There is a partnership, a bond between horse and rider; both take pride riding in the lead, a position they have worked hard for.

A golden glow settles over the plains in the dying light of late afternoon. On the long, slow walk back to the homestead, Bonnie chats easily with the stockmen but misses the company of her little dog. She ties up her horse and runs to find Annie.

'Annie, Annie, come here, girl,' she calls. She spots her pup's empty collar near the fence where Nick is leaning smoking a rollie.

'G'day, Nick. Where's Annie?'

He shoots her a quizzical look, turns to flick his smoke into the paddock with his thumb and middle finger. 'The dog got away, Bon,' he says quietly. 'I dunno where she is.'

Bonnie stares at him in disbelief, tears into the house to find Sara. 'Mummy, I can't find Annie. She's got off the lead. Can you help me find her?'

Sara turns away, her shoulders moving up and down, racked with sobs.

'Mummy, what's wrong? Tell me! Where's Annie? Where are the other pups?'

'Go ask your father,' Sara says. Her face is blotchy and red, her eyes empty. Her daughter's pain is unbearable and she can do nothing to help.

Bonnie feels a kick in her guts, deep in the pit of her stomach. With a blinding flash, she realises what has happened.

Charles is on the verandah reading *Newsweek*, with his feet up on another chair.

One of the stockmen, a blundering redhead with a dense, ignorant manner, asked him earlier why he bothered to read it at all.

'It's a month out of date by the time it gets out 'ere,' he sniggered. 'Seems like a waste of time to me.'

Charles levelled the stockman with a contemptuous glare before he humoured him with a reply. The question was as inane and stupid as the man himself. 'Because, young man,' he sneered, 'I like reading history.'

Now Charles glances up as Bonnie storms through the door, surprised by her vehemence.

'How could you?' she screams. 'You killed my dog!' Her jaw is set hard now, teeth grinding in fury. 'Why, Daddy, why? She was my friend!'

Bonnie's defiance startles him more than her anger. Hell, he didn't know she was so close to the bloody mutt. He shifts sideways in his chair, wishes she wouldn't cry. He hates it when women cry.

'Jesus, Bon, I didn't know she was your dog,' he says. 'Why

87

didn't you tell me this morning you wanted to keep her? I gave orders to Nick to shoot all the pups. You know they've been running around together, killing the piglets and hanging around the meatworks. I really didn't know you loved her.'

The earth is hard and unrelenting and it has taken hours to dig through with a spade. Bonnie's head is aching again, a roaring pain that she can't ignore. Nursing Annie gently for a moment, she lowers the pup into the rough grave. The earth splatters on her bloody fur.

'See you later, old girl,' Bonnie whispers.

The poddy calf is playful, with no fear of people. Bonnie wanders up to her, notices her horns are half grown, but strong. Catching Bonnie on the hop, the calf lowers her head and butts into the girl's ribs. The sudden assault takes Bonnie by surprise; turning for an instant, she clutches her hands to her wound and tries to back away. The calf will not be placated, lines her up for another hit, ramming her again in the buttocks. This one knocks her down, but the ground is a dangerous place to stay.

'You bloody thing!' Bonnie yells, struggling to get up and fight her off. It doesn't work; sensing victory, the calf keeps at her, pummelling with her feet and horns.

Les Wright, one of the station managers, hears the commotion and rushes out to find out who's in strife. He's not surprised to find it's Bonnie: this girl is always injuring herself, but by God she's got balls.

'Get off her, you bastard!' he screams, raising a horse rasp to shoulder height and swinging it wildly at the poddy's nose. The calf buckles, beats retreat as Les picks Bonnie up and carries her back toward the homestead. Sara, too, has heard the noise and rushed outside.

'Bonnie's hurt, Sara,' Les says. 'She's bruised and bleeding, but I don't think she's broken anything.'

Sara takes Bonnie in her arms, relieved to hear she is all right, but exasperated too. Why the hell can't she stay away from danger? Why is she always so reckless? Her impatience stems from another reason too. Sara is sickened at the sight of blood, and after automatic damage control, she invariably faints.

'You really should learn to be more careful,' she says, tending to the blood now seeping through her daughter's shirt. 'Why do you have to try and do a man's job? You need a lot of loving.'

Bonnie looks at her mother, surprised at her last comment. 'I don't need a lot of loving, Mummy,' she replies. 'I just need to learn how to swing a horse rasp like that.'

Bonnie is helping Dick in the workshop, watching as he drops bits of steel onto the master panel—a portable yard panel set up as a jig—and taps them into place with his toe. It looks easy enough, and they will never get finished if she just stands there looking. On the next panel Bonnie follows what he does, dropping the steel into place and whacking it with her foot.

'Jesus, that hurt!' she cries out, hopping around on one foot and clutching her injured toe. Dick looks down at her feet, then up again at her face. 'Steel caps,' he says, casually.

'What?'

'Steel caps, Bon. You can't do a man's job in sandshoes.'

The rain is pelting down, sheets of water that are hungrily devoured by the parched earth. The last vehicle has left Bullo, clattering over the rough track, its exhaust smoke belching as it races to cross the rapidly rising river. The station again has that eerie silence, so quiet it is almost mournful. Now virtually cut off from the outside world for the duration of the wet season, the only means of getting out is by aircraft.

Bonnie, Danielle and Sara are the only ones left at Bullo this year. Bonnie plans to spend the season fencing, driving the old Toyota out to remote corners and coming into the homestead only when she needs to. She tells Sara of her plans.

'Mum, I'll be out at number two bore for a couple of days. If I'm not back in by day three, could you come out and check everything's okay?'

Sara looks flabbergasted at the suggestion. She has been at Bullo River for nearly fifteen years, but has rarely ventured past the safety of the homestead. Whilst she now accepts this remote wilderness is her home, she has never grown completely comfortable with it. She prefers to leave the harsh vagaries of the bush, with all its terrors, to those who understand it. 'I wouldn't have a clue where bore two is,' she counters, 'let alone try to find you out there.'

Bonnie does a quick mental check. If something goes wrong out in the scrub, she will need someone to find her. Better to lose a day now than face the possibly disastrous consequences later. She pulls up a chair at the kitchen table, draws a rough map on a scrap of paper.

'Number two bore is straight across the river, about four miles from the homestead. Go upstream to the eight-mile crossing and then back down the other side. It's a really rough track, a two and a half hour drive from the homestead.' She looks at her mother for confirmation that she understands, but gets a sheepish smile in return.

'Bonnie, you've completely lost me. Can we start at the beginning?'

'God, Mummy, you're hopeless!' Bonnie laughs, redrawing the

map and pointing exaggerated arrows in the appropriate direction. 'You must have been out to this country at least *once*.'

But Sara only shakes her head. 'Afraid not,' she says. 'No. Can't say I have.'

'But what would you have done,' Bonnie asks incredulously, 'if there was no-one else here and you had to go and search for someone on your own?'

'Oh, that's never happened. There's always been someone here.'

Sara and Bonnie look at each other for a moment, then explode in a fit of uncontrollable laughter.

'Well, you'd better listen and learn then,' Bonnie says, finally catching her breath. 'This is wild country and if you don't know where to go, the chances are you'll end up lost while you're looking for the person who's lost. Worse,' she adds mischievously, 'you could be bitten by a snake!'

They spend the day poring over Bonnie's maps: where the Bullo meets the Victoria River, the bore sites, places to avoid in the wet season, paddocks and fence areas that are yet to be completed. With no interference from anyone else, the day passes quickly and easily. For the first time in years they are comfortable and happy in each other's company.

'Well, that's the theory lesson over,' Bonnie says when the rough maps are put away for tea. 'Tomorrow we'll do the practical stuff.'

Sara opens her mouth to protest. 'Oh, don't make me go out there, Bon,' she says. 'I can read your map.'

'Mummy, you'll love this country if you stop being so frightened of it. Honestly, it's magical. Come with me. Please?'

Just after first light the next morning, they pile into the Toyota to go bush, arriving back at the homestead on sunset. Under Bonnie's tutelage, Sara learns how to tie wire on a fence, how to drive the old Toyota. She teaches her the importance of checking fences, tells her why the station needs more cattle. Sara is easy to make enthusiastic, and what follow are happy weeks together. But it isn't to last. When Marlee returns, Sara retreats back to the homestead and the old resentments loom again.

Something is wrong with Titan. Normally gentle and placid, he is restless and agitated today, stumbling along the airstrip with graceless movements. Feed is in short supply at the end of the dry season and any spare cash is being spent on cement and building materials for the homestead before the monsoon comes in.

Bonnie goes over to Titan, rubs his sweaty flanks as she talks to him. 'What's up, old fella? Are you crook?'

Bonnie has raised Titan from a foal, but today he shows no recognition of her, lurching past, desolate and driven by an inner pain. His head is hanging down to the ground; his gait is clumsy, awkward. Bonnie notices his stomach is tucked up tight, his eyes large and glassy, his tail still.

He has the stench of dying.

She rushes back to the homestead for help, shouting as she runs: 'Titan has Kimberley Walkabout disease. Help me! I can't let him die.'

The native poisonous weed, rattlepod, grows wild around the river country. Cattle are immune to its toxic ravages but it is death to horses. Titan, desperate for feed, has eaten it ravenously before staggering back to find water. The poison works fast but not fast enough for the animals: within an agonising twenty-four hours, they die by lurching into a fence or drowning in a waterhole.

Bonnie returns to the airstrip. Titan is crippled with pain, and nothing can help him now. At twelve, she is too short to reach his ears without standing on tiptoe; he towers over her small frame. She buries her head in his neck, talking to him through her tears.

'Sorry, old fella. I'm really sorry.'

She stands tall on her toes, raises the rifle to his ears. Closing her eyes, she turns her head away and fires.

The hole for his grave is big enough now. Sara and Bonnie have dug it laboriously, working wordlessly through the heat of the day. Bonnie feels a bitterness gnawing at her; her teeth grind, her gums are flamed red and sore. She wants to scream at her mother; there is an obscenity in this. Titan didn't need to die, he should have been given decent feed. Her eyes are flint, she swallows hard. This is typical of the way things happen out here.

Sara returns, heartbroken, to the homestead. Bonnie places a handmade cross on the raised earth, sits on top of the grave, and weeps.

CHAPTER NINE

Bonnie is feeling out of sorts, with a strange, cramping pain at the base of her stomach. Tearful, too, which annoys her. She sometimes cries over sad poetry or when an animal is injured, but never for no reason, as she seems to be doing the past few days. Crying is a sign of weakness.

She feels uncomfortable, sticky, moves into the bathroom to find out why. She had better not be getting sick. Mummy is down south, this time for an operation; it seems to Bonnie that she's never around when she needs her. Marlee is looking after the homestead, her attitude cocky, and Daddy still hasn't fully recovered from pneumonia. There's a big muster coming up and Bonnie needs to be on deck.

She stares at her underwear, now a deep shade of scarlet seeping through onto her jeans. Alarmed, she searches for a reason. There's no point asking her sister—she doesn't give her the time of day any more—and she doesn't know who else she can ask. Puzzled and frightened, Bonnie throws the offending pants into the washing machine and wonders what to do next.

Julie, the latest secretary hand-picked by Charles, comes into the bathroom. Bonnie usually has to advertise for the staff and narrow the field from the mailed replies. Charles accepts her choice of male workers, trusting her judgement, but the women are different. They have to front to Bullo for a personal interview with Charles, and his reasoning sounds fair. 'Ah have to be sure they can tough out the isolation,' he says.

This one, a leggy brunette boasting extremely limited skills, obviously passed muster. Bonnie tried to persuade her father that the older woman who applied for the position was far more experienced and had spent time in the bush, but her arguments fell on deaf ears. Charles has made his choice, and that is that. Over a rum at the stock camp he tells the boys why he dismissed the matron.

'Ah told her,' he guffaws, never one to shy away from being offensive, 'I do thank you for comin' out here, ma'am, but the position has been filled,' he guffaws. 'She looked like a bush pig and ah wouldn't have known whether to screw her or shoot her!'

Julie prepares to throw some laundry in the machine, spies the soiled underwear.

'Jesus Christ, Bonnie!' she splutters. 'You can't just leave those in there like that! Take the bloody things out and wash them by hand. Anyone could have found them sitting in there!'

She storms out, her disgust hanging in the air. A few moments later she reappears with a softened expression. 'Bonnie, do you know what to do? Have you had a period before?'

Bonnie is crying hard now, humiliated that, even at fourteen, she doesn't know what's happening to her. Why hasn't anyone told her?

'No, I haven't,' she replies, keeping her head down so Julie won't see her tears.

Handed a packet of tampons, Bonnie is given brief instructions about what to do with them and how to wash her underwear. She sits on the bathroom tiles, looks at the strange wad of cotton in its clear wrapping, and wishes the floor would open up and swallow her.

When she arrives back at the station, Sara hears about Bonnie crossing the threshold into womanhood, and asks her if there is anything she needs to know. Bonnie shrugs, remains silent. It's a bit late now for answers; the horse, as they say in the camp, has already bolted.

'And you have to wash your bra sometimes too, Bonnie,' Sara adds. 'You can't wear it all the time.'

Still flat-chested, Bonnie feels no need to wear that uncomfortable harness Mummy bought her on their last trip to town. She thinks it's a ludicrous contraption, all straps and padding, and as soon as she got it she threw it on the floor next to her dirty jeans, wondering why girls bother with such unnecessary items of clothing.

Bonnie looks at her mother, wonders what the hell she is talking about.

'I haven't worn that bra at all yet,' she replies flatly.

The sudden somersault into womanhood confuses Bonnie. Until now men were her mates, people to knock around with on horses and with cattle, to talk to around a camp fire, but no more than that. No-one has ever discussed sex with her, and she can't ask her mother. She senses the subject is somehow taboo, but she remembers Sara telling her that children make you fat and ruin your life. From an early age, Bonnie has known she was an unplanned child. 'You were an accident of contraception,' Sara tells her. 'So were the other girls.'

Bonnie has often watched the mares foal, noticed the way they nurture and protect their young from the moment they are born, and she is determined that as soon as she can she will have her own baby to love. Contraception is not explained to her, nor the joys of making love with someone special. This is a man's world out here, and the girls will undoubtedly find out all they need to know soon enough. In comparison to Marlee, whom men find extremely attractive, Bonnie feels like an ugly duckling. To hide her growing need to be loved, she works even harder.

Sara's old dog, Hottentot, is dying. The Rhodesian ridgeback has been part of the family since Bonnie was a child, but now he can do little more than lie in the middle of the floor, his energy depleted. A new Alsatian has taken over his number one spot, and the old dog is confused and hurt.

'You will have to put Hottentot down,' Bonnie tells Sara. 'It's cruel to have him lying around like this. You must do something about it!'

Emotional and sensitive, Sara takes the easiest option, and does nothing.

'If you won't do it, Mummy, I will. This time, you have to think of the dog and not yourself.'

'I don't know how you can be so hard, Bonnie!'

'I'm not hard, Mummy. I have to be cruel to be kind.'

Bonnie loathes her mother's indecisiveness, her unwillingness to put the dog out of his misery. She carries him out to the flat, well away from the homestead, wishes someone else had taken this responsibility from her. She cries as Hottentot looks up with his big, brown eyes and she pulls the trigger.

* * *

Charles and Sara are pitched in another loud battle, screaming blue murder. Bonnie puts her hands over her ears to stop the noise, but she can't block out the vicious accusations that are being hurled. God, she's sick of this. She wishes her parents would come to some agreement about their marriage and be done with it. Charles storms out and locks the door of his room, and an uneasy silence enters the house.

Suddenly a pistol blast pierces the stillness, and Bonnie's heart leaps. 'Oh, God! she cries out. 'That shot came from Daddy's room!' She races up to the door, bangs loudly for him to open it.

'Please, Daddy, please, open the door!' Her sobs are short and sharp, and she can hear no movement inside the room. Running to the end of the wall, she squeezes through the gap between the post and flyscreen, sees her father sitting in a chair with his back to her. He is pointing the pistol out through the wire screen where he has fired the shot.

Bonnie's relief at finding he is alive is instantly replaced with a cold fury. She snatches the pistol from him, slams it down on the table and empties the cartridges onto the floor. She stands over him, barely able to refrain from grabbing him by the shoulders and shaking the living daylights out of him.

'How dare you!' she shrieks. 'How dare you frighten the shit out of all of us like that! Why would you want to do something like that? Why do we always have to bear the brunt of your fights with Mummy?' She tears out of the room, collides with Sara at the door. Her tears are rolling freely now, and she is shaking with shock.

'Daddy's fine,' she spits out in disgust. 'But I'm not!'

She slams the door behind her as she heads outside. She returns to the homestead hours later, and the ugly incident is never mentioned again.

After fights like these, Sara's threat to leave Bullo looms over the household for days. The final departure, euphemistically called a holiday, usually follows yet another screaming match and a lengthy, dark silence.

'The girls and I are going to Sydney for a holiday,' Sara quietly tells Charles, standing at the door with an aggrieved air and suitcases in hand. 'I don't know how long we'll be away.'

Their 'holidays' always follow the same course: a manic shopping spree, Charles sending more money, and Sara sulking until he begs her to return. This time, however, Bonnie and her mother have a hell of a row over their leaving. Tired of being dragged away, Bonnie's request to stay at Bullo falls on deaf ears.

'If you hate Daddy so much, why don't you leave permanently?' Bonnie screams.

Furious at being questioned by a teenager, Sara doesn't speak to her daughter for days. The tension is noticeable, hanging over the homestead like a shroud, and this time, even Charles deigns to comment.

'You know your mother has never loved you, Sara Lloyd,' he says.

Shocked and deeply hurt by her father's dismissive comment, Bonnie hopes he is being manipulative, playing sides. But doubt niggles at her.

The city confuses Bonnie with its noise and crowds. The parties are fun but she suffers cabin fever, misses the country and the vast expanse of sky uncluttered by tall buildings. She takes her frustration out in poetry, which finds no audience. When it's finally time to go back, she hastily throws her clothes into a case and waits impatiently for the taxi to arrive.

Bonnie's young horse, Bushlaw, tired and sluggish after a full day's muster, is too slow to move from the path of a raging bullock. The bullock's horns have run up the inside of his back leg, tearing the muscle, and his leg is awash with blood. They are too far from the homestead to go back; Bonnie has no choice but to stay with him in the scrub for the night.

A stockman gets word back to the homestead that Bushlaw is badly injured and that Bonnie is alone with him.

An hour later, Sara arrives with Ross Ainsworth who has flown out from Montejinni to help. He sews up the wound, but offers little hope that Bushlaw will pull through.

A full moon, golden and intense, hangs above them as Bonnie tries to stem the bleeding with her shirt. It is impossible; the river of red at her feet is testament to Bushlaw's terrible pain, and he is starting to waver.

'Please, don't lie down,' Bonnie pleads with him, holding one hand on the shirt covering his gaping wound and the other around his neck. 'I'll stay with you.'

'I think you're going to lose him tonight, Bon,' he says. 'The bullock has almost gutted him and he is losing too much blood.'

The sky is growing darker, and so is the light in Bushlaw's eyes. Bonnie, her mother by her side, looks up briefly as a shadow falls over the earth from the lunar eclipse overhead, feels her horse buckle at the knees and seek refuge from his pain on the warm ground. He whinnies softly as the shadows lengthen and the earth is plunged into blackness.

Bonnie picks up her shotgun, cries as its mournful blast reverberates around the scrub. Through the long, lonely night that follows, she commits her feelings to paper in a poem she names 'Eclipse'.

He stood there, dejected, without a sound,
His head drooped over to touch the ground,

And the only movement, that hot dread day,
Was his life's red blood just slipping away.

Relentless, steady with every drip
I felt my heart inside me rip;
The sweat had caked on white and dry
And every sign said he would die.

By his look of resignation I knew he was beat
I knew by the pool of blood at his feet
By the hawks that circled around his tree
By the feeling of doom hanging over me;

And that night as a full moon rose in the sky
I stood, gripped in terror, and watched it die
Watched it turn from gold to black, and many tears I shed
For when I turned around, my beloved horse was dead.

The station is shutting down for the wet again. The stock camp has gone to town, a weary band of men thirsty for a cold beer and a hot woman. A three-year-old mare stands in the paddock, unbroken, and Bonnie looks at her, weighing up the options. She has seen John Nicholson break in some wild ones no-one thought he could tame, but the only horse she has ever broken was her beloved Titan. Still small, she is looking for a challenge now the station is quiet. It's got to be worth a try.

She runs the mare into the round yard. So far, so good. The rope is tangled, keeps twisting in the loop; it's no stiff greenhide rope like they had in the old days, just a limp nylon that won't swing and catches on Bonnie's hat. The mare has wised up, darting around the yard and kicking dust. Bonnie tries for an hour, swinging the impotent rope, but it's an impossible task. She opens the bush gate and walks home through the creek, trailing the rope behind.

'Break a horse?' she mutters angrily to herself. 'You can't even catch the bloody thing!' She sits outside after dinner and contemplates the problem. What she needs is practice tossing that rope.

Three days later her hands are blistered and swollen from endless hours spent standing in the paddock throwing the rope at a post. At first it hung limp in the air, challenging her to do better. By day two there was a stiffening of the nylon but still no control where it landed. But she'd beat this bastard yet. Today, day three, the air is cloying, thick as a blanket, wet with the promise of rain. She stops to swig from a water bottle, goes back to the task. At last the rope hits the post. Her Akubra sails triumphantly through the air, caught in her bloodied hands.

'You bloody ripper!' she yells. 'I've done it!'

Heading back into the round yard, the mare looks at her before turning to walk in widening circles. Bonnie closes in, quietly drops the rope over the mare's head. The horse arcs with temper, nostrils flaring, sends dust spewing. Bonnie wipes the grit from her eyes, stays with her, walks round and round the yard. It is now day five and time to tackle the big one.

Shaking with fear, still unsure that this mare will trust her, Bonnie puts a foot in the iron, holds it for a moment and swings on for the first ride. The horse bucks furiously and skitters across the yard, then stops sharply, looking wild-eyed back at this girl who wants to break her spirit. Stubborn now; she will not move.

'C'mon, girl,' Bonnie urges. 'We can do this!'

The land is desolate; there's no-one around to help if the mare decides to throw her. A quiet rumbling starts over the escarpment— thunder before the big rains. If this mare doesn't move soon, they'll be riding in a downpour.

The horse looks back again, slowly starts to move. Bonnie works her up and down the fence for a while, stopping, turning, sometimes cantering. It's time to take her out of the yard.

Dick is watching from the Toyota, his last day before he heads to town. Bonnie has told no-one what she is doing, and he could swear that mare hasn't been broken in. They canter, then gallop, over the flat, and he gives a quiet chuckle. She's a spirited one, this one. Marlee always wears gloves to protect her hands and long shirt sleeves, but not Bonnie; she cuts her sleeves off so she can feel the warm horse flesh.

She returns at dusk, hands oozing from rope burn.

'It's your own fault,' Sara says, dismissive of her wounds. 'You should leave that work to the men.'

Dick, emaciated after years on the grog, is sitting in the corner of the kitchen, rattling with the aftereffects of the 'bush champagne' he has drunk the night before. Straining the crystals from the methylated spirits down a hot poker iron and then through cheesecloth, he mixes the deadly brew with sal vital.

It tastes like shit, but it's better than the DTs.

'Come here, love,' Dick says to Bonnie. 'Give us a look at your hands.' They are scorched sore, open and bleeding. 'Vinegar, Bon, put some vinegar on them.'

'Will that stop them hurting, Uncle Dick?'

'No, nothin' will do that. But it'll make 'em tough.'

Bullo during the dry is a complete contrast to the peace and solitude of the wet. In the dry season the place is always buzzing, and Saturday night is the biggest event of the week. It's the time when all the workers get together at the homestead over a few drinks and watch a sixteen-millimetre movie. A new pilot, suave,

103

tall and good-looking, is the flavour of the month, particularly amongst the girls at the meatworks who vie for his attention. They live in the quarters a kilometre from the homestead and are only too glad to accept the pilot's offer to walk them back when the movie is finished. With an affected swagger, he moves ahead of them, protecting them from the dark. Recent rains have flooded the creek they need to cross to get home, and their hero will stay in the middle of the group to ensure their safety.

Slim, one of the meatworkers, is suss about this pilot, figures he is too good to be true. He sprints ahead of the group and hides in the creek's long grass.

When the pilot is halfway across the swollen, fast-running creek, Slim, hiding in the dark shallows, imitates the unmistakable growl of a crocodile, closely followed by a thwack of his hand on the water. All pretence at heroics are lost as the pilot flails his arms wildly and knocks the girls out of his way as he tries to beat a rapid retreat. The girls go arse up in the creek. Phil, an apprentice electrician, bringing up the rear and generally forgotten in the shadow of the new pilot, rushes in to save the girls. As he does so, he hurls his can in the direction of the noise and collects Slim on the head. The joke is on the new pilot, and Phil's the new station hero.

Bonnie hears the story the next day and feels pleased for Phil, who had quietly accepted his lack of popularity, but had finished up in front at the end of the day.

At first light the pilot flies out of the station, and there is confusion at his sudden departure.

'He seemed like a decent person,' Sara says, shaking her head. 'I wonder what happened to him?'

Another dinner party is in full swing, and Charles is directing traffic.

'You sit here next to me, Gill,' he commands the new riding instructress who arrived at the station a few months before. 'Sara, sit the boys down the other end of the table.'

Charles has been drinking heavily this evening, his conversation littered with sparkling anecdotes and warmed by the candles' glow. Like moths, the guests dance around his flame.

'You'll all have to excuse mah appearance,' he says, drawing attention to a cut just above his lip. 'Ah've been fightin' with the baddest man in the district.'

That part is true: weeks before, Charles flew into Trevor Christianson's bush camp to sort out another dispute over the transgression of the muster boundary between Montejinni and Victoria River Downs. In one fell swoop, Trevor, a Golden Gloves fighter, downed Charles and his sidekick. Given half a chance, he would have pulverised the Yank. The cut would already have healed had Charles not deliberately nicked it while shaving. Now he wears the wound like a trophy to the dinner table, embellishing the story with every new audience.

'Come on, Sara Lloyd,' he says. 'Recite us some Banjo Paterson.' He relights his pipe, leans back in his chair and waits for his daughter to take centre stage.

She is coming along fine, this one: strong, resilient, with a will to work and an unflappable calmness that belies her determination. The spirit of this country is in her. Blessed are the strong, decides Charles, for they shall inherit Bullo. She's attractive, too, though she doesn't know it. Her lips are full and her curly, light-brown hair compliments her green eyes. And she has a boyish lack of inhibition: no prissy manners for her. At fifteen she has accepted his leadership baton and looks as though she will run with it.

Bonnie takes a mock theatrical bow, starts speaking in the curious half-American, half-Australian accent which is her trademark.

"'I had written him a letter which I had, for want of better knowledge, sent to where I met him down the Lachlan years ago; he was shearing when I knew him, so I sent the letter to him, just 'on speck' addressed as follows: 'Clancy, of the Overflow' ...'"

She loves reciting poetry, knows thirty of the best bush poems by heart, but lately they are becoming increasingly hard to mouth. Her jaw feels tight; even getting a fork into her mouth is painful, and those lacerating headaches are getting worse. Not even Disprin, which she hides inside the rim of her Akubra and chews on all day, takes the edge off the pain.

Charles looks around the room, notes the fellas at the end of the table are concentrating on more than just Bonnie's poetry. One has his eyes glued to her blouse, now revealing the hint of small breasts. Abruptly standing up, he calls a halt to the entertainment.

'Time to call stumps,' he roars. 'We've all got a big day tomorrow.'

Unceremoniously shepherded out, the fellas never understand why they had to leave so quickly. The party was only just beginning.

Gill has become good mates with Bonnie. She recognises her bush charms, knows there is more to this girl than meets the eye. Like her young student, Gill is a woman of few words, with a gentle smile and unerring capacity to be surrounded by bedlam yet rise above it.

'That woman seems to float in her own capsule,' one of the stockmen remarks. 'I wouldn't mind floatin' with her!'

Bonnie and Gill spend hours riding together in the scrub, stopping at billabongs to rest their horses and sharing quiet yarns about their life in the bush. Bonnie thinks the world of Gill, appreciates having another woman to talk to. Out here, friendship is hard won.

106

Today Charles is in the Beaver, warming the engine and waiting to take off. Bonnie has taken the meat invoice book back inside to Sara, and he waits impatiently for them to total it so he can be on his way.

'Be careful, Bonnie,' Sara says when they've finished. It's the same advice she gives every time her daughter goes near an aircraft, and especially with her father. God knows, they're a feisty team together.

Charles revs the engines, his head down, scanning the instrument panel and worrying already about the return flight. If they don't get moving, they will run out of daylight. Landing in the dark doesn't bother him, but it annoys the hell out of traffic control.

Gill has offered to run the invoice book out to Charles. The dull, monotonous beat of the radial motor fills the air. She bows her head, deep in thought, heads straight toward the aircraft. Bonnie has started to follow her. Suddenly she looks head up, opens her mouth to holler and watches in slow, slow motion as Gill's arm goes up, like a windscreen wiper, to stop the force of the propeller as it hacks through her neck and shoulder.

A blood-curdling scream dies midair, quivering, hovering around the valley, followed by a dull thud. Bonnie darts forward, stops in her tracks and sees Gill's head, completely severed, lying five feet from her body, the ground around her drenched in blood. Bile rises in Bonnie's throat and she chokes on her sobs as she stumbles backwards.

'Oh my God, she's dead, she's dead!'

Charles jumps out of the aircraft, hustles her away from the scene. Crumpled into his shoulders, she repeats, over and over, 'Why, Daddy, why did it happen?'

The propeller comes slowly to a halt, blood dripping from its blades. Overhead a single hawk, like death's kite, slowly wheels and

107

circles as the mournful cry of the crows echoes around the valley.

Sara is rooted to the spot, too terrified to move. She cowers, hiding from the hideous truth, imagining it is Bonnie out there. Overwhelmed to find it is not, she sinks to the floor when her daughter stumbles back into the room. But there is an anguished distance between them, and they cannot seek shelter in their shared grief.

Charles moves across to Gill and stands above her broken body with his fists clenched and jaw locked to one side as he farewells her with his tears.

The local policeman from Timber Creek, at Bullo for a routine visit, also witnesses the tragic accident. As a consequence, no inquest into Gill's death is necessary. Of all the tragedies at Bullo, it is this death which most shakes the family and which triggers many into believing that for all its wild beauty, Bullo is accursed.

Gill is buried under a bottle tree on the edge of the airstrip. A simple headstone marks her grave site.

CHAPTER TEN

The Aborigines call it piccaninny dawn—that time of day just before daylight when the sky is at its darkest, and the stars start to fade. In the east the sun lazily rises and the earth is wet with dew formed during the night. It is Bonnie's favourite time, peaceful and still.

All is quiet, not even a fish ripples the glass smooth pool.
This moment before dawn, nothing moves;
then slowly comes a change.
Hear the soft whisper of the passing wind so sharp and cool.
The rising sun, the light of life, floods the mountain range.
Spears of light attack the dark, the moon slinks in defeat.
Webs seem spun of silver thread where dew had touched
each strand,
And grey mist swirls in wispy wreaths about the ghost-gums' feet.
'Tis a beautiful thing to behold, the morning that comes to this land.

She opens one eye, feels her muscles are stiff and sore. Yawning, she throws back the swag and gets to her feet. There's no point lying here thinking about it, there's a lot of work ahead of her still.

For three days, she has been out fencing on her own, working so hard through the midday heat that her muscles cramp and perspiration pours from her. It's a job she hates, but it has to be done. The fences out here are in a state of such bad disrepair that the cattle trample over them, breaking out into the wild country. They urgently need to be fixed.

Working with a crowbar and shovel, digging through ground hard as rock, Bonnie knows she has found hell. It's the build-up, but at least when the rains start, the earth will become softer. In the middle of the wet, she will have to be extremely careful about getting back across the river. Last season, she was stuck for two days; only two miles from the homestead, it was a five-hour, four-wheel-drive-only journey back.

She hammers the pickets in, eight metres apart, adding five strands of high-tensile barbed wire and two droppers between each picket. Dehydration is a constant problem; the water in the jerry can is hot and there is no billabong nearby where she can cool off.

Danielle comes out with her when she can, but mostly she has only her dogs for company. They are good friends and also prove adept at killing the scorpions and redback spiders which crawl around the camp. Like everyone else at Bullo, Bonnie doesn't carry a first aid kit, so she is grateful for the dogs' bush skills.

The solitude suits her, and she is glad to be away from the constant noise at the homestead. The dogs are good hunters and supplement her dried food diet with a catch of goanna or wallaby. While she fences, the tucker slowly cooks in a fire with hot coals shovelled over it; after sundown, she eats the meal, washed down with a pannikin of tea.

Some days, when the heat is torturous, she drives back down to the river for a wash. Extremely wary of the crocodiles, she fills a bucket with water, dousing herself and her clothes with reckless abandon. When she runs out of food or energy, she rolls up the swag and heads back to the homestead.

Bonnie climbs into the Toyota Landcruiser; a tribute to Dick's engineering skills, this old girl is regularly given 'from the ground up' treatment. The chassis has an odd twist, easily remedied by strapping a forty-four-gallon drum on one side. When she fails to sit level on the ground, Bonnie knows the drum is almost empty. This is handy knowledge, as the fuel gauge doesn't work. Bush practice dictates that only a fool goes into the scrub without a full drum of petrol on the back.

Good head stockmen are hard to find, and the wages paid at Bullo aren't exactly a king's ransom. Some people, helping out during the muster season, leave in disgust when they find that their payment is only a slab of beer. Most find Charles almost impossible to work for, and Marlee, who has now extended her duties to relaying messages from the homestead to the camp, has upset the latest boss. Halfway up the road with a mob of steers, he has pulled the pin. This is nothing short of disastrous. The girls are now left with no option but to sort the mess out themselves. Bonnie starts up the Toyota and heads off into the bush.

The cattle, herded along the Bullo track, need to get to the trucks which are waiting on the highway—a three-day drove away. With the head stockman gone, Marlee announces that from now on she will give the orders, answerable only to Charles.

At the end of each day, Marlee retires to the homestead for a flash feed and a hot shower. Bonnie, instead, decides to stay out bush with the 'boys', Aboriginal stockmen of any age. They have been part of the show for as long as Bonnie can remember and are excellent with touchy horses and mustering cattle. Their bush survival skills are unsurpassed, and Charles' deep respect for them is now ingrained in his daughter.

As the dust settles in the evening chill, Bonnie and the boys pull up stumps around the camp fire. With a guitar and didgeridoo for accompaniment, they sing their favourite songs—'Trumby was a Ringer', 'The Pub with no Beer'—and laugh late into the night. Old Ginger, the camp cook, plays a mean tune on his sticks, pounding them on top of an empty flour drum. But he's not only musically talented, he's also renowned for cooking a damn good stew, using his secret recipe.

One particular day, walking back into the yard to find a sharpening stone to touch up the pocket knives they are using for castrating and earmarking the cattle, Bonnie spots Ginger emptying a swag load of fat, juicy witchetty grubs into the stew pot. He spies Bonnie watching him, gives her a toothless grin.

'Dey good tucker, boss, 'im make you strooong with plenty of munta!' he says.

That night, Bonnie tucks into the stew with a healthy appetite, but Marlee refuses to touch his cooking ever again.

Old Tiger, a camp cook with a glass eye, an ulcerated mouth and a raging alcohol problem, is hardly a sight for sore eyes. But his cooking is passable—when he's sober. But after a night on the grog, God help those who tackle his culinary delights.

A young girl from Darwin has asked if she can join the camp for a day or two. Bonnie doesn't mind, figures if she can handle the heat and dust and flies, she's welcome to come along. But the girl hasn't counted on old Tiger doing the cooking.

In the yard, the bloated, maggoty remains of a killer lie waiting to be carted out of the yard and downwind. Riding past, the girl looks aghast at the beast, clearly disgusted at the rank smell.

'Yuk, that looks disgusting!' she says to Bonnie.

Keeping a straight face, Bonnie replies: 'Oh, that won't do you any harm. Tiger cut the meat from it for dinner a few minutes ago. He'll be cooking it now.'

In fact the beef for their meal has been cut from a beast hanging high in a shady tree, but the girl isn't privy to that. Returning to dinner camp, she eyes the proffered corn beef with alarm, rejects the offer to eat.

'Ah, no thank you,' she says, with excessive politeness. Sickened, she notes that everyone else is tucking in with abandon; finally she decides to bite the bullet and eat some herself. She is extremely hungry and knows if she doesn't eat this, there is nothing else on the menu. Warily approaching the meat, she exclaims with horror that there is a blowfly dancing on the top of it. She turns green; any moment now, she will certainly throw up.

'Don't worry 'bout dat, missus,' Tiger says. Worse for wear after a night on the grog, he wants to get this dinner camp over with as quickly as possible. 'I pix dat. I pix 'em ply, look out!'

He pulls out a can of Mortein, sprays the blowie with a deliberate flourish at point-blank range. 'Him okay eat now, missus, no worries,' Tiger grins.

Steadfastly refusing to eat, the girl is starving by tea camp. She prays that beef is not the main event, but her prayers aren't answered. This time it is covered in a sea of white sauce, and Tiger won't be defeated.

'She'll be right, missus,' he says, urging her to eat. 'Dat white sauce hide da maggots, no worries.'

* * *

There is an early morning chill in the air as five stockmen on horseback open the yard gates to release four hundred head of Montejinni bullocks. These are big cattle, as wild as the Myall Aborigines who live in the nearby desert country and who still use spears to hunt their prey. Bonnie is aboard a rangy bay gelding that no-one else is keen to claim, and in line with the stockmen who have formed a blockade to slow the rush as the cattle come out of the yard.

A massive bullock dives past one of the ringers and heads off at breakneck speed toward the scrub. Instead of holding his place in the line, a stockman wheels his horse around to bring it back to the mob, leaving a dangerous gap between Bonnie's horse and the next. The bullocks turn toward this escape route and, in unison, start their mad dash to try and get out. In split-second timing, Bonnie spurs her horse forward into the gap to try and baulk the cattle. Confused at his sudden change of position in the line, her horse thinks he is at a rodeo and must do a feature impression. He drops his head as he dives forward; bucking wildly, he ignores Bonnie as she kicks her heels into his flanks to stop him. On the fourth buck, the girth strap breaks, sending Bonnie and the saddle plummeting to the ground in the path of the cattle who are now fleeing hell west and crooked. Bonnie hits the ground with a sickening thud; unconscious, she lies amid the spewing dust and in the line of the rushing bullocks.

Peter Fraser, an Aboriginal stockman, has seen her fall, and he bravely wheels his horse back, forcing his way through the front of the crushing mob. The other men can do nothing; carried away in the chaos, they are unable to contain the stampeding cattle. Peter prays he can get back to Bonnie in time; if he can't, she will be crushed where she lies. Buffeted by the bullocks, he reaches her inert body with just seconds to spare, standing his horse over her as the mob passes.

Out cold for almost ten minutes, Bonnie wakes to find Peter squatting beside her, quietly smoking a rollie and watching her intently. A fine horseman, he has perfected the art of rolling a smoke with one hand while his horse is at a gallop, licking his dry lips along the paper's smooth lines and spitting out the stray baccy strands at the end. He's a man of few words, but he has great respect for this girl.

He smiles down at her when she opens her eyes. 'Dat mob near kill you,' is all he says.

With a shoulder injury she still carries today to remind her, Bonnie never forgets that it was only Peter's courage and quick thinking that saved her life.

Ross Ainsworth, the darling of the Henderson girls, has fallen for a girl from Victoria. They've both had time to sow their wild oats, now it's time to settle down, and Ross brings Lynette up north to show her his country. It is her first trip to the Northern Territory. Fresh from an exotic world trip and swathed in silk, espadrilles and the lingering scent of Dior, she listens as Ross animatedly tells her about the Bullo girls and their lifestyle. She is longing to meet these wonders from the outback, and she doesn't have long to wait.

'This dusty old truck rumbled up and parked opposite our flat,' she recalls. 'Out jumped two hefty, braless, singleted creatures, with hair under their arms and the smell of men. They had two swags with them and four dogs of questionable breed. Without any further ado, they proceeded to unroll their swags and set up camp. Like the drover's dog they would guard their truck. Finally, when they had finished, they came to the door and announced their arrival.'

The three females look each other up and down, and Lynette wonders who these urchins are on her doorstep.

'They were the famous Bullo girls I had heard so much about! They had a quick spruce-up—nothing too flash—and as soon as Ross came home Bonnie handed around the rum. My first impressions were that they were strong, uncouth wildcats. Marlee was beefy; Bonnie very slim with fabulous jutting breasts, long shaggy hair, big thighs and hands like a man. Both had lovely smiling faces beneath dusty, hole-ridden, sweaty headbands, unmistakable onion breath and BO oozing from every pore. God, I thought, what the hell have I got here?

'And the dogs! I'm terrified of big dogs; mine was a charming, cavalier King Charles spaniel, but these things! Monster Rottweiler-cross types who came bounding into the flat, smelling nearly as bad as the girls and covered in revolting cattle ticks. The girls had come to town to have a night on the grog and to get the supplies, which they easily hefted onto this big old truck before they headed back to Bullo. It was all quite normal for them but an astonishing experience for me, who was used to women who looked—and smelled—like women!'

When Lynette finally visits Bullo, this magic place she has heard so much about, she is enchanted with the landscape and the isolation. But she also senses she has walked into the heart of a seriously dysfunctional family.

'Here is Charles,' she says, 'marching around the house with a rum in his hand, issuing orders and telling the girls that they should look feminine like me. I thought that was a bit rich when he also expected them to fulfil all the duties on the station that men usually had to do! Sara—gracious, queenly, the long-suffering wife—has forgotten that her daughters need to be taught how to be feminine. The girls, particularly Bonnie, are female Amazons. Young women stuck out in this man's world, they lack any social graces or sensitivity whatsoever. The truth about that place is a lot more unpalatable than the sanitised adventures that Sara describes in her books.'

Changing into her RM Williams boots, Lynette, like Ross, has to prove herself. The girls are determined to bring her undone, and suggest to Ross that they go on a pig hunt.

'The girls put me to the test, and I had to pass. With Charles, you had to constantly prove yourself intellectually; with the girls it was a physical challenge. Failure was not abided.'

Lynette, who has only ever trapped mice before, is sure she can handle this adventure. The happy troop set off into the scrub in the back of the ute: Ross armed with a knife in his belt like Crocodile Dundee; the girls with nulla nullas; Lynette in Gucci scarf and sunglasses; and of course the dogs. A ferocious, feral sow with piglets comes out from behind a clump of logs and the action starts.

'Ross drew the knife and stabbed the sow through the heart while the girls fell upon the darling piglets with their nulla nullas. The dogs went in all directions. I jumped off the ute to cuddle the squirming babies before they met their grisly end. It may have been their idea of fun, but it wasn't mine!'

Not be to daunted, Lynette accepts the next challenge to go on a horse ride. 'We were cantering back to the homestead on sunset and right near the yards was a big old pig. Bonnie yells to Ross, "There's a pig ahead on your right!" and, in the excitement, he pulls out his pistol, John Wayne style, and shoots it off between his horse's ears. He misses the pig completely, but the explosion scares the hell out of the horse who jumps sideways and almost dismounts his rider! We had hysterics as Ross' horse bolted for the scrub with him still on board, and the pig nowhere in sight. I had finally bonded with the girls, at the expense of our great outback hero!'

However, if Lynette could handle Bullo, her mother could not. On a flying visit, she is horrified at how ghastly and primitive it is. 'There was no privacy,' explains Lynette. 'All Mum could see were animal carcasses sticking out of the water trough; the generator went off at nine at night; it's stinking hot and the beef is so strongly flavoured and tough it makes her jaw ache trying to eat it. She has to sleep under a mosquito net with buzzing lavender bugs dive bombing all night. The poor thing didn't get a wink of sleep, and in the morning, she looks at the putrid kitchen, with ticks marching across the sofa from the dogs, and Sara asks her if she'd like bacon and eggs for brekkie. "No thanks," Mum says, "I'll just have a biscuit, if that's okay." She got out of there as quickly as she could!'

New blokes in the stock camp are always put to the test. They have to prove themselves and many, starting out with a swaggering confidence, come unstuck. The old boys stand back and watch as Bonnie puts one young fella through his paces.

'Can you ride a horse?' she asks. It's the same question every time, and it usually elicits the same indignant answer.

'Course I can,' the bloke replies. 'What a bloody stupid question, from a bloody stupid girl, too. I can ride anything.'

The old boys grin, wait for the action to start.

'Okay,' says Bonnie. 'Take that brown colt over there, let's see what you're made of.'

The new bloke squares up to the frisky young horse, prepares to saddle up. Impatient, the colt kicks dirt, the dust rising and settling on the rails. The horse twitches, dances sideways, spins away from the new boy then stops, dead, waiting for him to get on. The man is slow to raise his foot into the iron, the colt's hind leg comes up and slams his boot clean out of the stirrup. Then the horse

118

tears off around the yard, reins and leathers flying, snorting and bucking. The young fella is hunched in the corner now, sweating hard, fire in his eyes; a chorus of cheers and cooees come from the old boys.

It's time for the second half of the show. Bonnie steps up to the bloke, tries desperately hard to keep the grin from her face. 'Well, are you going to get on that horse or just stand there looking at him?'

The new boy glares at her; taking orders from a woman is bad enough, but climbing on that mad animal is worse. 'If you're so bloody smart,' he replies, 'you get on and ride the bastard.'

Bonnie's eyes twinkle; this is the answer she wants. She pulls the colt to the centre of the yard, waits until he pauses for breath. Quickly sliding herself into the saddle, the colt explodes under her, his head tucked tight, squealing and kicking. Bonnie stays seated, drops the strap around his flanks until he tires, trots him round the yard and stops in front of the new fella. She dismounts, hands him the reins.

'You're not scared of him, are you?' she asks, finally exploding with laughter.

The old blokes chuckle. No-one tests this girl twice.

Far from being gentle with the new boys, Bonnie goes out of her way to see if a rider can sit the buck. She knows that some of the horses are so toey you can't rattle a box of matches around them or they will drop the claw right away and start bucking. It is great sport to hook her toe under a new bloke's horse to see how he will react. She knows they have a good rider when he stays on board.

Many times Bonnie also comes adrift of the animals, sustaining injuries that slow her down for weeks. Galloping through sandy country, she belts her knee into a gum tree when her horse tries to sidestep a huge hollow. Dragged half out of the saddle, she literally hangs on for her life until her horse slows down. Eventually scrambling back into the seat, she can't straighten her knee for two months. But the unspoken rule is you get as good as you give: instead of offering sympathy, the boys get a great laugh out of it.

CHAPTER ELEVEN

Bonnie's headaches are getting worse and she can now barely open her mouth. Some days she thinks she will go mad with the pain, and her nerves are like live wires. In the quiet of a stock camp at the end of the day, she ties a piece of dark material over her eyes, prays she will feel better in the morning.

The latest drama involves the camp cook. Good cooks are hard to find, and even harder to keep. Most Bullo cooks are grumpy piss-wrecks with no culinary talents whatsoever. Now Marlee has gone and upset the new one, and there is bedlam in the air. A volatile Yugoslavian, Valentino doesn't take kindly to any criticism and is determined that revenge will be his.

'Don' you speaka to me like that!' he screams at Marlee, brandishing a long knife. 'You'a nothin' but a bloody bitch!' He takes a long, deep breath, his eyes bulging with anger as he prepares breakfast for the next morning. Before long, however, his temper subsides, and he smiles as he mixes the ingredients.

The curry is delicious, with an extra spicy flavour, and is hungrily devoured by all the crew. After breakfast the camp, with three hundred head of cattle, pushes on to the next bore where the crew will meet up with Valentino again at midday. They leave him humming cheerfully as he packs up the camp.

The morning stage is rough going; from Turkey Creek it is a gruelling eleven kilometres down the main jump-up onto the Auvergne flats. The sun is fierce overhead as they push on over rocky creeks, hills and gullies; over dry creek beds filled with leaves and sand, and then down onto the stinking hot black-soil plains. Small bush flies crawl over the riders' faces and the stringy tea-trees offer no shade. Everyone in the crew has a raging thirst—the curry must have been hotter than they thought. Men and beasts have been on the trail since four in the morning and are tired and irritable.

Suddenly Bonnie feels an uncontrollable urge to go to the toilet, but there's not much chance out here. In this barren country, there's absolutely nowhere to go. She jiggles uncomfortably in the saddle, looks back at Marlee coming up behind. Her face, too, is framed in a painful grimace; she obviously has the same problem. The Aboriginal stockmen have started deserting their horses in droves and are heading for the scrub, but there's a long way to go before the mob reaches Rooster Creek at dinner camp.

'What the hell's going on around here?' Bonnie yells, as she finally gives in to nature's call. 'Where are all you bastards going?'

The next bore is still a three-hour ride away, and they can't stop until they get there. Their thirst is now unquenchable, and they have drunk their entire water supply. Perspiring furiously and stopping every few minutes to empty their bowels, they are now dehydrated, and the boys still haven't appeared out of the scrub. Bonnie and Marlee, now alone, hold the mob together for several miles.

Bonnie's bum is red raw—nature doesn't provide soft toilet paper. She is livid. The first lesson in the bush is not to upset the cook. They struggle into the next camp for dinner, desperate for a drink of water. To Bonnie's horror, the camp is deserted. No cook means no water—the jerry cans are in Valentino's camp truck, and so is the food. Marlee is ropable, and so is Bonnie.

'This is bloody fantastic!' she yells at her sister. 'You've pissed the cook off so badly none of us get to eat dinner!'

Valentino has made his point: after putting Epsom salts in the breakfast curry, he has shot through to cool off his temper. Night camp is still another five hours walk with the cattle, and they have no fresh horses.

'We've got no choice but to push on, even if we are shitting through the eye of a needle,' Bonnie says.

Footsore, the cattle bail up under the scrubby trees for three hours before they can be seduced back onto the track again. Dehydrated and desperately hungry, the crew, now including the stockmen who have finally rejoined the girls, finally falls into night camp, where Valentino has deigned to show up. He shrugs his shoulders when Marlee screams at him.

'I no understand what you say,' he smirks, turning his back on her.

Fed up to the back teeth with the fights at home, with Sara screaming and Marlee constantly intervening, Bonnie now only goes inside when she has to. Tension and turmoil upset her and make her headaches worse. There is no longer any pretence at a marriage; the chasm between Charles and Sara is as wide as Bullo itself.

Marlee and Charles have had a terrifying row, and Marlee has skitched her Rottweiler dog onto him. This is no game; the dog, with bared fangs and mad eyes, bites him. Charles storms out of the room to where the firearms are kept and, in his temper, tries to jam 308 ammunition up the breech of a 30-30. In a fury, Bonnie realises what he is going to do, wrestles the rifle from his shaking hands.

'You can't kill that dog!' she bellows. 'You bloody fool! Why do you think she has the animal? To protect her!'

Charles glares at her, perspiration standing out on his forehead.

'If you want to get past,' Bonnie fumes, 'you'll have to thump me first.'

Their breath is coming in short, raspy bursts, and they stare angrily at each other. Bonnie senses she has won this battle; in all the years she has never known him to hit his children or Sara. He backs off, retreats to the verandah with a Bullo River Special, furiously smoking his pipe.

'You are a pacifist, but if ah ever get into a fight,' he tells Bonnie later, 'ah want you there.'

At fifteen Bonnie has come to recognise that men are more than just workmates. Sought after by them from early adolescence, she has always ignored their sideways glances, rolling up her swag and bolting into the quiet of the scrub. Sometimes, when the men get drunk and high-spirited, they look at her in that leering, lecherous way that drunk, high-spirited men do. But she doesn't take any notice of them, thinks they are silly bastards who will get over it when they are sober. If men see her as beautiful, she doesn't share their opinion. Feeling overshadowed by Marlee in the beauty department, her pubescent lack of confidence is reinforced by Sara. While her older sister is constantly told she is gorgeous, Bonnie's emergence from frail girl to eye-catching young woman is ignored. She has grown into a beauty, with a taut muscular body from fencing and stock work, and her outward toughness belies a sensuous nature.

Used to playing second fiddle to Marlee, who has always been very well aware of her appeal to men, Bonnie is at first taken aback by the male attention she starts to receive. While Marlee doesn't let her left hand know what her right hand is doing, Bonnie, open and honest, is incapable of subterfuge. If she fancies a bloke, she lets him know, focusing all her attention on his conversation or inviting him to arm wrestle her. Trouble is, there aren't many blokes out here to fancy.

Sara turns a blind eye to her oldest daughter's flirtations, but she notices Bonnie's. 'All you ever seem to do lately is chase men!' she tells her.

Bonnie doesn't bother to disagree. She's a long way from promiscuous, but she figures that's her business. There are men out here; relationships happen.

Charles pictures a fabulous union between his girls and big-name families: they'll marry a stockman over his dead body. Sara has simpler dreams, sharing romantic ideas about their possible beaus at kitchen-table conferences.

'They must be tall, dark and handsome,' she says. 'And rich. Make sure they are rich.'

Marlee giggles at the last comment, but Bonnie squirms uncomfortably. She doesn't care about money, and would hope the man she falls in love with has more going for him than just a fat wallet. Her ideal is a man with intelligence, someone with quiet self-confidence.

It's around this time too that Bonnie discovers what the older blokes around the station have always known: when the work is done, a strong, stiff drink puts fire back into the soul and relaxes aching muscles.

While the hardened stockmen drink bush champagne, or whatever else they can get their hands on, Bonnie cuts her teeth on OP rum—ten times stronger than the normal drink, it helps drown out the blinding pain in her head. But grog can also cause murder and mayhem and upset a tight ship. If the car breaks down because some drunken bastard has put petrol in instead of diesel, or the workmen are pissed on a savage home brew, it can ruin a whole operation. But the isolation is so extreme, allowances have to be made.

Sara, constantly policing the alcohol rations, fails to tell a new employee not to share her grog with anyone. A week after she starts work, she knocks on her office door.

'Um, it's about the beer ration, Mrs Henderson. Ah, actually, I don't drink beer. I've given it to Dick.'

Unceremoniously cut off from this unexpected supply, Dick suddenly comes up for a new bottle of aftershave lotion every second day. It is fifteen per cent pure alcohol, and good old Dick has a wonderful time wiping himself out every night. At least he smells reasonable—aftershave seeping out of his pores is more fragrant than metho and sal vital. But when Sara wakes up to what is happening, she puts the clampers on Dick's supplies; after that, he goes back to smelling of oil and diesel.

'Bullo was run on grog, sex and hard work,' Ross Ainsworth recalls. 'After dark, there was nothing else to do but roam about with a rum in your hand looking for mischief. You couldn't begin to perceive the excesses out there.'

Bonnie's first kiss stirs feelings she has never had before. She doesn't know what to do next, or if she is supposed to do anything at all. All she knows is that it feels good, and there is no-one she can ask about it. With no guidance and no rules, Bonnie often shares a swag with her mates. It seems a normal thing to do, and no-one questions her behaviour. For a long time swagging with a friend is purely innocent; later, when it involves sex, she can't understand why she is labelled as wild. While no-one questions Marlee's behaviour, it is Bonnie who cops the raised eyebrows.

She has no hang-ups about sharing a swag with someone; her guideline is, simply, that it be someone she likes a lot. Love does not have to enter the equation. Charles, by his own behaviour and standards, has taught her that lust and gratification is a good second to whatever is running first. Sex is part of the equation, and far from sacred. It is only later that she learns it can also be a sensuous pleasure, not just an athletic activity.

'Bonnie had blokes lined up from Bullo to Brisbane,' Danielle recalls. 'They saw her as good fun, a hard worker and she was good-looking too. She was a tomboy, and at work or play she strived to fit that label. That's why she always injured herself. Marlee liked make-up and was always centre stage. But if blokes got too close to Bonnie, told her they loved her, that was the end of that. She didn't want to know about it. Her life was Bullo.'

In the stock camps, Bonnie's dog, Fuzzy Bear, watches her swag, guarding it during the night. If Bonnie switches swags after dark, the dog follows. Sometimes he stays asleep when she goes back to her own piece of canvas. The stockmen grin: it's always a dead giveaway when a dog camps on someone else's swag.

Word has filtered back to the homestead about Bonnie's occasional swagging habits. Sara fixes her daughter with an icy stare, purses her lips in disgust. 'What do you think you're doing?' she rails. 'You will get yourself a very bad reputation if you're not careful!'

The hypocrisy of her mother's comment angers Bonnie. If no-one knows what she's up to, does that make it any better?

It takes Bonnie years to work out that Sara doesn't like her sharing a swag, not because she thinks it is immoral, but because she is a woman in a marriage that is, by now, virtually loveless. Still very attractive, the roughness of bush life has not killed Sara's charm. But Bonnie won't play her mother's game, won't hide her sexuality under a prissy air.

The army reserves are on exercise at Bullo. The weekend soldiers, waiting at the homestead for the radio operators to turn up, are growing increasingly impatient. They are two days overdue, and the wet season is roaring in with a vengeance.

'They're probably bogged at twenty-two-mile spring,' Bonnie tells them. She says it as a fact, surprised they haven't thought of it before. 'Do you want us to come over and help bail them out?'

They're bogged all right, the wheels of the Land Rover covered in muddy sand and water. Using a jack and timber under the wheels, it takes Bonnie and Marlee three hours to get them out of the slush.

When the vehicle is finally free, Bonnie sits back, triumphant.

'Next time you're in strife,' she laughs, 'don't call the army, call the girls from Bullo!'

The commander looks at her, digests her comment.

'Actually, you should think about joining the army,' he replies. 'We could use you as a bloody instructor!'

Charles is writing a note to Fraser, detailing a week at Bullo. In it, he spells out typical station problems, particularly during the wet season.

Monday: 46 Brahman bulls turned back four miles inside

128

*our entrance road due to bad creek crossing. Met by truck
which promptly broke down. Brahmans unloaded at wrong
yard and all went bush.*

*Tuesday: Neighbour came over with men and horses,
recapturing all but eight bulls.*

*Wednesday: Electric storm, almost 9 inches at homestead.
Generator struck by lightning. No power—again!*

*Thursday: Same storm bogged Buntine's roadtrain lifting
7000 gallons of fuel and wet stores. No fuel for wet and
truck's a total loss, with water over engines. The main
freezer blew up, containing 10 000 lbs meat.*

*Friday: Major alert for [my] lost Beaver aircraft. Bullo
River called Darwin radio—'Where's Beaver?' and eight
aircraft sent out to search. Had forgotten to cancel
Sarwatch [Search and Rescue].*

Saturday: Sara blew up.

*Sunday: Day off—except I had to work all day, as did
everyone else. This is fair dinkum and doesn't include the
minor problems. It will also, perhaps, explain why this
letter is a week late.*

'When Charles took over Bullo it changed from a small but slightly
profitable operation to a nightmare,' Gus recalls.

'Of course Charles immediately had grandiose ideas. He wanted
to establish a piggery, a fishing operation, an abattoir and a tourist
venture. Probably each of these was sound in principle, but in practice, it was a disaster. John Nicholson and Charles did not have a
happy relationship; John was basically a cattleman and didn't want
to become involved in other projects. Their arguments, over a bottle
of rum or numerous Bullo River Specials, became more frequent
and more violent. They often threatened each other and as they both

carried revolvers, I feared it might come to that.'

To stave off the approaching high noon, they reach agreement: Gus, now an independently successful businessman, who would later be honoured with an OBE for his contributions to business, will buy John out. It is, he comes to realise later, one of the more serious mistakes of his life.

Bullo's meatworks are being supplied with cattle from neighbouring Montejinni Station, purchased by Gus and Charles in 1977. The concept is simple: Charles will manage the property and, after improvements are made, they will sell.

'Needless to say it didn't work like that,' Gus says. 'He lost every manager he put on there because they couldn't work with him, and he insisted on mustering in January, a stinking hot month. By the time these poor cattle arrived at Bullo for the abattoir, up to half the herd had perished. Guess who had to foot the bill for that disaster?'

From the time they arrived at Bullo, Gus has been bailing the Hendersons out financially, a legacy of his enduring devotion to his boyhood friend. Interest free, much of the debt, which includes domestic bills—food, the girls' education, petrol—is not put on paper. It is, as the Maryland code of honour decrees, a gentleman's agreement.

'Eventually that debt was converted to a promissory note for $500 000, which was signed by both Charles and Sara,' Gus says. 'It became a sword of Damocles for Sara and she would do anything to get rid of it.'

On a bangtail muster every animal is identified as having been counted through the yard by cutting hair from the end of its tail. Mustering on horseback is slow and ineffective, and, increasingly, helicopters are taking over the job of mustering. But on a helicopter muster, the herd can stretch fifteen miles. Charles buys a Super Cub tandem seat tail dragger to help oversee the bangtail muster for the sale of Montejinni.

'It's time the girls learned to fly,' he tells Sara.

The prospect terrifies her. It's one thing for Charles, with his experience in the war, to fly that noisy, smelly aircraft; quite another for teenagers to have a go.

Bonnie looks at the Super Cub with fear and dread, desperately wanting to avoid these flying lessons, but Charles won't hear of it. If the girls want to stand up and be counted in the outback, he says, they need to get their wings. She sits in the pilot seat, staring in dismay at the instrument panel.

Charles sits behind her, shows her how to start the plane and point it in the right direction. They remain on the ground for days, for which Bonnie is extremely grateful. She has had only rudimentary lessons about what to do when they are airborne; the runway looms ahead of her and she knows that once she learns how to taxi in a straight line, takeoff must follow.

'It's time you got this bird off the ground,' Charles announces one morning.

Shaking, Bonnie opens her mouth to protest, but her father has strapped himself into the back seat and he obviously wants to see some action. She revs the engine, hits the throttle, and prepares to meet her maker.

'The hardest thing about a tail dragger is getting it off the ground safely,' Charles yells into her ear as the ground whooshes out underneath them. 'Give her some altitude!'

Bonnie feels a sickening lurch in her stomach as the plane stalls for a second and its wing dips sideways. Suddenly Charles clouts her around the back of the head and pulls her ponytail, hollering at her to concentrate.

131

'Get her back on balance!' he yells. 'Keep the ball in the centre at all times! Bring her around slowly and line up the airstrip!'

She does as she's told, gingerly turning the Super Cub until she spots the runway underneath her. The plane bounces and bucks furiously on landing, and Bonnie struggles with the heel brakes to bring the thing to a halt. Her legs, like jelly, feel as if they will give way any moment, and she glares at her father.

'That frightened the hell out of me!' she spits, as he stands and grins at her. 'Never again!'

Charles walks away, throws a comment over his shoulder. 'We'll have another lesson at the same time tomorrow. You can't work this country without knowing how to fly.'

She stares at his retreating back and clenches her jaw. No amount of pleading will make him change his mind.

'I'll show you, you bastard,' she hisses.

Doggedly, Bonnie practises taxiing up and down the airstrip, with Fuzzy Bear strapped in the back. She thinks about Bleep, the wild brolga they taught to fly when they were children. Raised by the publican at Timber Creek, he turned up at Bullo one day with the meat inspector, Bluey Lewis, who had put him in a cage for the journey.

'He's only a chick,' Bluey said, 'but he's got a long beak and he's taken to pecking at the hotel guests. The publican ain't happy!'

Running along the airstrip next to him, the children, in chorus with Bleep, flapped their arms as he flapped his wings. It took a long time before the bird summoned the courage to become airborne. Honking at the other brolgas who flew overhead, he suddenly one day decided to join them, sweeping majestically across the sky. He loved to entertain, showing off the beautiful brolga mating dance. Domesticated at heart, he slept under the aeroplane's wing when he deigned to come in to land.

But Bleep's old habits, learned at Timber Creek, died hard. When he started pecking at the piccaninnies down by the river, they stoned him to death.

Gradually Bonnie starts to love the challenge of the aircraft, and she becomes determined to exorcise her fear. It has some bizarre idiosyncrasies, this plane; its brakeage system is antiquated, and any sudden wind spins it round in circles. Often the wing tip comes to rest over the barbed-wire fence. Finally, elated, Bonnie proclaims she can taxi in a straight line. After several more weeks of lessons—stalls, spins, wingovers, precision turns at low level which are critical for checking bore tanks or shouting messages to people on the ground, and countless forced landing practices Charles is convinced she is ready to take off alone. She has no aero club polish or respect for air-traffic rules and regulations; he has omitted to teach her that, but who needs it out here in the bush? He is confident she has the necessary skills to control the machine and stay out of trouble long enough to gain some experience.

'Don't fly off our property!' Sara warns as Bonnie heads out for another day's practice.

It's magnificent up here in the sky, dodging underneath the clouds, with a bird's eye view of the Bullo valley. Peaceful, too; just her and the aeroplane, far from the troubles at ground level.

Bonnie flies low along the Bullo River, spotting crocs, practising tough landings by putting one wheel on the mud bank. Seeking new challenges, she passes the boundary and chases cars up and down the Victoria Highway, returning to the homestead only when she's low on fuel. When Charles grumbles and asks her where she's been, she tells him she's been counting cattle.

Her new-found love of flying eventually finds expression on the page.

I have the power in my hand
As I ride upon the sky.
For beneath me spreads the land,
How thrilling 'tis to fly.

To chase the dancing rays of light
And glide without a sound.
The great wide sky is blue and bright,
It's a highway without bounds.

To bank along a river's bend,
And dodge the frightened birds.
The power of flight can send
Me to a joy beyond all words.

I dance with some clouds then hurry
To seek some unknown goal;
And a feeling of eternity
Grips my soaring soul.

CHAPTER TWELVE

David has returned to the station and, now twenty-one, he is taller than Bonnie remembers. He has his father's eyes: intensely blue, they remain perfectly still when he is deep in thought, and dance when he is amused. Charles has given him some beginner's flying lessons, but he's not yet up to solo standard. No-one tells him Bonnie is taking to the skies alone.

'Come for a taxi with me, David,' she suggests. She's thrilled that he's back at Bullo, and the bond they shared years ago hasn't changed with age. 'I'll take you up and down the airstrip.'

Jaunty and confident of her new skills, Bonnie runs to the plane and waits for her half-brother to strap in behind her. For a few minutes she belts to the end of the airstrip, slows it down, turns, and then repeats the procedure. On the fifth taxi, she opens the throttle and soars into the air.

David, scared to death in the back seat, stares in horror at the disappearing ground. Below them, Charles is highly amused.

Bonnie has learned his rules well: he has given her the encouragement and confidence to believe she can fly, offered her the rudimentary skills and then expected her to do it.

The homestead is now just a dim speck in the distance.

'Where do you want to go to?' Bonnie yells, turning back to face her terrified half-brother. It's a perfect day for flying, and she's in no hurry to land.

He stares back at her, a look of stunned alarm on his ashen face. 'I want to go back down!' he stutters. 'Put me back down on the ground!'

When they reach terra firma, David shakily enquires how long Bonnie has been flying.

'Oh, not long,' she replies, casually, 'but it's great fun. Do you want to go up for another spin?'

Word soon spreads about Bonnie's flying adventure, and it becomes another game the Aboriginal stockmen play to put the wind up the new blokes in the camp. 'You'd better bin doin' wot she says or she put you in da back a dat hair blane an den you a goner!'

Alienated from her mother and Marlee, Bonnie finds solace and a quiet peace in her friendship with David. He is different from the other men on the station, doesn't need to prove himself with loud boastfulness. He refuses to swear around women and is a thoughtful, motivated worker. His arms, nut-brown from years working in the sun, ripple with taut muscles which are exaggerated against his lean frame. Bonnie watches him, intrigued, watches the way he sits a horse, deals with toey cattle, talks to the stockmen. He says little at the homestead in the company of other people, but in the bush, fencing or in stock camps, he talks to Bonnie all the time. They are relaxed in each other's company and share an unspoken understanding.

When they're not working, they go for long rides on their horses and play bush cricket, using a pandanus cluster as a ball and a hunk of dead wood as a bat. As the dry drags into the wet, they become inseparable. With David, Bonnie doesn't feel challenged or inadequate. He accepts her as she is, and finally she comes to understand her father's philosophy: you can't love someone you don't respect. With nowhere else to turn, they are the only friend each other has.

Working together for more than a year, they have a long time to get to know each other. Though they have been raised as virtual strangers, they find they share a lot of similarities. For the first time in their lives, both know what it is to have an unconditional friendship.

Danielle doesn't share her sister's enthusiasm for their half-brother. Still only a child, she remembers him as having a foul temper that went off like a bomb. 'He was skinny and sickly-looking from the rheumatic fever he contracted early in life. His temper was legendary. Once, he took hours to start a Toyota, and when he finally did, he deliberately rammed it into a tree in anger.'

If Sara or Charles is scandalised at the closeness of the friendship, nothing is said for a long while. But tension is increasing; in David's company, Sara's lips purse and her eyebrows appear to be permanently arched. Bonnie is starting to feel the heat. The unspoken reprimands confuse Bonnie; until now, there have been few moral boundaries.

Toward the end of David's time at the station, Bonnie and David reach mutual agreement that they wish they weren't related. For Bonnie, the realisation comes slowly, evolving over time. Growing up at Bullo, with its unique moral code, it takes her a long time to recognise that their feelings for each other overstep acceptable limits. The realisation comes like a kick in the guts.

'There was a huge shouting match between my parents and David, and he left,' Danielle recalls.

Many years later, in the preface to her autobiography *From Strength to Strength*, Sara writes, '… other parts [of my life] are so dark and dreadful that innocent family members would have to suffer the disgrace of other family members' actions …' Perhaps this obscure passage refers, in part, to her relationship with David.

Adrift from her family, Bonnie is in despair when he goes, feels an emptiness at the core of her being that not even Danielle can fill. She tries to replace what she has lost, becoming increasingly independent and ruthlessly self-sufficient. With no rules to guide her, she retreats into isolation, working herself into the ground, seeking sanctuary through physical exertion and trying to ignore her misery. No-one asks her what is wrong, and she couldn't tell them if they had.

The day before he left, David gave her a small gift.

'Look after him, Bon, give him lots of love,' he said, putting the wriggling parcel into her hands.

The animal, one of a litter from David's beloved old dog, nuzzled in to her chest as she waves goodbye to the disappearing plane. The dog is all she has left now.

Bonnie is seventeen and is packing up her school books for the last time. Apart from English and mathematics, the work bores her and she can see no relevance in it to her way of life.

'That's it, I've had enough,' she tells Sara. 'I'm quitting school, it's a complete waste of time. There's work to be done and I can't do both.'

Aghast, Sara tries to enlist Charles' help. 'Make her see reason!' she explodes. 'She can't just finish school because the fancy takes her!'

Charles ponders the dilemma for a moment, slowly offers a considered answer. 'She's old enough to make her own decision about that. If she wants to trade theory for practice, then that's okay with me.'

Picking up her hat, Bonnie whistles her dogs to follow her outside.

'If you're not going to finish school, you can help me in here with the housework,' Sara says, knowing there's no point in arguing the point further.

'Marlee's doing a great job of that,' Bonnie replies. 'I can find plenty of work to do out here.'

With her new-found freedom, Bonnie takes a closer look at the station's problems. With money in low reserves, the fences are non-existent or ineffective and the stock is badly mismanaged. It is the start of another muster season, and the place is a mess. For the past twelve months Bonnie has busied herself out of school hours rolling up the rusty barbed-wire fences that litter the station. Many times, galloping through the scrub on her horse, she has gone arse up, the horse twisted and tangled in the wire as she crawls out from underneath.

When she is at the homestead at night Bonnie tries to explain to Sara that maintenance on a property is vital. 'Perhaps if we spent a little less money on the homestead and a little more on fixing the problems outside, the station would run better,' she suggests.

Scratched, bleeding and bruised once too often from her battles with the barbed wire, Bonnie fills a hole, four and a half metres deep and six metres wide, with the junk lying around the homestead and in the scrub. Using a vehicle Dick lends her, she picks up the metal, and throws in into the pit. It takes months to fill the wire grave; when it's finished, she covers the hole with dirt and takes her horse out for a ride. At least now they shouldn't run into any more booby traps.

The mob of cattle consistently knocks down the laneway fence near the homestead, but no-one is fixing the problem. Using double twisted barbed wire, Bonnie rebuilds the fence, almost two metres high, working through the wet season. The effort earns high praise; not even a snake, Sara says, could get through that wire after Bonnie fixed it.

Bonnie flies the Super Cub out at first light to help supervise the muster. There are three choppers in the air, strung out for several kilometres, and she is on the wing of the mob, dive-bombing and blocking them from running up the gullies, calling to the helicopter pilots over the radio to head them out from under the trees where they have taken shelter. The plane stalls midair and she makes a radio call.

'I just ran the tank dry,' she says.

'Oh well,' one of the helicopter pilot says in a laconic voice, 'just let me know where you put the plane down and I'll come and bail you out.'

'You silly bastard,' Bonnie responds. 'I've gone onto another tank of fuel of course.'

Flying all day, she finally lands the Super Cub by the light of the full moon. A young chopper pilot, new to the company and having just weathered his first day at Bullo, offers her a rum and some sympathy.

'You must be really tired, Bonnie. You've been out there flying for twelve hours. I suppose you have a mustering endorsement?'

The old blokes choke on their drinks, but Bonnie keeps a straight face. 'No, actually I don't have an endorsement.'

'Well,' he says, 'you know you need to get one, otherwise you'll lose your licence.'

This comment is greeted with loud guffaws, and he looks with a bemused expression around the table before glancing back at Bonnie.

'You do have a licence, don't you?' he splutters. 'Please tell me you have!'

'Well, ah … actually … no,' she replies.

She waits for him to object, but he is too stunned to speak. Having come this far, she decides to push her luck.

She grins. 'I reckon if you don't live on the edge, you're taking up too much space.'

CHAPTER THIRTEEN

The Gourlays, wealthy Scottish landowners, have sent their sons to the antipodes for experience on outback stations before they return home to take up the reins. One son, Neil, a genial twenty-one-year-old giant, goes to Bullo after a stint breaking horses at Killarney Station, owned by the Tapp family. The Tapps, a strappingly handsome, wild and unruly mob afraid of neither man nor beast, are an empire and a law unto themselves. Their mother, June, nicknamed the Elizabeth Taylor of the outback for her violet eyes and indomitable spirit, is the matriarch who thumbs her nose at authority, fights to win, and cares not a whit about what people think of her and her brood. Everyone in the Territory, it appears, has a story to tell about the Tapps—their feudin' and fightin', their skill with horses and cattle, their father Bill's legendary capacity to drink and his eventual death from alcoholism

However, if the young Scottish laird finds the Tapps an eye-opener, he is in for even more of a treat at Bullo, where he finds himself endlessly fascinated with all the characters. Neil refines the girls' horse-breaking skills and notices that Bonnie has a natural aptitude for horses. Lustful and carefree, he has a wild fling with both sisters, but, captured by her free spirit, it is Bonnie with whom he falls in love. Sara and Charles are overjoyed when he asks her to marry him: his family are well connected, of the land, and rich. Neil, strong and self-assured, would make a fine partner and he is a good friend of Ross Ainsworth, which counts for much.

The house is silent, everyone in bed asleep except Charles, who has got up to go to the bathroom. He looks over at the dark shadows on the living-room couch, realises it is Bonnie and Neil snuggled up together asleep. He tiptoes back into Sara, rouses her from sleep. Describing what he has just seen, he asks, 'Sara, shall I be severe?'

She sits up in bed, yawns, and turns on the light. 'Were they doing anything untoward, Charles?'

'No. But they are cuddled up together.'

'Have they got their clothes on?'

'Yes.'

'Well, leave them in peace, Charles,' she says, snuggling back down into the bed. 'For goodness sake, just leave them in peace.'

Sara recounts the story to a bemused audience over breakfast the next morning, and in the months that follow, any drama is greeted with a loud chorus of 'Shall I be severe?'

Bonnie, with her usual habit of not allowing men to get close to her, pushes Neil away. Sex is one thing; love, quite another. However, he is not a man who was easily deterred.

'He told her that given she was only eighteen, he would wait for her,' Danielle recalls. 'He asked when she felt she might be ready to marry him. He even considered moving to Australia to live to be with her, leaving his own inheritance in Scotland.'

Bonnie asks her younger sister what she should do.

'I was only thirteen, and I advised her not to marry him. It was for purely selfish reasons—I didn't want her to live in Scotland. But the real reason she didn't marry Neil was she didn't want anything but Bullo. It was her whole life.' Danielle pauses, and adds reflectively: 'In many ways that property, Bullo, has been the downfall of our family.'

Increasingly, the boys start to call Bonnie *muligah*—boss. It's not a title she wants. Working hard and staying clear of the homestead is good enough for her, and she's happy being part of the crew.

'I'm not the boss,' she tells them one day. 'Why do you keep calling me that?'

The stockmen hesitate for a moment, fix her with a steady eye. 'You're not *muligah*,' one replies, 'but you should be.'

Charles, never fully recovered from the pneumonia that flattened him a few years ago, and with little money to keep the station books straight, has allowed Marlee to take over the role of camp manager. She keeps some distance from her employees and demands respect, but it is a demand that many find irritating.

Bonnie is shocked by how her father's health is deteriorating. At the end of the wet season, she throws all her energies into premuster preparations. The station is deserted, save for her, Charles, old Dick and Stumpy, the camp cook. Digging a hole for the gateway on the new fence line, Charles offers to help her.

'Pass me the crowbar,' he says. 'You have a go on the end of the shovel for a while.'

Bonnie does as she's asked, and watches with dismay as her father struggles to hold the heavy bar. Sadness overwhelms her. For the first time, she realises the cost of Charles' lingering illness. Once so strong and proud, he is now haggard and weak.

* * *

After holidaying in the United States with the family for Christmas, Bonnie returns home via Queensland, where Sara and Charles are continuing their vacation. Charles, in daily contact with Bullo, has some bad news, and is unsure how to tell her. Gaunt and unwell, he hesitates before speaking.

'Fuzzy Bear has gone missing,' he says quietly. 'She hasn't been seen for weeks.'

For six years the faithful dog has been Bonnie's constant side-kick, and she is alarmed by the news. 'Missing? What do you mean, missing?' Her heart is pounding, as she waits for Charles' reply.

'The dog's gone, Bon,' he says quietly.

Bonnie stares at her father, willing him to tell her he is kidding, but it is painfully obvious he is not. It breaks his heart that Bonnie has to endure yet another loss, and he can't hide that from her.

'Well, I'm heading straight back to the station to find her!' Bonnie says. 'I can't lose my lovely old dog!' As she is hurriedly throwing her belongings into her swag, Charles comes into the room.

'I'll come back with you. We'll look for her together.'

For weeks, Bonnie wanders the bush, searching everywhere for her dog. The day she finally accepts she is not coming home, she is inconsolable.

On a pig hunt shortly after, her second dog, Kimberley, suddenly disappears. Heartbroken, Sara scours the scrub trying to find some trace of the animal, but Bonnie knows there is no point looking. Wild pigs leave no clues behind them.

A few weeks later, Suzie, Bonnie's remaining dog, is sitting on the back of the trailer when Bonnie is carting portable yard panels out to the stock camp. Suddenly barking at the wind, Suzie bails out off the side and is crushed by the trailer's wheels. Bonnie hits the brakes, but she's too late. In six months, she has lost three beloved dogs; this time, she has no tears left.

145

* * *

Montejinni Station, purchased by Gus Trippe in 1977 for $800 000. has been sold for a substantial profit. From that, Charles receives a cool million. Gus, holding the chequebook, is adamant that his old friend pay out all his existing debts, bar what is owed to Gus himself.

'I insisted he pay out the bank mortgages for Bullo, which he did. The station under Bonnie's leadership was running like clockwork and Charles had enough money left over after his debts were paid to buy himself a yacht, which gave him the greatest pleasure.

Sara talks about being left with a million-dollar debt, but the truth is there was no debt, apart from the promissory note owed to me. I knew exactly what Charles owed, and the money from the sale of Montejinni was the first real cash he had seen in twenty odd years.'

Gus pauses to collect his thoughts, stares reflectively down the tunnel of time, back to the days when he was younger and friendship was worth more than money.

'Sara sold Charles' yacht after he died, which realised almost $80 000, and also sold a share of a gold mine in Western Australia which was worth a substantial amount. She puts the sudden cash flow down to having had a miraculous stock market win, and perhaps that's true, but I lived in the bush too long to believe that.'

After flying for years, Bonnie can no longer put off getting her formal private pilot's licence. The instructor sits behind her in the Super Cub, taking her through navigation exercises. After twenty minutes in the air, he instructs Bonnie to divert track and notify Kununurra of a change of flight plan and expected time of arrival.

146

Shouting at each other over the noise of the engine, Bonnie nods consent. This is a piece of cake; she was flying over this terrain before she could drive, and doesn't need to do the calculations on paper. After a quick mental check, she advises Kununurra of the changes and settles back to write a letter to Danielle who is at boarding school in Queensland.

Twenty minutes later, the instructor taps her on the shoulder. 'What's taking you so long!' he shouts. 'Are you still working out the flight plan?' There is no way, he thinks, that this girl is ready to get her licence.

'I've already advised ETA,' Bonnie yells back.

'Well, what are you writing, then?'

Bonnie waves the letter to her sister over her shoulder. 'Oh, this, you mean? It's just a letter.'

'So how did you work out ETA?' he screams back, fast losing patience.

'I did it in my head.'

Now incredulous, he demands Bonnie practise a forced landing. 'And do it by the book!' he shouts. They are flying over the Victoria Highway, and Bonnie lines up the Super Cub, raps in the throttle and prepares to bring her in. The instructor taps her on the shoulder, more violently this time.

'What do you think you're doing now? You can't land on the highway! I only meant for you to show me you knew how to do it, not to put it into practice!'

'It's pretty safe out here,' Bonnie grins. 'Not a car within cooee!'

For the rest of the exercise, the instructor insists she fly below five hundred feet. At this level, a pilot can't see enough of the terrain to map-read accurately and must concentrate instead on compass readings and wind direction.

'How did I go?' she cheekily asks him when they land.

147

'Yeah, well, I was a bit worried when you wanted to bring it down on the bitumen highway, but still, you passed with flying colours,' he says.

It's time to draft the horses, brand the clean skins and castrate the stallions. The fire is stoked and the irons hot, and for the ringers this is a chance to show off their skills with a rope and knife. It is a job that requires great skill: a horse can die of shock if it loses too much blood, and an animal that is cut proud—left with one testicle—is nothing but trouble.

The first horse is run into the yard, eyes wide with fear as he desperately searches for a way out. Bonnie feels for the animals, but it is a job that has to be done. A ringer in the centre of the round yard swings the rope, waits for the horse to settle into a steady trot, pushes the animal's nose between the rails. In the next yard, the other horses wait, and the stallion sends a shower of dust flying as he tries to get back to them. The rope swings silently to the rhythm of his trot, settles with a whoosh on the base of his neck and slides up sharply as it tightens behind his ears. Snapping his head back, the horse brings both front legs forward to strike. The ringers are working more quickly now, passing the head rope through the rails and holding it fast. The animal fights to breathe, his heart pounding and his flanks heavy with a white lather of sweat. The leg ropes fixed, the head rope is loosened and flicked over to the ringer in the centre of the yard. The horse leaps forward, believing he is free; as the leg ropes pull tight, three hundred and sixty kilos of flesh hits the hot bulldust.

'Grab 'is head, hold 'im, hold 'im, git that rope on 'is other foot!' the ringer yells. The free hind foot hits the bottom rail before it too is fettered by a rope. The hind leg is pulled hard against the

148

horse's girth, and the animal is now almost beat. A ringer kneels behind the head, puts a knee and full weight into his neck, hooks his elbow around the nose and twists the horse's head back.

Bonnie moves in, knows she must be quick and take deadly aim. A horse's scrotum is close to his body and some are able to retract their testes admirably. The horse, quivering with fear, tries to move, and she takes a deep breath, using the blade to nick the flesh just to the right depth. A ripple of pain surges through the animal; he whinnies, strains against his muscles and rope. Bonnie digs her boots into the loose dust, fights to keep her balance and her grip. She cuts the testes and membranes, stretching the main blood vessel tight in short sharp motions to reduce the bleeding. The struggling, jerking horse aids the separation and, finally, the bond is broken.

The ringers nod to her in a sign of silent respect, and prepare to brand. The smell of singeing hair and burning flesh fills the stock yard for a brief moment before the horse, his head cradled in Bonnie's arms to keep him still, is given a whack on his rump with a hat to get him back on his feet.

'Bush gate!' Bonnie yells as the horse moves uncertainly toward the mob, his legs splayed slightly, his head dropping and his dark coat dull with caked mud and blood.

She wipes the perspiration from her forehead, takes a gulp of water. 'Bring in the next one,' she calls.

It is Marlee's job to check the steer paddock fence. The only way to check the last three kilometres is to drive an extra ten kilometres down and then back up because the creek is impassable at the fence line. The other option is to ride a horse around the entire length, which takes up to three hours. Extra effort is required to check the last three kilometres and occasionally it's a task that is passed over.

Bonnie takes the boys out to camp draft the top line of three hundred steers which are to be sold later in the week. After two hours mustering, when they're finally blocked up in the bottom corner of the paddock, it is evident many of the larger steers are missing. Bonnie is exasperated; it is impossible to round up the cattle who have fled back to the freedom of the bush paddock and are now most probably mixed up with 5000 head of cows. Short of mustering the whole of the lower country again, they are gone until next season's muster.

Riding back along the fence line, she finds the tracks of the cattle and broken wires where they have pushed out under the floodgate at the creek crossing.

'Jesus Christ,' she mutters to herself, 'that lazy bitch hasn't restrung the floodgate properly after the last high tide two weeks ago. Marlee knows the fence needs to be checked twice a week. We've lost some of our best steers.'

Returning to the station, Bonnie has to front Charles with the news that she is well short of the anticipated number for the sale. This is not going to be easy; always reliable on her estimates of the number of stock, she knows he will demand an explanation. She also knows that the ultimate rap is going to be on her shoulders. If she issues an order that isn't complied with, she wears the responsibility.

'At least one hundred and thirty steers are missing, and I've found cattle tracks leading under the floodgate,' Bonnie tells her father. Charles hits the roof: they are counting on this mid-year sale to finance the remaining season's muster, and there are endless bills to pay.

'Bugger me, how the hell did they get under the floodgate!' he demands. 'Murray-Lee checks that fence twice a week.'

150

'The wires are loose and haven't been restrained since the last high tide,' Bonnie counters. 'It's our fault, Dad. You can't blame Marlee. We have clearly given her a job that she is not up to.'

To the west, Bullo borders Newry Station—rugged, untamed country which boasts wild and woolly scrub cattle. Bonnie's recent musters are on the boundary area here in a feeble attempt to clear some cattle. She chooses various yard sites along the road, where the trucks have easy access to the mob. Bonnie directs the entire operation, shifting the yards at night, the time when the cattle are most oblivious of movement.

The helicopters swing wide to wheel the flighty herd back into the gully. Looking for escape, the cattle turn sharply, but there is no way out; amid swirling dust, they channel en masse into their holding area. It is hot, dusty, dangerous work, and slow going. After many hours, they score only a miserable few hundred cattle.

The chopper pilot is running out of shotgun shells and the boys are complaining to Bonnie that they are fed up with rerigging the yard.

Bluey Lewis, now a stock inspector, knows this country and the cattle in it like the back of his hand. Bonnie trusts Blue absolutely. He's a man's man, and he looks it. At a hundred and eighty-three centimetres and weighing more than a hundred kilos, he has a shock of flaming red hair and sports a big hat which covers his face. Born in Queensland, he moved to the Territory and worked as a ringer before joining the Agricultural Department as a meat inspector. As tough as old boots, he also has a reputation as a softie.

As the former inspector at Bullo, Blue had an unenviable job. He continually bailed Sara and Charles out of trouble with their meatworks operation. As government regulator at a station where

rules were often ignored, he tried to offer the most liberal interpretation of the statutes. His job was difficult enough, but he had a
love–hate relationship with Sara and Charles, who always wanted to
take more than they could get. At every opportunity they took maximum advantage of his generosity; where Blue was prepared to bend
the rules, they expected him to break them.

Unlike Charles, who directs operations from a distance, Blue is
a hands-on man. In this isolated outpost, he brings in supplies, parts
for broken-down machinery, helps truck cattle, and fixes mistakes.
While the girls were still young and inexperienced, it was Blue who
did the work until they were old enough to help. A constant in a
world where people flit in and out, he later taught Bonnie and
Marlee station-hand jobs: how to slaughter and bone a beast on the
flat, and salt the beef. When Dick goes walkabout, with flash
dreams to travel to the big smoke, he invariably ends up, drunk,
dishevelled and disorderly, at Blue's home in Timber Creek. After
Dick spends days on the grog, culminating in the DTs, Blue, in despair, throws him in a truck and drives him back to Bullo. It is an endlessly repetitive pattern, but Blue never closes his door against him.

On a personal level, Blue plays an equally important role at
Bullo. The sounding board for all the schemes, he is also a shoulder
for Sara's troubles and a permanent fixture at the dinner table. When
the bush telegraph whispers that his role goes even further than that,
no-one blinks an eyelid.

'There are nearly 2000 head in that country,' Blue, sitting on
his haunches in the dust and pointing his finger into the scrub, says
to Bonnie. 'The government has offered a new incentive, as part of
the BTEC campaign, to shoot them out. It's worth quite a few
dollars per head.'

Bonnie supports the Brucellosis and Tuberculosis Eradication
Campaign which is aimed at removing all feral stock and

establishing some control over the spread of disease, but she cringes at the prospect of a shoot-out. If she has another year, and a few more fences, she is sure she can get those cattle out by muster. Newry and neighbouring Legune Stations have brought in some of the highest TB test results in the area, and are taking advantage of the scheme. But Bullo is clean and Bonnie hopes they don't have to resort to such brutal tactics. However, she also recalls reading the journals of the early explorers who described the Victoria River Downs as mile after mile of waving Mitchell grass. Now, after years of feral cattle, it is desolate, eroded and worn out. At least BTEC, with its culling of cattle, will allow regeneration of this country.

Bonnie decides to defer to management, but hopes Sara will back her up and the cattle can be saved. It has been a good season, she argues; she has stuck to budget, her predictions for cattle numbers and breakdowns have proved remarkably accurate, and all they need is more time.

'It's easy money for the cost of three hours chopper time,' Charles deliberates. 'We can shoot a hell of a lot of cattle in three hours.'

Sara sighs, but capitulates. 'Well, I suppose it has to be done.' Bonnie has been outvoted.

Working in tandem with Charles, who, as usual, is orchestrating from behind the scenes, Bonnie does all the work necessary to keep the operation running smoothly. With her crew of boys, they shift the yards every five days, moving where she knows the cattle to be. The program encourages testing of the herd that goes through the yards, but with a holding period of seventy-two hours, many are lost, perishing from heat stress or choking on dust. In areas too rugged to be mustered, and when cattle can't be tested, money is paid to shoot-out.

One poddy calf, his mother destined for the meatworks, is given little chance of making it through the night. Her mother will not accept her, and does not give her the first drink vital to her survival. Under the program, cattle's ears, chopped off and sent to the powers that be, fetch up to seventy-five dollars. Danielle, flat out working with Bonnie and with a yard full of cattle, pleads for the poddy to be spared.

'Yeah, okay, Danielle,' Bonnie agrees. 'But she is very weak, and you may lose her.'

Ten kilometres from the homestead, and with no fresh milk, Danielle nurtures the poddy on weak tea and sugar until he is strong enough to stand alone. He sleeps between their swags, and proves as faithful as a dog. Danielle nicknames the poddy 'Ears'.

The eventual shoot-out tally, for 1200 head, brings a handsome cheque, which is received quietly. The program is a godsend for Bullo station, ensuring they can now improve the quality of their stock. Out of the proceeds, and from the money from the sale of Montejinni, Charles buys himself a yacht, the *Mary Blair*.

It is the end of Bonnie's first season running the camp, time for checks and balances, an overview of successes and failures. There is no doubt it has been a good year, helped considerably by the economic boost of the BTEC program, but Bonnie knows she can't judge her own achievements; that must be left to others. She sits on the verandah at the homestead, knocking back a rum with Ross and Bluey, watching as the rain washes over the valley and settles the dust and turmoil of the past hectic months. The pressure has been enormous: she has had to organise helicopters, ensure the cattle trucks are where they are meant to be, dismantle and move the yards, oversee the horse plant, test the cattle in the holding yards and keep the lid on tempers. Most important, she had to come in on time and on budget.

Bullo tradition dictates that when the last yard gate shuts, it is time for the cap of the rum bottle to be thrown away. As early evening settles, the talk turns to goals for the following year— which fences need to be completed, projected stock figures, the future for BTEC. Bluey toasts a successful year, asks Bonnie what her next twelve-month plan is.

'There's no point asking me. You'll have to talk to Marlee. She's the boss next year.'

'Like fucking hell she is!' Bluey storms. 'You've done a fantastic job and everything's running like a Swiss watch. If you're not camp manager again next year, I want to know why.'

Rum in hand, he marches in to talk to Sara and Charles, demanding to know why Bonnie will be demoted to underling again. 'The boys respect her, she runs a good show and the figures tell the story,' he insists. 'No-one is going to be happy if there is a change of manager. For Christ's sake, leave it as it is.'

Charles has to agree. He and Bonnie are an effective team, and he respects the decisions she makes. He has given up telling her what to do; experience has taught him that while Bonnie listens to him, she inevitably goes her own way in the end if she feels her way is better. With his big dreams, Charles would prefer to spend his time pondering how to move Hong Kong to the Ord River. Bonnie is more practical. 'Before you put that grandiose scheme into action, Daddy, do you think you could order the trucks? I need them. Tomorrow.'

Bluey is right on another score, too: she has built up a strong muster team, blokes who like and respect her. Out here that's half the battle.

Marlee, initially furious when told Bonnie has usurped her

role, is finally placated by Sara, who wagers a compromise. Marlee will be bought a Toyota in compensation.

These early 80s are wild times for Bonnie. She has come into her own. Confident, intelligent and a team leader, she inspires her crew to try harder, do better. She spends the wet in preparation for the muster season—fencing, breaking horses, preparing yards, flying around in the plane to check waterholes and pick yard sites, writing up a plan and working out the budget. During the muster season, she sits up half the night drinking rum, singing with the boys and spinning yarns. A hangover never stops her working; up at four in the morning, she runs the show from a helicopter, flying until dark. She has good eyes in the scrub. Hanging out of the harness and peppering the cattle with shot to get them out of the cover of the trees and into the open, she shoots over her left shoulder with a semiautomatic twelve-gauge, sometimes going though three hundred shells in a day. With the cattle settled in the yard overnight ready to be drafted in the morning, they crawl into their camp and party all over again.

CHAPTER FOURTEEN

The station mechanics have ordered some spare parts, and the truck delivering them is due in at Kununurra.

'I'll fly the Super Cub in to pick them up,' Bonnie offers. She doesn't want to tackle the trip by road; apart from the fact that it is painfully slow, she hates driving. Besides it's a good excuse to give the fencing a miss for a day. A few of her mates from the flight service are in town, and this will give her a chance to catch up with them.

The truck hasn't arrived yet. Bonnie saunters into the bar at the local Kununurra pub to find her friends; there's nothing else to do and she has to wait until the spare parts get here. The sun is raging overhead and the cold beers go down well. If the truck doesn't get here soon, she won't be able to fly anywhere.

It arrives midafternoon, four hours behind schedule, and Bonnie sizes up her options. It's tempting to stay, but she had better get back. The mechanics need the parts by tomorrow morning. Her legs feel a bit unsteady as she heads toward the aircraft. She stops halfway across the tarmac, lines it up in her sights.

'Either that thing's moving or I'm more pissed than I think I am,' she says out loud. She knows she is lucky to be in Kununurra and not controlled airspace in Darwin: she would never get away with flying in this condition up there. A howling cross-wind buffets the plane as she fires it up and prepares for takeoff. She has forgotten to remove the wheel chocks and the aircraft jumps over them on full power. There is a twenty-five knot wind on the nose, and airborne, Bonnie heads straight for the wind sock.

Her mates in flight service watch the plane bank around for Bullo, and shake their heads. After putting up with Charlie Henderson all these years, they've now got his daughter to contend with. Obviously she has learned only too well from her old man about flying the Henderson Highway. They hope she isn't as honest about flying while under the weather as he is. But they know she's inherited his wicked sense of humour and doubt she would defer to bureaucrats any more than he does. They are still chuckling about a recent conversation Charles had with a very proper, very pompous Department of Civil Aviation delegate.

'What's your position?'

'Search me, son, ah haven't a clue.'

'Don't you have maps and navigating equipment?'

'Sorry, can't afford them.'

'Is it true that you drink when you fly?'

'Of course ah do.'

'Why? Don't you realise there is a strict regulation forbidding pilots to drink?'

'Why? Because the more ah drink, the more careful ah am. Safety is mah guide.'

'You mean, when you're sober, you're careless?'

'Too right! Now, sir, for this heinous crime, could you tell me whether you plan to deport me, or just ground me!"

The job of the flight service operators isn't to control aircraft movement but merely to monitor radio calls and give flight information. Bonnie's mates are more than happy to be able to turn a blind eye to her antics.

By the time Bonnie hits Bullo, the beer has really taken effect. Too plastered to land, she flies around for another hour and counts an awful lot of cattle before she feels confident she can bring the plane in.

Bushfire has come to their doorstep, leaping flames of gold and copper furiously running with the wind. The fires have raged for days, like Dante's inferno, and the stockmen, weather-beaten and weary, have fought them relentlessly. This is a hard land, built for hard men. An eerie stillness now sits heavy on the night air. Bonnie can smell the heat, the burning trunks of ancient trees and the oil from their leaves, the smoke that drifts and the scorched ash. She can hear the bush animals scurrying for cover, away from the furnace, and the squeals of those who can't escape. She remembers old Mary's dreamtime story about fire, told to her in that gentle singsong voice, one of the many stories that lulled her to sleep in her childhood.

In early times people had no fire because it was kept by two friends, Koorambin the water rat and Pandawinda the cod fish, in their underwater home amongst the river reeds. All efforts by the people to obtain a spark of fire failed.

One day the two friends cooked a large heap of freshwater mussels on the riverbank. The fishing eagle noticed the smoke from the fire and, soaring high in the sky, he magically caused a strong wind to blow the fire amongst the dry reeds. The two friends desperately tried to put out the fire, but the eagle caused a whirlwind to blow the fire in all directions so that it reached as far as the forests which grew thickly at that time on the plains bordering the river. The forests were burnt out, and that is the reason for the immense bare plains; but the people were able to get as much fire as they wanted and have kept it ever since.

Flying over the property's border the next day, Bonnie sees the desolate land far below her, black and bleak and barren. It is still smouldering with singed stumps and shrivelled carcasses. When the rains come, it will regenerate; the grass will grow and the creeks flow. But now, it is a dead, torched land, with a dead and ghostly silence.

The mickeys—young wild bulls—have to be castrated and branded. It's a tricky job, and dangerous. The bulls, frisky and quick, take deadly aim when they kick. Like everyone else, Bonnie knows to move fast if one looks particularly vicious. She has already had a few near misses this season, which adds a bit of spice to the work. While dehorning cattle, a cow slipped out of the steel head brace and came out looking for trouble. Heading straight for Bonnie, he just about took her shirt off, and left a graze mark right across her stomach. It is a lesson she is determined not to forget: always sidestep, stay out of their way.

'Sometimes you have to move only a foot to save your life,' a ringer tells her, 'but move that foot you must! And do it fast!'

Today the yard is full of cleanskins and there is a big mob to clear before they can start to tail out the steers and cows, test for TB and move the yards. Bonnie thinks about her father's expression 'chop chop, no walla walla', meaning cut the talking and get to work, and moves into the yard. They are already behind schedule and have a long way to go.

Grabbing the knife, she rests on her haunches and prepares to cut the bull's testicles. This one, weighing two hundred and fifty kilos, is restless and cranky, kicking up the dust next to the other ten head that are jammed in next to him. Bonnie grabs him, tries to keep him steady as he lowers his rump and pinions her wrist underneath him. Waves of pain shoot up her arm; instantly, she jabs the knife in his side to get him to move off her. She picks the knife up again, realises she has no strength left from the crushing weight of the bull. There are still one hundred and fifty left to cut and not much time to do it in. Ambidextrous, she makes a deft switch. Now using the knife in her injured left hand, she castrates the remainder, using her stronger right hand to grip the testicles.

The next day her left wrist, which has swollen during the night to the size of a tennis ball, is excruciatingly painful. The vet, arriving at camp the next morning, takes a look. 'What the hell have you done to it, Bonnie? It looks in terrible shape.'

He makes a rough cast from plaster of Paris, offers some sage advice. 'If an animal was in that much pain, I'd make sure it slowed up,' he says. 'You're going to have to have it checked by a doctor, regardless of how busy you are. Go back to the homestead.'

'I'll be right,' Bonnie answers. 'It's not that bad.' She grinds her jaw, takes a slug from the pannikin, feels the rum warm her and hit the mark. 'This is man's best friend, next to a dog,' she grins. 'Takes the edge off any pain.'

The Disprin she has taken has no effect, and the swelling is still intense. Reluctantly, she finally admits that in the two weeks since she injured her wrist, there has been no improvement. Using her good hand, she guns the Super Cub down the airstrip and heads the aircraft to Darwin.

161

The doctor, Wal Tracey, used to rough and ready men from the bush, shakes his head when he examines her wrist. As a family friend and regular visitor to Bullo, he has known Bonnie since she was a girl, and chastises her. 'You should have been brought in as soon as you hurt it,' he admonishes. 'It needed to be plastered properly, to set it back into shape, instead of being in that cast for a fortnight. It's broken, and it's a complicated fracture. You'll need to keep it strapped for six weeks.'

Bonnie groans, thinks of the schedule ahead of them back at camp. 'What a pain in the arse,' she says.

Wal has noticed something else about her too. Her mouth barely opens when she speaks, as if it is painful for her to move it. She has avoided light since she entered his surgery, turning her head away and shading her eyes with her good hand. Clearly she is not well.

'Bonnie, do you have a headache?' he asks her. He watches closely for her reaction, trying to gauge the source of her pain. She squints back at him, ripples of light dancing in front of her eyes.

'It's not really like a headache,' she answers. 'It feels different to that. Worse.'

Wal immediately recognises classic migraine symptoms, but he's unhappy about the lack of movement in her jaw. 'How long have you been restricting your jaw muscles, Bonnie?'

'About ten years.'

'Ten years? So you've had it since you were a child? Have you ever had it checked?'

'Mum took me to a doctor once, a long time ago, but apart from that, no,' she replies. 'I don't come into town that often.'

Wal pulls up a pethidine shot to ease her migraine, advises her to seek specialist help for her jaw as soon as she can. 'You can't muck about with your health like this, Bonnie. You've put up with the pain for 10 years too long already. What do you take to ease it?'

162

Bonnie stifles a laugh. What does he think they take in the bush—a cup of tea and a Bex? 'I drink rum,' she says. 'That helps.'

He glances at her, disapproval written all over his face. 'It might help short term, Bonnie, but it's no cure.'

'Maybe so,' she responds, 'but it's better than any other cure that's offering right at the moment. And besides, there's nothing like a good hangover to let you know you're alive!'

It's time to round up another stock camp. Bonnie, raised side by side with the Aborigines, shares the same respect for them as Charles does. Like him, she wouldn't give two bob for the white 'rednecks' of the north who refuse to work; people referred to, in Maryland, as 'po' white trash'. But she is deeply saddened by the breakdown in Aboriginal society, a disintegration most evident in the men and women she has known all her life who haven't drawn a sober breath in years. Many of them now look like malnourished refugees, skinny, with weeping sores and forlorn eyes. The tribal leaders can't control them any more, and know that an honest day's work is the best way to keep them on the straight and narrow.

Bonnie, like her father, recognises that an Aborigine doesn't need a university degree to prove he's bright: most of the fellas she knows are courteous, intelligent, brave and loyal. If a man can track a lizard and sit a wild horse, he deserves respect, has earned it. Everyone, she believes—from the highest dignitary to a beggar in the street—should be judged by their character, not by their background or education.

Some of the Aboriginal stockmen go back to their communities after a muster season, but most head to town, living in camps and spending their wages on grog. If Bonnie is to get a good crew again this season, she has to get them sober.

163

She pulls the Toyota up outside the camp, nods g'day to Albert Croson Montejinni, who has taken his grand name from the station when he worked as a ringer long before Charles and Gus owned it. He's getting old now; in his seventies, his brown eyes are milky and weeping from the cataracts that blind so many of his people. He squints through the afternoon glare, recognises who has just spoken to him. He has known Bonnie since she was a piccaninny; he trusts this one. Reaching into his shirt pocket, he pulls out a pristine white handkerchief and wipes away the perspiration and grime from his gnarled hand. He puts the handkerchief back in his pocket, extends his grip to Bonnie's in a solid grasp. She smiles: Albert may be losing his eyesight, but he will never lose his dignity.

She swings into the camp, asks a group where she might find young Peter Arwon, who proved himself a tireless worker in the last camp. 'Hey, mate' she says. 'You know me, from Bullo River. You know that fella, Peter Arwon—where 'e now? I want boys for my stock camp, we work maybe five weeks and I bring them back for Kununurra rodeo.'

The oldest bloke in the group recognises the newcomer amongst them, points to her with a grin. 'You Charlie Henderson's daughter,' he says. 'I bin knowin' you since you was only a girl. Dat Peter Arwon, 'im not 'ere, but I bring you my cousin and my brudder, dem good blokes, we go fin' dem.'

It's more a command than a question, and he saunters off ahead of her through the camp, talking to her as he goes. 'My brudder he bin in dat nudder camp now. We bin find 'im.'

Peter's whereabouts still remain a mystery, and Bonnie ventures to ask again where he is. 'Where Peter? 'Im at the pub, 'im working? Where Peter now?'

The old bloke looks at Bonnie, as if he had already answered her question. 'Oh, he bin in jail.'

164

Bonnie knows better than to enquire how long he's been serving time at Her Majesty's pleasure, or when he's due out. Time has no meaning for these people; years of working with them has taught her that it is measured by the sun and the seasons. It is also selective: many have an uncanny ability to know, without asking, when it's pub opening time.

On the last camp, while sitting on their horses tailing a mob of cattle—keeping them together in a group but allowing them to wander and graze a little—Bonnie had asked Peter what time it was.

He'd looked at his watch, shook his head. 'Don't know what time,' he said. 'Watch is having a camp.'

He looked up at the sun, gauged its position in the sky. 'It's four o'clock,' he'd ventured. He was spot on.

'You tell that Peter Arwon,' Bonnie says, 'when he gets out he come and see me. I'll come pick him up, take him out to Bullo River.'

The answer obviously pleases the man. 'Yeah,' he replies. 'You take 'im out dere, make 'im work on dat station and stay 'im out of trouble, dat Peter Arwon.'

It is still dark, and the damp chill of a dewy dry-season morning settles over the canvas of swags. Sparks fly from the camp fire and the smell of ironwood leaves drifts in the air as flames slowly start to leap in the glowing embers. Bonnie opens one eye, sees Stumpy, the cook, bending over the fire, stirring the coals with a stick. He makes a small hollow by the log that has been burning slowly all night and puts the billy on. All around, the flat is covered by the shadow of the boys hunkered low in their swags. Last night's stew pot is pushed closer to the heat and soon its sweet aroma mingles with the smell of the smoke.

The camp is stirring now: the clatter of tin plates and pannikins in chorus with the crackle of the fire, quiet morning greetings and the mournful bellowing of the cattle in the yard. The rattle and clank of the portable yard's panels echo on the air, and the thought of handling those cold steel rails on this chilly morning sends up a collective shiver. Everyone moves closer to the fire and hands wrap tighter around the hot tin mug of strong, sweet blue-black tea.

Last night, the helicopters finally chased the cattle up the wings, forcing them through the gates in a mushrooming cloud of dust. Spewing over everything, the fine bulldust can choke or suffocate young or weak cattle; to prevent this, the yards are sprayed with water from a small tank hooked behind the tractor and filled with water pumped from the river. The cattle mill around, hot and temperamental from being stirred by the choppers. Bonnie climbs up on the rails from where she can see the entire mob, and does a rough count in her head. It will take all day tomorrow to draft this lot; there are some big bullocks and the trucks will have to be ordered for the day after that. First, they need to settle and cool off overnight.

Early morning light streaks across the horizon as the camp tucks into stew, damper and tea before heading down to the yard. Every man knows his job: three blokes in the back yard push the mob up to the forcing pen while two work the round yard gates. Bonnie is on the drafting gate, checking them one by one as they run past, instructing which gate each is to go through.

A huge bullock comes crashing into the small round yard. 'Meatworks!' Bonnie calls. This bastard has been on the loose for a long while; as big as a thoroughbred horse, he spins around the yard looking for a way out. The boys are quick on the gate as the bullock dives through into his designated pen.

'We'll have trouble loading him,' she yells. 'His horns are too wide for the ramp.' There is no way they can take even a few inches off his horns; she has seen many bullocks just lie down and die when they are cut.

She feels sad for the old scrubbers, has written about them.

... They broke an iron spirit when with sticks they beat him hard
When they roped and tied and trucked him to the
wooden railed yard
For now he stands, just barely, the pain shows in his face.
And he knows that he has run his last and final race.

But there is no time or room for sentiment in the stock yard.

Snorting and crashing, the next mickey is run in. This one has obviously never been in a yard in its life.

'Cleanskin!' Bonnie yells. The cleanskin pen is a wild affair. Restless and reckless, the cattle refuse to stand quiet, and when a new one runs through there is a rush to the back. In the mayhem, they knock each other over and crash into the panel. Bonnie has to keep an eye on them: there are a few big ones that missed last season's muster and who will trample on the smaller ones and cause a pile-up if the crew is not careful. After a few days in the yard, branded, hand-fed and watered, they'll settle down.

Bonnie marks each one as it comes through, recording three hundred and eighty head on the tally sheet by dinnertime. It's too slow: she will have to make sure they get through a lot more by teatime. They pull up in the heat of the day, water the stock and hose the yard down, take note of the troublemakers at the back of the pens. Hopefully they'll cool off by the afternoon.

The portable yard is dangerous work. Panels shift as a scrub bull crashes into the rail below Bonnie's feet and the horns lock under and start to lift. She leaps off the other side of the rail, returns with a short pipe to whack the bull on the nose. Spinning wildly, the bull lifts a heifer clean up over his back; bellowing, the young cow hits the ground and scrambles up with blood coursing from the wound in her side.

'You bastard!' Bonnie yells. 'Get him out, quick!' This bull, a massive five hundred and forty-five kilos, has eluded the yard for years, and has no intention of staying in there. As the gates swing open, he jams another steer against the side of the yard.

'Hunt him up, fast!'

An Aboriginal stockman jumps down into the gateway, drops to all fours. 'Hey, bullie, come and get me,' he taunts.

The scrubber wheels about, his head drops and foams flies from his mouth. The boy flicks a handful of dust up and instinctively leaps sideways as the half-ton of beef goes hurtling past. The gate clangs shut.

'You didn't hang around long in there!' Bonnie laughs. 'Are you scared of that little bullie or something?'

There never seems to be enough time: it's all rush and tear, chasing the clock, organising the choppers and trucks, shifting the yards and the wings, moving drums of av-gas to a lonely place in the scrub prearranged with the helicopter pilots. But there is a sense of belonging, great pride in a job well done, in teamwork and in knowing this vast country.

CHAPTER FIFTEEN

The SAS have chosen Bullo to practise survival missions. The country is perfect: remote, hot and with dense scrub, it will put any man to the test, even these elite army boys. For two weeks they have to supplement their small rations with bush food, find a way out from where they have landed, and remain undetected by the imaginary enemy. The night before their exercise starts, Bonnie wagers a bet with them.

'This is the deal,' she says. 'I bet I can crack your hiding place within half a day. If I do, you owe me a couple of bottles of rum. If I don't, the shout's on me.'

The army boys have heard of the Henderson women—there have been other army exercises at Bullo—but they are very rarely seen in public, except at outback rodeos or when they get their stores in town. The boys look at each other, give a sly grin. Seems the easiest way they know to score a few bottles of free grog.

'Okay, you're on. Give us two days to find our spot, and then you can try and find us.'

This country is tougher than they expected. The rivers are swollen and infested with crocodiles; the heat is savage and so are the spiders and snakes that crawl and slither around them. Exhausted from trying to negotiate their way, they finally hunker down under thick scrub and make camp for the second night. This part of the country is so dense, no-one could ever find them.

At first light Bonnie takes off in the Super Cub, flying low, looking out the side window for any sign of the troops. They obviously know their stuff, have hidden themselves well. She knows they would have to be in scrub country and that they are wearing camouflage gear. The only way to find them is to put herself in their shoes, work out where she would go in the same situation. They wouldn't be too close to a river because of the crocs; wouldn't be too far away either, because they need water and need to be in country where they can catch animals to eat. That narrows it down a lot …

Bonnie heads the plane toward the Victoria River and senses she is on a victory trail. They couldn't have covered any more area than this by foot in two days, and beyond here, the country becomes less dense. She's got to give it to them: for strangers to this part of the world, they have worked out their position well. Dropping down to below fifty feet, she scans the bush, notices the faint trace of human shadows. This is a great game. She circles, looks for a place to put the plane down, then saunters over to their hiding place.

'G'day, fellas,' she laughs. 'Who's got the rum?'

They spotted her plane flying over earlier, kept their fingers crossed. It is bad enough to be cracked at all, let alone to be cracked by a woman. If word of this gets out, they'll be the laughing stock of the army.

The commander shakes her hand, gallantly admits defeat. 'I don't suppose you want a career change, do you?' he asks.

Sick of their bush rations, the troops accept Bonnie's offer to send a vehicle out and bring them back into the homestead for breakfast. Eggs and bacon have got to beat the hell out of what they've been eating, and what army headquarters don't know won't hurt them.

Bonnie's reputation for having inherited her father's legendary flying style has spread through flight services. Like Charles, she often flies with her feet up on the instrument panel, reading a book or writing a letter. The bureaucrats on the ground, with their sticky rules and regulations, are more an annoyance than a help. Whilst Bonnie is flying to Darwin with Charles, the radio roars into life with the obstinate demand from flight service to advise her track for destination. Neither she nor Charles has bothered to work that out; they know this airspace and know where they are going. Shouting over the din of the radial engine, Bonnie asks her father for advice.

'They want to know our track,' she yells. 'What do I tell them?'

Charles leans back in his seat, affects a serious air. He purses his lips, as if deep in concentration. 'Ar, well, ask them what they suggest.'

Bonnie loves this game. When she is flying alone, she gives them wild and fanciful excuses about why she hasn't tracked direction: her map has flown out the window; she has to sign off because she is losing radio contact and will get back to them later; she has spilled her flask of coffee and is busy wiping it up. She gets on the radio, goes through the preliminaries, and hits them with the question at the end. 'What do you suggest for our track?'

The response is always the same: demands to report in when they get on the ground, furious allegations of irresponsibility.

'I don't think they're very happy, Daddy,' Bonnie laughs as she signs off. 'They've got no sense of humour, those blokes.'

RM Williams, born in rural South Australia six years before the start of the Great War, could not have foreseen the empire he was later to build. As a young man, he left home and hearth, humping his swag through virgin country in search of a dream. They were tough, wild days in which he mixed with tough, wild men; through the bleak depression years, he often relied on the generosity of strangers and his own guile to put food in his mouth. More often, camped on the outskirts of a town, he was asked by the local constabulary to move on or be booked for vagrancy. Through his young life, he worked as a well-sinker, stockman, tea planter, cattle trader and drover.

In 1933 Williams got the break that would change his path in life and indelibly print his name on the Australian psyche as a visionary; a man who proved that with honesty and hard work, dreams could become reality. Starting a small manufacturing business, he sold a handmade pack saddle to Sir Sidney Kidman for five quid. Kidman, renowned for his miserly spirit, was impressed with the handiwork and with the man who sold him the saddle. An empire was born.

Bonnie, kitted out in jeans and pigtails, goes to Adelaide to observe the saddle-making section of the RM Williams factory. Almost twenty-one, she takes with her only her swag, her ability to learn by listening and not talking, and a boyish charm. Dresses, perfume and lipstick are not for her; she is happiest sitting on the floor, a pannikin of tea close by, messing about with leather dyes and needlework. Romance is a long way from her thoughts; she wants to learn how to make saddles, and then get back to Bullo. She feels at odds in the city.

Susan Seppelt, RM's granddaughter, notices this girl from the bush. 'She was intriguing: sometimes silent, sometimes loud and earthy,' she recalls. 'The thing that struck me most about her was her honesty. There was no guile in her; she never said a bad word about anybody. Partly for that reason, people loved her. You instinctively knew you could trust Bonnie.'

Susan's uncle, Peter Williams, also notices Bonnie. Seven years his junior, she fascinates him, the way she focuses on the task at hand, how she moves among people and, in a few short sentences, makes them feel good about themselves. She's beautiful, too, her skin clear and brown from years in the sun, with a full, sensuous mouth and green eyes that hint she's game for fun. He has only ever seen her in her Levis and covered in leather dye, but he senses that, dressed in feminine clothes, she would be a knockout. He is right. At a family dinner she wears a skirt and silk top, her hair loose around her shoulders. If she notices the attention she receives, it isn't obvious: charming and attentive, she draws people to her like a magnet. She obviously isn't wearing a bra, either, which amuses him. You can take the girl out of the bush, but you can't take the bush out of the girl.

Many nights Peter and Bonnie sit over a bottle of rum and talk. He loves Bonnie's company, her sharp wit and lateral thinking, and it doesn't surprise him to learn she has almost a genius IQ.

He is right about another thing, too: she does like to have fun, and her earthy mannerisms belie a passionate nature. Most of all, she likes to cuddle, to snuggle in next to his chest and feel his arms around her. By the time she has to return to Bullo, Peter, gentle and intelligent, has fallen in love.

* * *

The party is in full swing. Gone are Bonnie's pigtails and jeans; tonight she wears a white dress and her hair long. Peter has arrived from Adelaide and has asked her to marry him. She has said yes and her parents are thrilled. If Bonnie has doubts, they are swept away in the heat of the moment.

Lynette Ainsworth, at the party with Ross, is one of the few to sense that all that glitters at Bullo that night is not gold. 'I don't know if anyone really bothered to ask Bonnie whether she loved Peter,' she says. 'They seemed to meet one minute and become engaged the next. Charles visualised a glorious alliance between the Williams and Hendersons, and it appeared that it would come to pass. Bonnie, his favourite daughter, raised in isolation and free from outside influences, is to marry the son of one of Australia's best connected families.'

An ABC crew, at Bullo filming a sequel to a documentary they made there years earlier, turn their cameras on the party. It is a wonderful setting: food and grog is in copious supply, music hums in the background, and friends joke and chat.

Susan, injured in a car accident in Adelaide, has come to Bullo to recuperate. She and Bonnie have become good friends, and it is a friendship that strengthens over the years.

Living so close to the family, Susan has witnessed the conflicts first hand. 'Charles loved young girls with good legs and, as a result, Sara tended to see them as a threat. He deliberately created conflict, arranging the seating at the dining table to suit himself and his preference for that evening.'

Although Charles' philosophy—to build strength of character through adversity—is accepted without question at Bullo, Susan finds it disconcerting. 'It shaped a very dysfunctional family and there was

174

always a lot of tension and turmoil in that household. Charles wanted his girls to be as good as a man in everything they did and then, at night, to play the feminine role. He was intolerable to live with in many ways, particularly when he was bored. Bonnie was the station manager when I was there and she and Marlee never shared the same stage; it was an unspoken rule. I have heard Charles tell Bonnie, "You know your mother never loved you," and there were obvious conflicts created by that statement. Charles played favourites with Bonnie, and Sara did the same with Marlee. It wasn't positive parenting.'

The ABC producer, an Irishman with a strong brogue and gift for making people feel at ease, seeks perfection in his filming. Bonnie, stitching a saddle, does not stop working as he talks to her, the camera rolling. Intent on her saddle making, she keeps her head down when he asks her what attracts her in a man.

'Oh well,' she says quietly, 'intelligence and then, I guess, self-confidence. If he isn't strong in mind and body, I can't respect him. If I can't respect him, I can't love him.'

Asked where she would like to live after she is married, she replies, 'I'm happy right here.'

Repeatedly, the producer asks the family to redo a performance for the camera. 'Ooo, that was foin, terrefec,' he says, 'but would ya moind jest doin' it one more toim?'

Bonnie is delivered gift-wrapped to Peter in a sheet. She feels silly, dressed up like this, wonders what she will have to do for an encore at the wedding.

'There you are,' Charles says to Peter. 'We've been trying for years to get rid of her.' The comment is meant as a joke, but Charles' sister, Margaret, is less charitable when she sees the film.

'I shuddered; here was this lovely young girl being handed over in a bedsheet to her prospective husband. They may as well have added, "Here, take her."'

Bonnie hands Peter his engagement present—a handmade saddle on which she has worked for weeks—and waits for his response. This saddle, the first she has made, is special. During the wet season two years before, she pored over books on how to make them, working at night when no-one else was around. She found an old saddle of Marlee's that had been sitting gathering dust for years; the brown leather had deteriorated, and mould covered its American insignia. Bonnie checked with Sara that she could use it, pulled it apart and started from scratch. Dyed black with white stitching, the end result was superb and she is very proud of it. It is a saddle fit for a king. Marlee was furious when she returned to the station and found the saddle remade.

'That was mine!' she said. 'You had no right to pull it apart!'

This time, Sara came to Bonnie's defence. 'That saddle has been sitting there forever, Marlee. That's a ridiculous attitude for you to take.'

Now the saddle has been handed to Peter, and Bonnie badly wants him to love it. For a moment she recalls the bridle she made David for his twenty-first, using the treasured awl blade that an Aborigine on the station had given her after he saw her struggling with the pointed end of a pocket knife. David loved his gift, used it all the time.

Peter accepts the saddle, smiles a shy thank you, and puts it aside.

Well after midnight, with the effects of the rum now kicking in and a feeling of vague disquiet about her impending marriage, Bonnie kisses the producer goodnight. Suddenly her old spark returns; in a loud voice she says to him, 'Ooo, that was foin, terrefec, but would ya moind jest doin' it one more toim?'

Before long, Peter knows something is wrong. Bonnie is one of the boys at the stock camps, and the pair don't seem to spend many intimate moments together any more. When he finally asks her what she's thinking, she kicks at the dirt and avoids his gaze.

'I suppose it was all a bit quick,' she answers. Out at Bullo, the differences between them are patently obvious. He comes from an isolated existence where men are gentlemen; Bonnie comes from a place where men are men, and the women have to work like them.

Later she confides to Susan the real reason she broke off the engagement. 'Peter's a wonderful bloke, but he's too nice for me. I need someone who offers more of a challenge.'

Lynette remembers the episode as another bizarre chapter in the life of a family who made its own rules. 'The film crew picked up their cameras and went home; Peter picked up his swag and went south, and Bonnie picked up her old way of life and got on with it. And that, as they say in the classics, was that.'

CHAPTER SIXTEEN

Charles' double pneumonia has weakened him considerably, and in the face of his physical weakness, his solution is sheer arrogance. Now, instead of earning respect, he demands it, working on an even shorter fuse than normal and expecting superhuman efforts under supertrying conditions. The debilitating illness saps the energy he needs to fly the aircraft and deliver the beef, and it affects his decision-making. He is drinking more, sometimes demolishing a bottle of rum a night, using alcohol to spark his flagging spirit, fire his imagination, help him sleep. It's a cycle of self-destruction that is painfully evident to those closest to him, but he refuses to capitulate, to take the rest he so desperately needs.

His illness has taken much of the light from his eyes, and he is losing control of his once legendary dinner parties. He occasionally retires to bed earlier than usual, but his expectations that others do the same are increasingly ignored. If Sara once followed him without question, guests note that she now lingers at the dining table

Amelia, Bonnie and Hattie.
Janette Wilson

Bonnie riding her first bull.
Janette Wilson

A hard-earned thirst after Bonnie's first bull ride.
Janette Wilson

Hattie and her blue cattle-dog pup.
Janette Wilson

Hattie, and Julia's foal, Willo.
Janette Wilson

The hub of the household — Bonnie's workroom.

An example of Bonnie's fine saddle work.

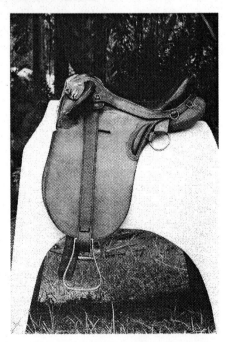

Learning to throw a rope was a hard slog, but it has
been an invaluable skill.
Janette Wilson

First contact. Bonnie uses the gentle approach with Anna.
Janette Wilson

One of the many things Bonnie inherited from her father was his irrepressible love of life.
Janette Wilson

well after Charles has gone to bed. His displeasure is written on his face as he takes his lone departure.

But even with Charles away sailing the tension at the station reaches extremes. This season the build-up to the wet season is suffocating and tempers are short. Increasingly interested in aerobatics, Bonnie escapes by spending as much time in Darwin as she can. The freedom of aerobatics interests her: flying upside down, surrounded only by air, with the noise of the engines blocking out everything else. In twelve hours she learns every manoeuvre in the book; after fifty hours, she seriously thinks of competition flying. The boys at the aerobatic club know her well by now: she flies like a jet jockey and is a natural.

'You're not a bad pilot, for a girl,' they tell her. It's high praise, and Bonnie knows it: Australian aerobatics has always been a man's domain. Few women have proven themselves capable, and none has ever taken a title. Bonnie hangs around the club so often she has become part of the furniture, and she's not afraid to get her hands dirty.

Lying on her back, cleaning the undercarriage of the aircraft one day, she notices two pairs of feet stop in front of the plane.

'Bonnie, come out here for a sec.' It's Guido, her aerobatics instructor.

Covered in grease, Bonnie wheels herself out and wipes the oil from her hands onto her jeans. The bandanna around her forehead hasn't stopped the perspiration trickling into her eyes, and she squints through the harsh sunlight as she extends a grubby hand to the stranger. 'Hi, I'm Bonnie Henderson.'

The man returns her grasp, speaks in a modulated, smooth voice. 'Arthur Palmer. Pleased to meet you.'

'You shouldn't be,' Guido interrupts. 'This girl flies better than you do!'

Bonnie laughs. Guido is an extremely competent pilot who has flown on the Australian team and instructs her—and Arthur—in aerobatics.

'I've got to finish working on this plane,' she says. 'See you later, Arthur.'

He watches her as she disappears under the aircraft, thinks she'd be gorgeous if she wasn't covered in grease.

Bonnie is at the hangar again, sitting on some boxes and drinking a beer with the boys. Arthur saunters in, head held high and a confident swagger in his slim hips. He heads over to speak to Bonnie, but she is embarrassed. For the life of her she can't remember who this bloke is.

'We met last week, when you were cleaning the aircraft,' he prompts. His brown eyes have an intensity she finds daunting. They move restlessly, taking in everything around him in a quick sweep, and the exaggerated tone of his voice hints that whatever he has to say should be listened to carefully. Occasionally his hands move to punctuate his conversation, as if he is conducting an impromptu play.

Bonnie has to admit he's attractive. Slim, with brown hair flecked with blond, the shadow of a smirk flickers around his mouth. He has an arrogant, cocksure manner, is obviously intelligent, and knows it. She stares back at him, and his eyes are teasing now, laughing. She suddenly remembers what Guido said to him: 'This woman can fly better than you can,' and she smiles to herself. Score one for her.

'Would you like to go for a drink somewhere?' he asks. The invitation is extended casually, like a throwaway line, but Bonnie senses he is not a man used to knockbacks.

'Yeah, righto,' she answers. She's going out with a few different blokes at the moment, none of them serious, and that's the way she wants to keep it. She doesn't intend to repeat the close call she had with Peter. They keep in touch, are still good mates, but she knows if they had married, it wouldn't have lasted.

'Are you heading off, Bon?' one of the fellas asks. Bugger Arthur Palmer, he thinks; he had wanted to ask her out himself.

Born in mid-April, 1953, Arthur Beau Palmer was raised virtually as an only child on a farm west of Toowoomba in Queensland. His sister, born ten years earlier, was already away at boarding school and Arthur's place in the family, as the son and heir, was protected and secure. From early childhood he displayed many typical Arian character traits: idealistic, arrogant and egotistical, his outwardly self-confident demeanour masked a fierce drive and determination to win. His father, a RAF pilot during World War II, is an Aussie gentleman, and his mother, with an English finishing school education, is graceful and charming. Neither of them had any knowledge of how to manage their mixed dairy, sheep and crop farm when they first began, but perseverance and hard work paid dividends. At ten Arthur was sent to the exclusive Brisbane Boys College. Dominant and forthright, he is a leader not a follower and clings tenaciously to his belief that he is smarter than the next man. He will not suffer fools.

Having gained a diploma of Fine Arts, Arthur, with youthful visions, undertook a career as an anthropological consultant working for Aboriginal land rights. Whilst he fights to realise their land claims, he views the Aborigines with a curious mixture of respect and disdain. There is fire in his speech as he talks of their appalling living conditions, their diet, and their helplessness in fighting the diseases which decimate them. But he has seen too much: children living in filthy camps and trailing tapeworms from

181

their bottoms; open sewers running through Aboriginal communities, attracting blowflies and disease; new houses reduced to shanties within weeks. He is moved more by frustration than pity. His field work, investigating ways to eradicate tapeworm in the dogs who eat and sleep with the Aborigines, takes him years, and he knows the winds of change must start blowing in Canberra before they blow through to the north. He sits for hours, crosslegged on the earth, discussing problems with the tribal elders whom he greatly respects; but if he is among them, he is not of them. Arthur Beau Palmer is a white man, and as a white man he has more power.

Blessed with boyish good looks, innate charm and a fine grasp of the English language, which he uses at every opportunity, Arthur likes to win. From women he expects and demands a high degree of loyalty and an equal degree of independence. When he tires of a partner, the ice in his voice reflects the cooling off in his ardour. Later, Bonnie is to learn she has more to fear from his ice than his fire.

Their relationship starts slowly. Darwin, now risen from the ashes of Cyclone Tracy, is still a relatively small city, where tongues wag. Arthur, living with a woman, needs to be a little careful. He and Bonnie catch up over dinner or drinks when she is in town, talk about life in the bush and Australian poets. Arthur often marks out pages in poetry books for Bonnie to read, but if there is a flame between them, it is yet to ignite.

'I was thirty years old, owned my own house, had the most successful anthropology consultancy in Australia, enjoyed flying and flew well, and had no intention of getting married,' he recalls. 'Bonnie and I shared interests, but there was nothing happening between us in the beginning.'

Following a trip overseas which lasts several weeks, Arthur flies one of Bonnie's boyfriends down to Bullo. The boyfriend, uncouth and shabby in comparison with Arthur, may as well have stayed on board the plane. Bonnie, hanging on Arthur's every word, can't take her eyes from him, and he can't help but notice. There is only one way to read that look.

'Arthur kept flinching all the way through the dinner that night and I wondered what on earth was wrong with him,' Lynette recalls.

Bonnie looks exceptionally attractive tonight. Horrified at how primitive the girls are, Lynette has given them all a haircut that morning. It is one thing to live in the bush, she tells them, quite another to advertise it with ghastly haircuts that are ten years out of date.

Ross and Lynette have been living in Katherine since they were married in 1983. Their wedding was decorously planned around another premiere social event—the Brahman breeders' dinner. Many of their guests, including big-name Territory pastoralists, would be in town for that weekend and, as getting men of the land off their properties requires much foresight and planning, it seemed the perfect opportunity. Charles had decided against attending the wedding—these formal events really weren't his thing—but Sara and the girls were looking forward to a weekend in town.

The outfits they had chosen were eye-catching in the extreme, prompting a city girl to remark they looked like extras from *Gone with the Wind*. Sara wore a full pink chiffon skirt over taffeta, complete with picture hat; Marlee and Bonnie were in matching numbers, one in aqua, the other baby blue. But if their costumes created sidelong glances, what followed was nothing short of a spectacle. On opposite sides of the room, both Marlee and Bonnie proceeded to get roaring drunk on rum and grapefruit juice. Never renowned for her social graces, Bonnie really hit her straps, becoming increasingly loud and garrulous.

Always the queen of tact, Sara was mortified, apologising profusely for her daughter's behaviour and glaring at her to settle down. 'I am so sorry, Lynette,' she said. 'I suppose the girls feel as if they are losing something that is theirs. Ross.'

Lynette, who had by now embraced the Territory and its way of life, found the incident amusing and regarded it as a meeting of two different worlds. Her southern friends, wide-eyed at Bonnie's antics, took photos to enrich their retelling of the story back home. In typical Territory fashion, the reception continued until dawn when the guests stumbled out into the dusty, quiet street to make their way back to their respective hotels. The girls had lost Ross, and Lynette had won, and sometime during the evening, they had decided to strike a happy truce.

'Before that night Arthur was a dinner guest,' Lynette says, 'I'd been hearing about nothing but cows and steers for the past eighteen months at Bullo, so it was wonderful to have someone different to talk to. What I didn't realise was that Bonnie had made her move and was sitting across the table from Arthur playing with his feet. Needless to say, her boyfriend didn't hang around long after that.' Arthur had arrived, as it were, and was another eccentric amongst the eccentrics.

Sara watches the budding relationship between her daughter and Arthur with concern. Taken with his intelligence and wit, she is also afraid for Bonnie. 'He doesn't have the character strength you need, Bonnie,' she tells her. 'I don't like the influence he is having on you.'

Bonnie ignores her mother's advice, irritated that Sara is suddenly taking so much notice of her. She suspects her mother has an ulterior motive: knowing Arthur could never fit into station life, she thinks he would ultimately prove a poor choice of partner.

In many ways, Sara recognises that this man is Charles' double: smooth, well-read, with big dreams and an attitude that he is born to greatness. She doesn't know how long Bonnie can hang on for the ride, but she does know it won't be smooth.

Charles makes his opinion of his daughter's choice of beau perfectly clear. 'That guy is a smartarse, and Bonnie had better watch out,' he fumes.

Charles tests Arthur mercilessly, as he does everyone else, and has to admit to a grudging respect for his brilliant mind. But that doesn't mean he likes him. He accepts, however, that while Bonnie spends so much time with her aerobatics practice in Darwin, it will be hard to keep them apart. He can only hope their relationship doesn't become any more serious.

Danielle, privy to the frequent discussions Charles has with Sara about Arthur, says he made no bones about his feelings. 'The plain truth of the matter was that Daddy loathed him. If he could, he would have put a hit on him. There is no question of that.'

If Arthur notices Charles' petulant attitude, he chooses to ignore it. What he does notice is that Charles is an extraordinary person of considerable substance, with a quixotic personality that requires very careful management. This man, he recognises, wouldn't miss an opportunity to offend someone, not even to save his own life. He notices, too, the tension in the household, the vast chasm between Sara and Bonnie.

'They are such different people, and it showed in virtually everything they did. But Charlie and Bonnie were on the same plane—they could both break things down to their essence, had the unerring ability to demystify and decomplicate.'

On the occasions Arthur is at Bullo, he is careful where he treads. 'Out there, I was like Caesar's wife—not only appearing to be above reproach, but actually being above reproach,' he says.

But the pecking order, which inevitably starts with Charles, rattles his cool exterior. 'You can't take a shit around here without his permission,' he complains to Bonnie.

* * *

Arthur is watching Bonnie eat, and he is alarmed. He has noticed the way she clenches her teeth all the time, notices, too, that everyone else appears to ignore it.

'For Godsake, Bonnie, you can barely get a morsel of food past your teeth. Have you had it checked?'

She is loath to admit she hasn't. Since the time she went to the doctor in Darwin, she has been extremely busy working on the station or practising aerobatics.

Arthur, used to dealing with Aboriginal health issues, realises Bonnie's problem is not a congenital condition. But finding out from Bonnie what is causing it is not easy. She has, he believes, built enormous emotional brick walls around herself; treated as just part of the plant and equipment at the station, the problems with her jaw extend back to the tensions and strains she suffered as a young child and into adolescence. It was patently bloody obvious she was in pain, he says, so why didn't anyone else notice?

Frustrated at Bonnie's reluctance to verbalise her problems, Arthur slowly pieces together the missing links in the puzzle, eventually forming his own conclusions. 'Bonnie was placed under impossible strains for a young person, and most of the variables—the weather, unpredictable people, broken-down vehicles, the isolation —were outside her control. Her work required enormous competence, leadership and the ability to take risks, and she was filling multitudinous roles normally shared by a lot of people. The expectations placed on her were far too great. She was the one who worked until exhaustion in extreme conditions and who worked with constant pain. She virtually ran that station single-handedly for three years. Her big downfall was that she cared. She passionately cared about the level of success, or lack of it, at Bullo, and she took it personally.'

186

Bonnie has felt a little off-colour for weeks; not sick, but run down. She is sometimes tearful for no reason and her breasts have gone into overdrive, tingling and sensitive. She misses a period and, with a mixture of foreboding and elation, she waits for her next one. It doesn't come.

She has never been interested in marriage, but from early adolescence has wanted to have children. Despite Sara's advice to her that they ruin your figure and disrupt your life, Bonnie is sure motherhood would be a great adventure and that children bring their own love with them. She has watched mares with their newborn foals and can't understand how it can be so perfect and natural for them, but not for a woman. Contraception, never discussed or offered to her, doesn't cross her mind. It's hard enough getting through the day without also having to remember to take the pill. Besides, life in the stock camps isn't exactly conducive to lugging along feminine toiletries.

Bonnie turns to her mother, giving Sara the information she needs to lead to the conclusion she is pregnant. Disappointed and worried, she is nevertheless supportive and understanding, but the idea of Bonnie keeping the baby is never raised.

'You are so young, Bonnie,' she says. 'I will keep this information from your father, tell him you are going to Darwin for women's problems. I will stand by your decision to terminate your pregnancy.'

Bonnie also instinctively knows better than to suggest to Arthur they should keep the baby. He has made it clear that at this stage of his life, children are not on his itinerary.

For the next week, while the arrangements are being made, Bonnie goes through the subterfuge of inventing sudden pains in her stomach whenever her father is in the room. If Sara is understanding, she also recognises that Charles may not be, and she wants to protect Bonnie from that.

Later, Bonnie comes to recognise that if she and Sara had talked about it a little more, perhaps there may have been mutual happiness about her keeping the baby. It is an abortion she now bitterly regrets, but for which she holds no-one responsible but herself. For Sara and Arthur, it is the beginning of the end of any relationship they had shakily started to build.

In contrast Arthur and Bonnie's relationship becomes increasingly serious, and everyone can feel the heat. Returning to Bullo after a dinner in Darwin with Arthur and Danielle, Bonnie guns the truck and leans out the window as she turns toward the highway.

'Hey, Arthur,' she mouths, 'I love you.'

The outburst surprises him—she has never said anything like that before—and he is taken aback. He feels protective of her, admires the depth of potential in her which he finds awe-inspiring, her ability to spend the day pulling bores, shifting yards, organising a stock camp and then cook an enormous meal for twenty people that night. But he also knows once he commits, it will be a serious responsibility.

'I mixed professionally and personally with artists, writers, lawyers and anthropologists,' he says. 'I was the head of land claims with the Northern Land Council. I had no interest in getting married. But Bonnie had a look, more than a physical presence. When I realised I wanted to see that look on a child of my own, that's when I got serious. It's that look in which you instinctively understand that person will never back away from an issue on your behalf, that when it gets really tough they will still be there. That look that makes you realise that without this person in your life, they will be lesser years. Once I crossed that Rubicon, there was no going back.'

Bonnie has her own bridge to cross and right now, standing in the middle, she is unsure whether to go back, move forward, or jump into the swirling current. Her relationship with Arthur is

188

exacerbating the existing family conflicts, and creating some more besides.

Charles, who left Bullo at the beginning of the wet season, is now sailing around the Pacific, issuing orders from the middle of the ocean. Sara, with a martyred air, is furious she has been left to run the homestead alone, but Charles will not return. The salt air is helping to clear his lungs, and the sea is his passion, his escape. The stock camps are running like clockwork under Bonnie's command and are economically viable, but Charles is becoming increasingly agitated about Arthur. Using his iron will, he tries to bend Bonnie to his way of thinking.

'You can't run the camps and a love affair in Darwin at the same time,' he yells down the phone. 'Ah know you want to fly aerobatics and ah will support you in that, one hundred per cent, but please, get rid of that man.'

Startled at his determined tone, Bonnie is also angry. She is twenty-two years old and will make her own bloody decisions about her love life. God knows, her father does. 'What is it about him that bothers you so much?' she yells back. 'Everything is going well at the station, we're on track as we wanted to be, and I'm having as much flying practice in Darwin as I can in between. What is the problem?'

She can hear Charles' breath labouring as he tries to keep his voice firm. 'He will never make you happy, Bonnie. Ah know it's hard for you to see that, now, but trust me on this. Please.'

The phone line has gone dead, just a hissing static. Bonnie stares at the receiver in disbelief, slams it down on its cradle. Sara and Marlee are chatting in the kitchen, and she slips out past them to go for a ride on her horse. This is one conversation she doesn't care to explain. Now that Charles is away, she is under enormous pressure to do more work and produce better results. She is getting tired of it, tired of defending her daily decisions, tired of fighting for more fences to be built, tired of the prolonged silences between herself, Sara and Marlee, and tired of playing the devil's advocate between Arthur and her parents. Most of all, she is tired of living with the constant pain in her head.

CHAPTER SEVENTEEN

The weather is perfect for flying: little cloud, no turbulence and a clear, sunny day. Arthur and Bonnie are heading to Ballarat in Victoria to pick up a plane; the plan is for Bonnie to fly the new aircraft, a single-seat Pitts Special, back to Darwin alone, meeting Arthur back there after he visits family in Queensland.

They are giggling like schoolchildren, happy to be on their own, swapping jokes and reciting poetry from memory. Up here, they have a wonderful sense of freedom, and trust each other's abilities as a pilot. The world is theirs to conquer, and they are in love. Arthur leans over and kisses Bonnie, whispers to her to let the plane fly itself for a while. He doesn't have to ask twice. Arthur has ignited her sensuality, made her a woman, and together they are a raunchy team. This is a lot more fun than reading a book at 3000 feet.

Arthur flies out of Ballarat ahead of Bonnie, organising to liaise with her in Darwin in a week's time. The weather is nasty, with low cloud and a front moving through. The only thing Bonnie knows for certain is that the VHF radio in the Pitts is limited in range and, with no electrical gear, the plane needs to be started by hand. Her experience flying the Super Cub at Bullo has given Bonnie confidence with dead reckoning navigation—flying on compass and using maps. She plots her course: to fly until she sights the Murray River, and from there to Renmark and on to Leigh Creek. Confident she has passed the first rule of dead-reckoning navigation—to make sure you're flying in the right direction—she heads the plane toward the Murray.

The aircraft, sheet metal with no lining and a thin canopy, is noisy and freezing cold. By her calculations, she should have hit the river after one hour and ten minutes, but it has been longer than that. Something is amiss. Turning the plane sideways to see the ground, she wonders where the hell she is. There has increasingly been less chatter on the radio and now she has no contact at all. She checks her watch, decides to keep flying for another fifteen minutes before turning the plane sideways again to check her bearings. There is nothing underneath her except salt bush scrub; this is remote, barren country, not a river in sight. She turns the plane sideways again, fights to keep it from going straight over on its wing tip. Perspiration gathers on her neck, despite the cold; panicking now, she cruises at 10 000 feet, feels the cabin's temperature plummet even lower. Christ, she needs to see a landmark soon; she is unsure how much fuel is in the long-range tank. It isn't fitted with a gauge to calculate litres and fuel flow. She holds the map above her head, reading it as she flies, and realises she is bushed, miles off track. She doesn't know precisely how much longer the fuel will last and is determined to establish her position before it becomes critical.

In the distance, Bonnie spies an old homestead with a runway next to it. She breathes a sigh of relief, heads straight down, but is quickly disillusioned. The homestead is abandoned, and the runway covered in barbed-wire fence and pitted with yawning potholes. Her descent has cost her the height and safety margin, but there is no way she can land here, in the middle of nowhere. Gaining altitude again, she frantically searches the horizon for signs of life. As far as her eye can see, the landscape is deserted.

Shaking with the cold and with increasing fear, she wills herself to stay calm. She has been flying again for another twenty minutes, and the situation is desperate. Suddenly, in the distance, she sees what appears to be a fielding paddock. She heads towards it, lines up the aircraft on the bush runway.

The farmer, ploughing his paddock, has watched the small aircraft approach. He's lived in these parts all his life but this has really got him tossed. He turns off his tractor and scratches his head. What the hell is a plane doing flying around out here? Bonnie jumps out of the cockpit, and his jaw drops to the ground. A female pilot, to boot!

'Can you tell me where I am, please?' she asks in a sheepish voice. She is pushing the map toward him, and he looks at it, then back at her with a quizzical expression.

'Is this the map you is usin'?' he enquires. He is scratching his head again, shaking it from side to side.

'Yeah, same map. Why?' Bonnie kicks at the dirt, plunges her hands in her pockets and glances up to the sky. If he doesn't answer her soon, there won't be enough daylight left for her to go anywhere.

'Well ...' he drawls, 'have youse got the other page of the map? Youse won't find these 'ere parts on this one.'

Bonnie wants the earth to bury her. She is not only lost, she has been flying for the three and a half hours since takeoff in the wrong direction. Her compass is thirty-five degrees out, which she knows is a classic pilot error. It is a must always to check the compass with runway heading prior to takeoff. Also, when she had turned up to take delivery of the Pitts, it was fuelled and waiting; she had taken the exact number of litres in the tank on hearsay. With the lack of fuel gauges on board, the rule to fuel your own aircraft is particularly vital. She hasn't put in a full reporting flight plan either; in typical Henderson style, she is flying on Sartime—search and rescue time—and no-one would miss her until that expires in eight hours. She should have been flying on full reporting, where her position would be known at all times. Worst of all, she has ignored her father's first lesson: look at the ground to find your bearings before you get well and truly bushed.

The farmer fills her tank with fuel and waves a dismissive hand when she offers to pay for it. 'You're right, lady,' he says. 'I 'ope you make it safe now.'

Bonnie gives him the thumbs-up sign as she flies overhead, and makes a vital decision. This trip could have been a disaster; the fuel tank was virtually empty and it was only sheer chance that she had found somewhere to land. Never again will she take a 'she'll be right' attitude. Next time, she might not be so lucky.

Aerobatics manoeuvres originated during World War I, when flying aces dodged enemy aircraft guns with spectacular turns and rolls. For those pilots it was a matter of life or death, and it is still not a sport for the faint-hearted. These are not devil-may-care pilots with a death wish; labelling carefully executed aerobatic manoeuvres stunts is akin to calling Olympic gymnasts circus acrobats. The aim in competition is to demonstrate an ability to skilfully handle an aircraft through a set sequence of manoeuvres which requires both practice and a thorough understanding of physics.

Bonnie is excited and nervous at the prospect of entering her first aerobatics championship. No other woman in Australia has ever attempted it and she has less than sixty hours practice time behind her. She has to get the aircraft from Darwin to Griffith in New South Wales, and this is not an easy plane to fly across the continent. With no starter motor, someone has to pull the propeller for takeoff; the cockpit is too small even to unfold a map; if it starts with the throttle advanced, the tail can lift off the ground and put the prop in; and most of the time Bonnie is out of radio contact. Tagging along behind another plane, she flies for ten hours on the first day to get to Longreach in Queensland. During the long monotonous crosscrountry flight, Bonnie thinks about training and competition practices, and the fact she is too scared to go below seven hundred feet, despite having a five hundred feet waiver; when she attempts to drop lower, the ground whooshes up to meet her. On the second day, she flies into Gatton for a week's training before the competition starts.

'What are you, scared of the ground?' an aerobatic team member asks her on her first flight. 'You're going to have to do better than that if you expect to compete!'

Summoning all her courage, Bonnie finally gets to five hundred feet, just two days before the competition starts.

Through a haze, a combination of excitement and adrenalin, she notices the reluctance of the aircraft to respond in the pull-up and right-hand rolls. She blames herself and her lack of experience and doesn't suspect it may be mechanical failure of the wing; she is determined to keep going. She badly wants to do well: Sara and Charles are in Griffith to watch her, and her father gives her last-minute advice.

'Play mind games with your competitors,' he says. 'Psych them out before you go up.'

Sara is terrified as Bonnie climbs into the cockpit. All eyes are on this first female competitor. Over a three-day period, she has four programs to complete, each one twelve to fifteen minutes duration. All twenty manoeuvres, judged from one to ten on the precision of lines and angles and style, must be contained in a 1000 metre cube of air. Bonnie has entered the toughest category—unlimited—for which the lower limit is three hundred feet and for which she needs to execute a four-minute freestyle manoeuvre.

She goes up, gives the judges a wing wag—a wave of the aircraft wings—and feels like she is in a tumble-drier. With split second timing, she manoeuvres through vertical ups and downs, rolls, spins, and executes high and low speed stalls. The view from the cockpit is blurred, and she loses all sense of up and down or left or right. The world becomes a line between sky and ground. She must stay a whisker ahead of where she wants to be, and know where she wants to be before she gets there. If she starts to fall behind and lets the force of gravity overtake her, she runs the risk of blacking out through lack of oxygen. The higher the acceleration, the higher the G-force; travelling at two hundred and fifty nautical miles an hour, positive-G can be a killer. She knows, too, that if she overloads on negative-G, she will get pain in her head from the pressure being forced into her brain. Adrenalin can disguise the pain from negative-G, and the result can be burst blood vessels in the eyes, blown eardrums and stressed muscles.

To impress the judges, Bonnie needs to watch the wind direction so as not to be blown out of the box, fly within the lower limit and not go below it, which would bring immediate disqualification. Finally, she has to drive the aircraft home, in total control. Grace and style are the keys: aerobatics competitors don't stagger around the air. Her adrenalin is pumping; she has flown well, and she knows it.

She waits impatiently for the scores and is thrilled and proud when they come through. In her first competition, she has come third overall. The male competitors shake her hand, and congratulate her. They will have to watch this girl from the bush very closely from now on.

Flying out at daylight the next morning with a hangover from hell, she goes straight to 10 000 feet. Dehydrated and suffering from lack of oxygen, she has four hours flying ahead of her before she can stop and get a cold drink and an aspirin. Her head feels like it is going to split open, but she can't stop grinning. One day, she will be number one.

In Darwin, her aerobatics instructor takes the plane for a test run. When he gets back on the ground, he checks the internal wiring on the wing.

'All the bracing wires have pulled through the main wing ribs,' he says. 'The wing could have collapsed at four-G, but you were pulling over ten-G. You flew in that competition with the wing like that! It's amazing that you could manoeuvre the plane at all, let alone get third place. That's one hell of an effort, Bon!'

The last muster of the season is organised, just before the build-up starts with a vengeance again. The team is ready to go; the wings—star pickets and wire, which are easy to assemble and dis-assemble—are up. Starting at the yard gate, the wings are placed on either side to form a funnel shape, and long lengths of hessian hung on wire to make it look solid. Now all that is necessary is for the choppers to be booked. The Queensland State aerobatic titles are in a few days, and Bonnie has everything organised, nothing is left to chance; she will fly down for the championship and return to Bullo in time for the muster.

She stands in the kitchen, swag under her arm, and gives Sara last-minute details.

'The muster's ready, and I'll be back in a week.'

Sara does not wish her well in the championships. It's bad enough that Charles is swanning around the ocean without Bonnie taking off and swanning around the skies.

Bullo is just a speck in the distance when Arthur presses Bonnie to see a specialist in Brisbane about her jaw. 'You can't keep putting it off, Bonnie. Just let him look at it, at least, to see if there is anything that can be done.'

Like her father, Arthur is extremely determined when he makes up his mind, and Bonnie knows it. Right now, the championships are uppermost in her mind and require undivided concentration. She doesn't need a battle of wills with Arthur as well.

'Yeah, righto,' she agrees. 'He can have a look, as long as I'm back in time for the muster.'

The specialist has finished his tests on Bonnie's jaw—an extremely painful procedure—and asks her to take a seat in his surgery. Sharp and to the point, he doesn't mince words.

'You are in bad shape. Essentially, you have been living with a crushed cartilage in your joints for the past fifteen years. In the space between your jaw and skull sits a cartilage which acts as a cushion. That cartilage has nerves connected to either end. Stress and the action of your teeth grinding have damaged, crushed and pushed the cartilage and nerve endings. The cause of your migraines is extreme pressure on those nerves. Your restricted jaw movement is from tightening of the muscles and has created intense pain. Why nothing has been done about this before is beyond my comprehension. It has gone far beyond preventative action, and an operation is now your only recourse.'

Bonnie's hands have suddenly become clammy, and she is close to tears. The specialist continues talking.

198

'Could you just briefly explain to me when you think it started? I have your doctor's referral notes here, but I would like you to tell me in your own words.'

'I remember being crook from about the age of eight,' she replies. 'I always got into trouble from that time for not chewing my food properly or for being disagreeable because I was in pain. My jaw seized up gradually until, when I was sixteen, I couldn't put a finger between my teeth.'

'And you told your parents about this?'

'Yes, but out where we live we're a long way from medical care and I suppose they got sick of me complaining about it. Mummy took me to the doctor a long time ago but in the end I just put up with it. I used to sneak pain killers so they wouldn't know. It's not their fault. You have to live at Bullo to understand.'

He puts his pen down on the desk, moves back into the seat of his chair. 'Yes, quite,' he answers. His tone makes Bonnie nervous and she senses he is not at all convinced. 'I would like to operate immediately, Bonnie. Do you have any objections to that?'

'Well, yes,' she replies. 'There's a muster about to start and I need to be back for that. Can't we do it another time?'

There is no mistaking his attitude now. He leans toward her, staring hard. 'It is my professional opinion that you have waited long enough. Can you reorganise your schedule?'

'Well, yes, I suppose,' she says. 'Everything's ready to go for the muster, so it's not impossible.'

Her brain is swimming. She will have to call Sara and ask her to arrange the helicopters, but Bonnie is sure that will be fine. In the past three years she has organised a great muster team and they are extremely competent. They can get through this once without her.

'I will book you into hospital. You won't know yourself after you have this operation. You will be pain free.'

When Bonnie calls her mother, Sara is livid. The muster is looming, and now Bonnie is on the phone telling her she won't be there for it.

'This is just great, Bonnie,' she seethes. 'You've known for ages we had this planned and now you're telling me you won't be here for it?'

'The doctor told me I should have this operation now. Why don't you support me on this?' She is disappointed at her mother's attitude, but annoyed with herself too. She knows from hard experience that if you expect something from someone, you set yourself up for a fall.

'All you have to do is organise the choppers,' she persists. 'Everything else is done. It's not that hard!' But it is clear that Sara feels Bonnie has let her down.

Shapes are slowly coming into vision, and Bonnie can hear voices. She realises she is in the intensive care unit, tries to move her head, but the pain is unbearable and the post-op anaesthetic is making her feel sick. She can smell hospital disinfectant and touches her face, realising it is bandaged on both sides. It is too hard to try and stay awake, and she drifts back into an uneasy sleep.

When she wakes, they are preparing to move her into a ward, and her specialist is chatting with a nurse.

'Hello, Bonnie, you've finally decided to join us,' he smiles. 'The operation went very well, but you will feel the effects of it for a while. It took three hours, and we had to open your entire jaw to remove the broken cartilage. It has been replaced by suturing sylastic onto the skull to act as a cushion. There is a scar from your temple to the bottom of your ear lobes on both sides, but don't worry about that, it will heal. You will need to stay in hospital for at

200

least a week and then undergo some post-op therapy to get your jaw working again. Beyond that, you'll be as right as rain. Don't try to speak for at least a few days. The nurses are moving you up to the ward now where you will be more comfortable. I'll see you tomorrow.'

Arthur, who returned to Darwin prior to the operation, is persuaded by his father to go back to Brisbane to be with Bonnie. Gentle and caring, he is concerned that no-one is with her. 'She needs you there, son,' he says. 'This is a major operation. Go back.'

Sitting on the side of her bed, Arthur tells Bonnie he is going to slip out and ring Sara to let her know the operation was a success. He is not looking forward to this conversation, not after the reception Bonnie got earlier.

'Sara, it's Arthur here,' he begins. 'Bonnie is fine, everything went well, but she will need another few weeks to recover and to have post-operative therapy.'

He pauses, realises she hasn't spoken one word yet. 'Hello, Sara? Are you there?'

'I'm here all right!' she screams. 'Are you aware of how much work there is to be done up here? Tell Bonnie from me to get home!'

Arthur can feel his anger rising, tries to keep it out of his voice. 'Your daughter has just had major surgery, Sara. She is not well enough to go anywhere at present, let alone back out to Bullo. Try to be reasonable.'

'I don't need your advice, thank you very much, Arthur,' she shoots back. 'I have told you what to do. Tell Bonnie to get back up here to work.'

Arthur explodes, now oblivious to the people walking past in the hospital corridor. 'This is utterly scandalous!' he yells back. 'Bonnie is not your working dog, and your attitude amounts to nothing less than sheer neglect! She will stay here, under doctor's orders, until she is well enough to return! Thank you for your support!'

He slams the phone down on its receiver, shaking with fury. If he didn't know what Sara thought of him before, he is under no illusions now.

Sara is talking to Charles, trying to finish sentences before he interrupts again. Always impatient, he is incredulous about what he is hearing, and not in the best of tempers. Just recovering from a cataract operation, he doesn't need any extra problems on his plate.

'Well?' demands Sara when she has finally finished telling Charles why Bonnie won't be back for the muster. 'What are you going to do about it?'

'Ah'll tell you what ah'm goin' to do, Sara,' he finally responds. 'Ah'm goin' to give her a choice. She either chooses Bullo, or she chooses that boyfriend of hers. There is no middle line.'

Charles paces the floor, restless and edgy. Goddamn, Bonnie has been given every opportunity and he knows it is her work and iron will that keeps the camps running so smoothly. They need her, but if she chooses to follow her heart, there will be no turning back. He will not tolerate disloyalty, and this amounts to insubordination. He expects the same loyalty he demanded from his men during the war. What he can't understand is why she would leave them in the lurch right at the last moment. It is so unlike Bonnie not to follow a project through to the end. He will find out why she has done this, make it clear to her that she is risking her inheritance. She won't turn against him, he is sure. Charles can feel a duel coming on, and it cheers his spirits. There's nothing like a good fight, particularly one he knows he will win.

* * *

Recuperating in Darwin, Bonnie's recovery from the operation is slower than she had hoped. The swelling still hasn't completely gone from her jaw, but she can now speak and, to her amazement, the migraines have stopped. She has had no contact with anyone at Bullo since she returned to the Territory and is reluctant to spend yet another wet season breaking in horses and building fences on her own. Charles is about to leave for Maryland to visit Bomma, and without him at the station the situation is untenable. Her dream is to compete in the world aerobatics titles, and she hopes to spend this wet practising.

She has moved in with Arthur in Darwin, and it feels odd to rattle around a suburban house with little to occupy her time. He keeps asking whether she has spoken to Sara or Charles, and the answer is always no. One morning, however, she meets her father at the aero club; their conversation doesn't start well, or finish well either.

'Sara Lloyd, what the hell is going on?' Charles demanded. 'Why aren't you back at the station? What do you think you are playing at? Why weren't you there to oversee that muster?'

'You know why, Daddy,' she replies. 'I went to the State titles and after that I was in hospital. You know that.'

Charles looks stunned, and there is a long pause before he answers. 'What do you mean you were in hospital! In hospital for what? Are you sick?'

'No, Daddy, I'm not sick, I had my jaw operated on in Brisbane and had to spend a week recovering before I came back here for further therapy. I thought you knew that.'

Charles puts his head down, and Bonnie suddenly realises he is crying. She hates him to think she has let him down, is saddened that no-one thought it important enough to tell him where she was. The recognition hits her hard; her father is not as strong as he once was, is losing his grip on this family. She is crying now, too, trying to explain.

'I would never let you down, you must know that. But there are other things I want to do, Daddy, instead of hanging around the station doing all the bloody work myself. I want to fly, and to do that I need training.'

'I understand that,' he says, touching her arm. 'But I also understand that we need you at Bullo. You're the only one who can run the camps properly, and you know it.'

'Marlee's there, Daddy, and she's run the camps before. There's a good team down there to help.'

'They're your team, Sara Lloyd,' Charles reminds her. 'They work for you because they want to. What are you suggesting, that you're not coming back at all?'

Bonnie takes a deep breath, knows that she must be very careful what she says next. 'It's not that I'm not ever coming back, Daddy. I love Bullo, you know that. It's just that I don't want to come back at the moment. I've done my fair share, and a lot more beside; you know that too. But other things are important to me now.'

Charles understands she is not just talking about flying. 'You're not telling me that you've decided to stay with Arthur?' He can't hide his disgust, doesn't even attempt to. 'We've talked about this before. You're going to have to make a choice now.'

'A choice? A choice between what?'

'Between the station or your boyfriend. It's up to you.'

She can't believe he is doing this to her, that Sara hadn't told him she was in hospital, that she is being forced into a corner and manipulated like a puppet. This time, she won't back down.

'You're excommunicating me, is that it?' She follows her question with a bitter laugh, but she is dangerously close to tears again. 'Surely you're not serious?'

'Ah've never been more serious in my life, Sara Lloyd. It's up to you.'

'Well, go to hell then!' she snaps. 'I'll choose Arthur.'

With the lines now firmly drawn, Bonnie and Arthur fly to Bullo to pack her swag. Charles, in Sydney before he travels to America, is devastated he has lost the battle, but he tells no-one that. Instead, he uses reverse psychology: Bonnie is to be treated as a persona non grata; disloyal to the family, she will be ostracised as a stranger. He is sure that one day she will come to her senses.

There is a distinct chill in the air as Bonnie packs her few belongings, and awkward silences. Someone has to say something.

'I think I've got just about everything.' Bonnie is speaking to Sara, but her words seem to echo around the kitchen, coming back to slap her in the face.

'Here are your Christmas presents. I'll be off now.'

Danielle, close to tears, hugs her sister. 'I'll miss you, Bon,' she whispers. 'Take care of yourself.'

'I'll be okay, Danielle,' Bonnie replies. 'I'm coming back to get my horses in a month, and we'll talk then.' Bonnie couldn't bear to leave the horses behind. She loves them and would be lost without them. Marlee is furious she is taking them and levels her with a bitter stare when she arrives.

'Trust you,' she spits. 'You cause all these problems and then want the horses as well. I'll be glad to see the back of you!'

Bonnie is shuffling, uncomfortable now, wanting to put

distance between herself and the icy tension. 'See you later, Mum.' For a second, she hesitates, wondering what to do next. Sara is obviously not going to make a move in her direction; as far as she is concerned, Bonnie has made her bed and she can lie in it. They have reached a turning point in their relationship, but both are reluctant to admit it. It's better to say nothing, for there is nothing more to be said.

Bonnie walks across the airstrip, and climbs into the plane. When they circle overhead to turn toward Darwin, she wills herself to look down. There isn't a soul in sight.

'God, you could have cut the air with a knife back there,' Arthur says, trying to break Bonnie's reverie, dispel the black clouds that have descended over her since they left Bullo. 'Anyone would think you'd committed a mortal sin. Have they forgotten people have a democratic right to free choice?'

Bonnie isn't in the mood for his philosophies, but she would hate to hurt his feelings. She adores Arthur and couldn't imagine living without him now.

'Sorry it was so unpleasant,' she says. Her voice has dropped, soft and low, as it always does when she is upset. 'I'm sick of the shit fights! I need a rum!'

Arthur is angry she has been made to feel like this and angry at her response to it. 'You don't need a rum, Bonnie, you drink too much. You drank to stop the pain, but you can't use that as an excuse now. The plain truth of the matter is that if you hadn't had that operation and I hadn't got you out of there, you would not only have been a physical wreck, it is quite likely you may not have survived.'

Bonnie sighs. She is slowly starting to understand that Arthur has the unerring capacity to take credit for everything.

* * *

Pain-free for the first time in years, Bonnie can finally think clearly—and has to. Determined to make selection for the Australian aerobatics team for the world championships in England later in the year, she focuses on training. The only way she can make the grade is to increase her practice hours.

She pulls the car into the carpark of the Darwin hangar, heads toward her aircraft, a Pitts Special. Charles gave it to her a couple of years ago in lieu of wages, and later Sara asked her to sign it over to the company, Bullo River Station Pty Ltd, for tax purposes. It is still in the company name, but is Bonnie's, nevertheless. She loves this plane; over the past twelve months it has taken on an identity of its own, and she is sure that between them, they can make a winning team.

The president of the Northern Territory Aerobatic Club is standing in front of the Pitts and he greets Bonnie with a sour look.

'G'day, Ossie,' she says. 'You don't look very happy. What's up with you?'

He ignores her question, gets straight to the point. 'You can't take this plane out, Bonnie.'

'What do you mean, I can't take this plane out? It's my bloody aircraft, I can do whatever I like with it!'

He is leaning in front of the cockpit, arms folded, glaring at her. 'I'm telling you, this aircraft is dangerous and it won't leave the ground!'

'Pig's arse, Ossie,' Bonnie says, moving closer to him. She looks down, sees the prop and wheel lying on the ground.

'What the hell are you doing? Why are these bits out here on the ground?'

Her good humour is rapidly diminishing. Any minute, this bloke is going to wear one.

'Put the wheel and prop back on, Ossie,' she says. Her mouth

207

is barely moving, but her eyes are blazing. 'There's nothing wrong with this plane, so put it back together!'

He glowers at her, smiles smugly. 'Get stuffed, Bonnie. The aircraft stays as it is.'

It happens so quickly, he doesn't see it coming. Bonnie's right fist sails through the air, crunching into his nose. He staggers for a moment, then slumps to the ground. His cheeks are crimson with humiliation.

'Would you like to get up again, Ossie?' she asks. Her temper obviously hasn't abated; her eyes are wild and her knuckles clenched. This is one fight he is not at all confident of winning. He grabs a piece of cloth lying nearby, furiously blows his nose and wipes away the blood. She looks down, thinks he doesn't look so smug now that she's decked him.

'Righto, now put the prop and wheel back on my plane!'

He does.

It's a short-lived victory. Sporting a bruised jaw and equally bruised ego, Ossie pronounces the plane mechanically unsound after Bonnie lands, and grounds it until further notice. The hold-up serves only to make Bonnie more determined; flying to Brisbane, she uses a friend's aircraft in which to practice.

The next thing Bonnie knows, the plane has been sold without her knowledge or consent, and she receives the news grimly.

'It might have been nice if my mother told me she was going to sell my plane,' she tells Arthur. 'How dare she! It is my aircraft that Daddy gave me! It's as if I don't exist.'

Their friend, Steve Hart, buys the Pitts and immediately resells the aircraft to Arthur so that Bonnie can keep practising.

* * *

Charles, desperately ill in a Sydney hospital, has asked to see Bonnie. In typical fashion, he plays his cards close to his chest and shares his change of heart with no-one. He misses her; they have been great mates over the years, and he believes it is time for a reconciliation.

'I am sending you the airfare to get to Sydney, Sara Lloyd. Bring Arthur with you. There are many things I need to discuss.'

Recovering from an operation to improve the use of one lung, Charles still believes he is invincible, but Bonnie is devastated to see how he has deteriorated. He is greyer than he was, his eyes, sallow and dull, have lost their sparkle, and his conversation is halted by hacking coughs that render him unable to talk for several minutes. But he hasn't lost his spirit and is determined to prove it.

'Sara Lloyd, when ah get out of here, ah want you to come sailing with me. The salt air is good for mah lungs, and we can do the Sydney to Hobart yacht race together. What do you think?'

'That's a great idea, Daddy. We'll do that,' she replies.

Tired from his exertion, Charles settles back against the pillows, surveys her with a sad smile. 'Ah knew you wouldn't let me down. Ah just knew it.'

Bonnie sits outside his room on the hospital verandah, staring into space as he and Arthur talk business. She smiles, realises that, as shaken as he is by his operation, her father is still ordering his troops, still fighting to win.

'Arthur,' he begins in that voice that she knows so well. Whatever he is about to say, he means business. 'Ah want you to promise to marry my daughter. Where ah come from, that is the gentlemanly thing to do. Do you love her? Will you promise to do that?'

In some ways, Bonnie is not surprised at her father's apparent change of heart. She knows exactly how he feels about Arthur, knows, too, that he will never change his mind about that, but he does want her to be happy. He is also as wily as an old fox and right at the moment, he needs some things done.

Thoughts of marrying Bonnie have recently crossed Arthur's mind a great deal, and he has no qualms answering the question honestly. 'Yes, I'll marry her, if she'll have me,' he says. 'It would be my pleasure.'

'Ah would like you to start to instigate divorce proceedings on my behalf,' Charles continues. 'When ah am out of here, ah will take over the proceedings. There are some other arrangements ah would ask you to organise …'

He riffles through a pile of papers on his bed, issues instructions. Now, Arthur has some of his own business to discuss.

'As you are aware, I brought the aircraft for Bonnie after it was sold to an acquaintance of ours. I paid $42 000 for it and did so to assist Bonnie with her flying. The aircraft was Bonnie's, which you gave her in lieu of wages at Bullo. It should not have been sold, but the sale was able to go through because it was signed over to the station for tax purposes. What is to be done about it now?'

Charles pulls out a chequebook, writes his signature with a flourish.

'Ah am writing a cheque for $50 000, to cover the cost of the aircraft and expenses for Sara Lloyd to go to England for the world championship. Ah had every intention of doing this, which is part of the reason ah asked you both down here to see me. If she wants to fly, ah support her one hundred per cent. But don't cash the cheque for two weeks.'

Arthur realises the cheque is not only a financial settlement; it is Charles' gesture toward reconciliation.

When Bonnie re-enters the room, Charles makes an effort to sit up straight, but he looks tired and old. 'Ah will see you when ah get out of the hospital.'

Bonnie hugs him goodbye, hears the wheezy rattle in his chest. 'You have to take good care, Daddy. I'll see you soon.'

'Sara Lloyd?' She turns at the doorway, and he is smiling. 'Remember: always buy your round in life. Never walk out when it's your shout.'

She quickly leaves the room, before her father sees she is in tears.

Charles has organised for a bank loan to cover the cheque and to pay Gus Trippe in cash instead of cattle, the money he is owed. The bank contacts Sara to advise her of the loan, and it is stopped. Whether it is because of the circumstances which follow, or whether it is deliberately stopped by Sara, Bonnie never finds out.

The bank manager doesn't like being questioned, and particularly by a woman.

'I'm telling you, Miss, ah'—he looks down to read the name, glances up again—'Miss Henderson, there is no money to cover the cheque your father made out.'

'Don't be ridiculous, of course there is!' Bonnie storms. 'Daddy wrote it out, in full, when I visited him in Sydney, and gave it to my boyfriend. My father may be many things, but he is not given to writing cheques that he knows will bounce. This is ludicrous. Please check the account again!'

The manager sighs, spreads his hands out in front of him on the desk. He looks over her head at the clock, a gesture to signal their appointment is fast coming to a close.

'You are quite obviously not understanding what I am telling you, Miss …'

'Henderson!'

'Yes, Miss Henderson. The cheque was cancelled.'

'Cancelled? You can't possibly be serious! Who cancelled it?'

He ignores that question. 'There is no money in the account to service the cheque. Do you understand?'

Bonnie stares at him, open mouthed. 'You're telling me that I won't get my money? You must be joking!'

'Well, may I suggest you take that up with your parents,' he says, standing up. 'Now, if you'll excuse me, I have another appointment.' He extends a limp hand, which hangs in the air for a moment before he drops it back to his side.

'Good afternoon, Miss …'

'Henderson!' Bonnie rejoins, glaring at him with a thunderous look.

She storms out of his office, leaves the door wide open in her wake. He shakes his head. What an angry young woman.

CHAPTER EIGHTEEN

Her blistered hands, stained with tannin, are raw and painful from moulding the stiff, unrelenting leather. The late afternoon sun has lost none of its intensity; perspiration drips down the back of her neck and her clammy fingers leave a nut-brown smudge mark where she wipes it away.

'Christ, it's hot today,' she mutters, leaning over her makeshift workbench and wishing, again, that someone would answer the bloody telephone that's been ringing interminably. That seems a vain hope; impatiently she props the saddle against the wall and moves toward the phone.

'Bonnie Henderson,' she answers, in a crisp tone. She hates the telephone at the best of times and particularly when she's busy.

A familiar, genteel drawl, greets her. 'Bon, it's Gus here. Are you okay?'

Something in his staccato breathing and his voice, grappling for composure, stops her in her tracks. She pulls a piece of cloth from her back pocket, wipes the sweat from her forehead. 'I'm fine, Gus, keeping busy. What's up?'

His muffled sobs echo down the phone line. Bewildered and frightened, Bonnie demands an answer. 'Gus, for Godsake, talk to me! What's happened?'

He takes a deep, slow breath, fights hard to keep his voice from wavering. 'I'm so sorry, Bon,' he says. 'I assumed your mother would have already told you. God, I'm sorry. Your daddy died this morning.'

The world spins on its axis, and Bonnie's mouth is suddenly parched and dry.

'Oh, no, no!' It is an anguished wail which strangles in her throat and seems to her a long way off. The phone dangles on its cord as she slides, falls, between wall and floor.

Bonnie cries as if her heart would break, through all of that night and all of the next morning. She cries like there is no tomorrow; sometimes soft tears born of wry, gentle memories; sometimes hard and agitated sobs, bitter and tormented. She should have been with her father at the end, should have been warned he might be dying, should have been given the chance to say goodbye. Death has reached out its hands close to her before; she has felt its pain before, but it never felt like this. This heartache is unbearable.

She rings Lynette, tells her the news in a flat, monotone voice. 'Daddy died yesterday. I don't have any clothes for the funeral. Could I borrow some of yours?' Almost as an afterthought, she adds, 'It's very cold in Sydney. I will need a dress and coat.' Her voice is low, almost inaudible, her face drawn in a desolate mask.

As Lynette riffles through her wardrobe, she glances at Bonnie, come to collect the clothes, slumped on the floor, and wonders if her strength of will will drag her through the next few days. God knows she is going to need it: she is facing a lonely time.

Bonnie seems to have aged overnight, and she has obviously had no sleep. Introverted and silent in her grief, she goes through the motions, but she can't hide her shattered heart.

If Lynette Ainsworth has tried to keep her own counsel on the idiosyncratic Hendersons, she is outraged that Bonnie is not told of her father's death by Sara.

'It is unforgivable that Sara didn't make the effort to put aside their differences and tell Bonnie her father had died. Bonnie had only Ross, Arthur and myself to help her through that ghastly time. She suffered in the extreme, made worse by her alienation at the funeral. I can't understand how Sara can be so harsh to Bonnie. As a mother myself, I know that children need you, regardless of their age. Surely that is the overriding factor—that you help your children. You don't spurn them, and certainly not publicly, as Sara has spurned Bonnie. It is an outrage, and a disgrace.'

Her borrowed clothes don't quite fit; nothing seems to fit any more. She would rather be anywhere but here, rather be sitting in the saddle than on this hard church pew, sitting in the saddle where the dust hangs at stirrup height; instead, ashes to ashes, dust to dust.

Outside, a wintry Sydney sun attempts a bleak salute, and military guards of honour are framed in the cathedral doorway like frozen marionettes. All this pomp and ceremony bothers Bonnie; she is sure her father would have preferred a knees-up wake, Glenn Miller blaring out 'In the Mood', his friends quaffing Bullo River Specials and spinning yarns about this mad Yank who conquered Australia's outback.

It is raining now, inside and out, and Bonnie reaches for another tissue. Her feet are cramped in these unfamiliar shoes and she tugs at her black dress, notices her fingernails are dirty underneath. There was no time to scrub them before she came south. Daddy would have been amused by that; Mummy, if she noticed, would be mortified.

Bonnie stumbles to follow the words in the prayer book, stumbles to reconcile that shiny coffin with other memories: Charles, always the devil's advocate, holding court at Bullo or marching around wearing long johns and a red smoking jacket, bellowing orders. The weeks he taught her to fly, daring her to rise to the challenge and slapping her around the head if she made a wrong turn. That faraway look when he remembered the death of his tiny sons, a heartache from which he never recovered. His grand ideals; the love he had for the tough, unforgiving outback; and his last dream—that his wheezy, emphysemic lungs would again fill with salt spray and he would sail the oceans with Bonnie.

They are reciting the final prayers now. 'Our Father who art in heaven', and she has a fleeting thought: are you, Daddy? Are you in heaven? He had never believed in God, though he told everyone he did. Here, in this vast cathedral, Jesus watches paternally from the Cross, Son of the God whom Charles denied until his dying breath. Now the tissues are sodden and she realises there are no pockets in this damn dress to hide them.

It is cold inside the church, cold from the bitter winter, cold from the funereal music. Sara is standing near Bonnie, dry-eyed and as frozen still and upright as the guards outside. Flanked by Marlee and Danielle, she keeps her eyes locked on the casket and will not look at Bonnie.

The coffin is moving out of the church now, past the heads bowed in mourning, past the military swords crisscrossed under the arch. Bonnie stands in the street, watches as her two sisters slip into the mourning car with Sara. She feels isolated from them, even though Sara has tried to include her by covering her travel expenses for the funeral, as she did for her other two daughters. Bonnie shivers as the rain slides down her cheeks, pulls the coat higher around her neck. She wants to scream, 'It is too soon for you to die, Daddy, too soon, too soon.' Instead, she searches the crowd for a familiar face, someone she can talk to. They are moving away, saying respectful farewells, disappearing.

Bonnie turns to leave, suddenly recalls what people say of her: 'She's her father's daughter, that one; afraid of nothing, afraid of no-one,' and realises that at this moment, she has never felt more afraid in her life.

Bonnie is listening to Sara speak, trying to grasp the meaning of what she is saying. She has asked to see a copy of Charles' will, but has been told that won't be necessary, there is nothing in it of any interest to the children. Scrambled thoughts chase each other, a mixture of shock, anger and disbelief. Surely this isn't right, that Charles has left nothing to his children? She thinks about the boys, whom he loved and who worked so hard over the years at Bullo to ensure his dream came to fruition. Why wouldn't he leave them something, even if it was only a small memento? What about Danielle; has she been left out too? Why would he ignore his youngest daughter? And Marlee, who is still living at Bullo, does she get nothing?

Bonnie hesitates to include herself in the equation, still unsure whether Sara knows that she and Charles reconciled before his death. One day she will tell her, but it's not the time now. Her mother has that pinched look again, is shutting down in the face of Bonnie's questions. It is obvious this conversation will be cut short very soon.

'What are you telling me, Mum?' Bonnie asks. She tries to keep her voice even, for fear she may explode. 'Are you saying Daddy deliberately ignored all of his seven children, that he wanted us to have nothing of his?'

Bonnie understands her mother was seeing another man before Charles died, and that the marriage was all but over. What she can't understand is the cloak of silence surrounding the will.

'Your father didn't leave anything in the will, Bonnie,' Sara replies. Her tone is flat, definite, the tone Bonnie knows only too well. 'I know that may be hard for you to accept, but he left nothing, except a huge mountain of debt.'

Bonnie shrugs, realises there is no point continuing to probe. The distance between them is now wider than the Grand Canyon, and right now it looks doubtful whether it will ever be bridged. She feels an immense sadness about that, is deeply wounded that it has come to this. But she realises there never has been a final nail in the coffin of their relationship; the nails have just slowly been hammered in over the years.

Bonnie stands up to leave, hesitates, wanting to ask more questions. Why did Daddy leave the hospital when he was so ill? Did he die at peace with himself and the world? Did he say anything, leave any messages for anyone? Did he tell Sara he and Bonnie had planned to go sailing together? Was her mother aware he had asked Arthur to instigate divorce proceedings because he was too sick to do it himself? Did Sara love him still, or had that died too? So many questions, but they all remain unspoken, hanging heavy in the air.

A final boarding call has been made for Bonnie's flight to Darwin. She shakes Sara's hand, but can't look at her, walks away without turning back.

* * *

Despite feeling some bitterness toward Sara—exacerbated by their disbelief that not only had their father apparently not left a will, but also that they weren't offered any personal mementos such as his war medals—Charles' sons promise him before his death that they will look after her if she needs them. It is the Maryland code of honour, and they are honourable men. Their gesture needn't have been made: like Bonnie, they both become persona non grata after their father's death.

At his home outside Washington, Fraser reflects on his father's death and on the lack of a will. Extremely diplomatic, he weighs his words carefully, mentally juggling them before he speaks. 'My understanding was that Dad left behind a huge property, which was well stocked with cattle, a yacht, condominium, stocks, bonds and a gold mine. Sara was wise in the way she dealt with these considerable assets. I think Dad left her a great deal.' If he is tempted to say more on that subject, he refrains. Charles may be dead, but the Maryland code of honour is not.

In Maryland, Charles' son Hugh writes his father's eulogy. In parts, it reads: 'He dreamed of building his own society, far away from the ravages of the ultraliberal sixties ... and he did it, too ... He played for the sake of the game itself. The monetary rewards were purely consequential. Despite the remarkable material gains throughout his life, he was actually far from being materialistic. His domain was achievement. His life was a quest for excellence, and challenge. The human spirit was his domain. But the thing we will all remember most was his intense charisma and energy ... He would scale any wall or simply crash through. Above all, he dreamed of a better world ... and this is perhaps where he has handed the torch to his children.'

There is a different mood at the Darwin memorial service. In a letter to Bomma, now in her nineties and unable to travel to

Australia, Gus writes: 'This is a sad time for all of us but, of course, especially for you. I arranged a memorial service in Darwin because many of Charles' friends were not able to fly to Sydney, as I could not. Jack and his family came, as did Bonnie and her fiance. In Charles' honour, we drank Bullo River Specials and reminisced about the man we all knew.'

Surrounded by friends, Bonnie takes the floor, rum in hand, and starts the Banjo Paterson recitation her father loved best. 'There was movement at the station, for the word had passed around, that the colt from old Regret—' She stops midsentence, in tears.

Gus, reading from the eulogy he has composed, pauses when he gets near the end. With Charles gone, he feels like a ship at sea, wonders if he will ever get over the loss. His wife, Nancy, holds his hand as he speaks the last words.

'In Australia, Charlie's adopted country, he became its greatest advocate, its greatest defender and its greatest critic. He refused to accept mediocrity or half best in any circumstances. There is no doubt we have lost a great friend, husband and father.'

Raising his rum and grapefruit juice, he adds: 'I know you all join with me in wishing him well wherever he may be. God bless you, Charlie.'

Jane Newbecker, one of the all-female crew who sailed with Charles, is tired out after his death. A qualified nurse, she barely left his side from the time he became ill. She is bewildered and disgusted that in Sara's book, *From Strength to Strength*, there is innuendo that their relationship went further than friendship.

'We got on well. There was no more to it than that. He treated me like a fourth daughter,' she says.

Jane's mother, Noel, believes Jane's role in looking after

Charles during his final illness should have been filled by his wife and daughters. 'Bonnie was in Darwin; Danielle was too young to help; Marlee was at Bullo, and Sara was in Queensland,' she says. 'Jane was left to cope virtually on her own.'

Noel cannot disguise the bitterness and contempt she feels toward the Australian Hendersons, describing their family's association with them as a sorry chapter in their lives which they now wish only to put behind them. The tragic turn of events which follow Charles' death undoubtedly colours her thinking. Accepting an invitation to visit his family in America—an invitation in part extended to thank her for her kindness in looking after Charles—Jane spends much of her five-month stay with Bomma at Lloyds Landing. Stepping out from the sidewalk one day, she is hit by a car, a shocking accident which has long-term repercussions. Returning to Australia with her devastated parents, the young, vibrant woman still retains some brain damage. Charles' sister, Margaret, says it was her brother's wish that Jane have the boat on which they enjoyed so many hours sailing. Instead, it is sold after his death.

Charles had kept the *Mary Blair* on his friends Carl and Caressa Crouch's moorings at Palm Beach in Sydney. Nine years after his death, Bonnie receives a letter from Caressa, whom she has never met. It reads, in part:

I have been prompted to write to you after reading an article on your flying. Congratulations on your terrific results ... I just wanted to write to you to let you know how much your father touched our lives. He would tell us of his problems with you, his rejection of your chosen marriage partner ... telling [us] you were the spitting image of him. But mostly he was always so proud of you and your sisters—but mainly you—and would always be describing something you had done with great pride.

We keep in contact with Jane, who is very depressed at her head injury. Although an employee of your father's, she was protected and controlled just like one of you—as you can imagine, it was 'Jane, do this' and 'Jane, do that'. Having had two children myself in the intervening years, I can now see how young Jane was when your father died. At the time, I put it down to her nursing experience, to be able to cope with renting the house by the beach so Charles could see the Mary Blair *as he didn't want to stay in hospital any longer. He hated it. Although he didn't last long after that, he knew where he was and was happy. Jane was there for all that.*

Charles always promised Mary Blair *to Jane after his death but of course Sara sold it and said she would buy her a smaller boat instead. [That did not happen.] I haven't been able to read any of the books your mother has written, as I have been so disgusted at hearing on radio the innuendo about his nurse, Jane, and Sara only talking about her* two *daughters. I just wanted you to know that when I read the article on you, I thought: that is Charles Henderson III's daughter and how incredibly proud he would have been.*

CHAPTER NINETEEN

Selected for the Australian aerobatic team to compete in England for the world title, Bonnie takes her place amongst the world's best pilots with great pride. She is flying in the Pitts, her favourite aircraft, but she realises it is outdated for international competition. The Russians are flying in Sukhois, which are far more advanced. Bonnie vows to fly a Sukhoi one day herself.

Just before the competition, she and her team-mates cut kangaroo shapes from contact paper and stick them in the middle of the Soviet stars on all the Russian aircraft. The Russian pilots and mechanics think it is enormously funny, but the KGB don't share the joke. When the Soviets make a bouncy landing and the media cartoonist draws a picture of a Soviet SU26 hopping down the airfield, they explode.

'You vill remoov dose kangerooz right now!'

Staring into their thunderous faces, Bonnie has visions of being shipped to the Gulag post-haste, and missing the competition.

She wants to tell them to lighten up, but thinks better of it.

Struggling to keep up the pace in her Pitts against the superior Russian aircraft, Bonnie doesn't score well. Pilots must fund themselves for competition; already underfunded, this is the last aerobatic team Australia will field for eight years. Disappointed in her overall performance, Bonnie is determined to do better next time, with the philosophical approach: 'Anyone who says winning isn't everything is a liar.'

The travel agency is advertising fares for Bali.

'Would you like to go there for a holiday, Bonnie?'

She pauses, thinks about the things she has to do. 'Yeah, that would be great, Arthur. But when? We're both fairly busy at the moment.'

'Oh,' he smiles, 'I thought we might make it our honeymoon.'

'Is that a proposal?' She is staring at him, hands rammed into her pockets, her green eyes a flame dance.

'Yes, it's a proposal. What do you think?'

Her arms are around his neck, her mouth against his ear. 'I think,' she whispers, 'that Bali sounds wonderful.'

Arthur slips a beautiful engagement ring—a cluster of rubies set on a simple gold band—on her finger. The ring is a family heirloom, which Sir Arthur Palmer, Arthur's grandfather, had brought back from India.

Bonnie asks Lynette to be her matron of honour but, only two weeks from having her second child, Lynette graciously declines. Instead, she offers to be the official mother of the bride which, for two reasons, she believes is far more appropriate.

'I wanted Bonnie to be the most beautiful bride, and didn't think that pictures with me, cumbersome and pregnant, would really fit the part. Also, it was patently obvious that Sara would not be attending her daughter's wedding. Someone had to stand in as a representative in her role. It was to be, after all, a wonderful day for Bonnie. Nothing must ruin it.'

When Arthur asks Bonnie where they should hold the ceremony, Bonnie replies, 'I always promised my dad I'd be married in a church.' The cathedral is booked.

To save money, Bonnie accepts the loan of a traditional bridal gown. 'She had been away from the station for months,' says Lynette, 'and her hands, for once, weren't rough and calloused, and her skin was clear. She was also extremely slim, which complemented the tight-fitting gown. There was no question that she was going to be a beautiful bride.'

In a last bid to try and salvage some familial relationship, Arthur sends Sara a letter and invitation to their wedding. But if he hopes his gesture will bring about a reconciliation, he is badly mistaken. Bonnie knows that even if he had got down on his hands and knees and begged, Sara would never have relented.

The letter reads, in part: 'I would have hoped that our marriage could be a focus for reuniting what could be an extremely effective family team … If you choose to abdicate your role as mother for this ceremony, after we have entreated you so, then you also irreversibly abdicate any role as grandmother and mother-in-law for us for all time.'

The letter is ignored.

Not a champagne drinker, Bonnie soothes her nerves with rum and water before the ceremony. Lynette does her make-up: a hint of gold powder on the lids, and glossy lipstick. She curls her long, lustrous hair with hot rollers, which are brushed out in waves and finished with a halo of frangipani. Bonnie isn't sure about the rollers: it is the first time she has ever had them in her hair.

It is a long walk up the aisle of Darwin's cavernous cathedral. Pausing at the doorway, on the arm of Gus Trippe, Bonnie radiates inner dignity. Her nervousness doesn't show; she hides well the butterflies which are dancing in her stomach and the aching realisation that if Charles were alive, he would have given her away. Familiar faces crane to watch for the bride's approach. Bonnie has hoped that Danielle would somehow be able to attend her wedding but, caught in the family politics, she has stayed away. Sara, too, is conspicuous by her absence. From the back of the church, Bonnie notices that Arthur is well represented by his family members, sitting in the front pew. In contrast, the pew for her family is almost empty. Only her half-brother, Jack, is here.

Bonnie looks exquisite. Her white lace dress complements her natural tan. Tucked in at the bodice, the gown shows off her small waist and falls in a scalloped effect around her ankles. A long train trails on the cathedral's floor, and her hair, swept high and curled on the crown, is interwoven with flowers. For once, her fingernails are perfectly clean—no sign of leather dye or grease underneath.

She keeps her head straight, eyes locked on Arthur. Resplendent in a dinner suit, he has turned to watch her walk toward him. Arthur's parents beam as Gus Trippe gently lets go her arm, steps back as she moves beside her fiance. Bonnie suddenly remembers the time at Bullo when she was led to her fiance draped in a sheet. At least this time she feels more elegant.

The service is short, but sweet; after fifteen minutes, the minister blesses the union and pronounces them man and wife. Bonnie is grateful they have reached that point quickly: this year's build-up to the wet is particularly steamy and uncomfortable, and the eighty wedding guests are in danger of expiring if they don't get out of the church quickly. Outside, Lynette bathes the couple in white and yellow frangipani petals as they step into their car.

The sun is sitting on the horizon as they reach the sailing club where the reception is being held. A cool breeze fans the palm trees and white caps dot the aqua sea. Charging their glasses with champagne, the guests listen and occasionally heckle as Gus proposes a toast to the bride and groom.

'The only sad thing about today is that Bonnie's father couldn't be here to give his daughter to Arthur,' Gus begins. 'He was very proud of Bonnie and her many achievements. She was his favourite. Bonnie has accomplished much in her young life; in fact, she has excelled in every task or objective she's attempted. You all know that she has become one of this country's leading aerobatic pilots; she is also a top rider and can hold her own with any man I've ever known. She has learned and developed skills in station management, cattle husbandry and in the full range of jobs required to run a cattle property. She is an artist who can draw and sketch to a high standard and a poet who paints vivid images with words. A superb saddle maker, she now has more business than she can handle.

'I now turn to the groom and find myself confronting an equally talented young man. But before proceeding I'd like to quote Shelley, who asked, "Have you heard that when a man marries, dies, or joins the country liberal party, his best friends hear no more of him?" Arthur, let this not happen to you. Arthur is a third generation pilot. His grandfather flew in World War I; his father was an ace in World War II; and Arthur flies in his own war between the mining companies, the pastoralists and the Aboriginal groups. I first met him when he was acting for the Aborigines who had put in a claim for a portion of Montejinni Station which Charles and I owned. We were defending; Arthur was acting for them. The judge and court were in session. I saw this serious and angry young man racing from one

Aboriginal group to another. He had organised truckloads of Aborigines from Wave Hill, Hooker Creek, Victoria River, even Bathurst Island. I don't think it mattered to him where they came from, as long as they were Aboriginal family groups who looked at home at Montejinni, with children swimming in the Top Springs waterhole and generally acting as if they had been there all their lives. He had organised a magnificent luncheon, special tribal ceremonies. The judge was impressed; Arthur won their claim.'

Looking around the room, Bonnie feels perfect contentment for the first time in her life. Arthur has repeatedly told her she deserves to be happy, and right now she is. Their future holds myriad promises: love, friendship, intense physical chemistry and shared interests in flying.

The only moment of discord happens when Bonnie's mother-in-law says to Lynette, 'It is a shame, dear, about the thickness of Bonnie's ankles; hopefully it won't be passed to her children.'

The comment is met with a sarcastic rebuke. 'Do you mean,' replies Lynette, 'it might lessen the breed?'

'Bonnie was not from landed gentry,' Lynette explains now, 'and it would have taken some time for Arthur's mother to accept her. Perhaps there was a thought that Arthur had married outside his class. And after all, one just doesn't do that, does one?'

Just before midnight, with the reception in full swing, the bride and groom say their farewells. The guests will stay on and party: Territory tradition dictates that while there is beer left, it must be drunk. It has been a memorable, happy day, but the newlyweds are tired and want some time alone. Tomorrow they start their honeymoon in Bali; but when they return, they have a battle royal to face. Bonnie must begin seriously to consider whether or not to fight Bullo River Station for her lost wages. Preferring to maintain a nonconfrontationist approach, she has so far managed to avoid tackling the problem.

* * *

A year after Charles' death, Bonnie and Arthur are overjoyed to find
she is pregnant. Deliriously happy with her husband, Bonnie nevertheless feels hemmed in in town, filling the house with saddles and
heading down the track to watch on polocrosse practice days. She
misses Bullo badly; the country, the lifestyle and stock camps; but
that is another world, and she is determined to make her way in her
new life.

Bonnie enjoys her pregnancy and radiates happiness. Her skin,
always clear, glows with good health and she swells with pride as
the baby grows. The prospect of her forthcoming labour doesn't
frighten her. She has known Aboriginal women to give birth where
they are, falling away from their tribe, finding a secluded spot and
squatting on their haunches for the delivery. Soon after, they move
on to find their group, proudly nursing their newborn infants. She
has watched animals give birth countless times, nuzzling into their
foal or calf with loving attention from the moment they are born.
When Bonnie's labour begins, she faces it with ease. However, after
the baby does an unexpected roll in the birth canal, Bonnie's calm
vanishes.

'God, I'm dying!' she thinks as another contraction hits her full
force. In the darkened room the midwife monitors the labour, but
this one is moving exceptionally fast. Within forty-five minutes the
baby appears, but something is wrong. She is choking and blue—
the umbilical cord is wrapped twice around her neck—and the
doctor doesn't waste any time.

'Push the baby back in to the birth canal while I cut the cord!'
he says.

Once freed from her restraints, their daughter enters the world
on 13 March, 1988. They call her Amelia, a family name and a

tribute to Bonnie's heroine, aviatrix Amelia Earhart.

Motherhood does little, if anything, to change Bonnie's sense of self. She refuses to accept that being a mother can limit her in any way. If she is naive, she doesn't see it that way. Amelia, her little shiralee, simply goes with her.

Ross and Lynette, now managing Tipperary Station, owned by media-shy mogul Warren Anderson, have set up a polocrosse team. Anderson provides the ponies and the head stockman from Tipperary is dispatched to Victoria to 'test drive' them. The Top End clubs are developing the Darwin showground's rear lots into a polocrosse field and, with a great sense of anticipation, the team from Tipperary heads up to Darwin to watch the polocrosse carnival.

It is the end of the wet season. Low cloud hangs overhead and the humidity is oppressive. Steam rises from the red clods of the newly-ploughed field, a stinking heat that would drive people to the cover of air-conditioned amenities—if there were any. The horses are covered in sweat and foam; mud cakes everything, and the flies crawl like black dots over every face. The showground is a far cry from the hallowed playing fields of England, and there is no decorum here. This is polocrosse, Territory style.

'Imagine our surprise, on arrival, to see none other than Bonnie and four-week-old Amelia there,' Lynette recalls. 'Bonnie's horse float was attached to the four-wheel drive and Bonnie is ready for action! Her breasts are the size of inflated balloons from which milk continually squirts, but she has no embarrassment. She is here to play polocrosse, and nothing will stop her. Amelia, the fattest, most contented little bundle, is asleep in her carry basket under the shade of the float, Bonnie's Akubra keeping the flies from her face.

'Bonnie's out there playing chukkas in the sun and humidity, and in time out, she nurses and feeds Amelia before she taps the shoes on her horse's feet! Instead of drinking water to rehydrate, she gets stuck into the beer, just like one of the boys.

'The next day I phone and Arthur takes the call. Bonnie is bed-ridden, suffering sunstroke, dehydration, exhaustion, the works! She stays that way for days. She had no idea of what being a mother was all about, and certainly had no guiding hand in that direction to help her. She had an image to maintain, and it never occurred to her to change her lifestyle to accommodate the demands of mother-hood. What a girl!'

Arthur is pacing the floor restlessly, trying to make Bonnie see his point of view. She has been putting off this decision for a while now.

'You worked like a bloody dog at Bullo for years and got absolutely no financial gain from it at all! You are entitled to your wages, Bonnie; it is your inalienable right to have them.'

'Yes, I know,' Bonnie says. She is tired of this conversation, and it always comes back to the same thing. She does deserve to be paid, but in order to do that, she must sue Bullo River. The director of that company is her mother.

'Arthur, it is a huge step to take. I don't know that I can do it.'

'Your father would have wanted you to get what is yours, Bonnie. Do you at least agree with that?'

'Yes, I do. Mum worked out my wages for three years' work, said they came to $12 000, then Daddy buys me the aircraft in lieu of them which she sold for $42 000. Then the cheque he gave me to cover the cost of the plane was stopped. I know all that, Arthur, but to take the company to court? God, it's a horrible thought.'

Arthur throws his hands up in resignation. 'Look, it's ulti-mately your decision, but you know my attitude. You are fighting only for what is yours. What are you going to do, just lie down and let people walk all over you? Make up your mind and let me know what your decision is.'

Bonnie wanders around the house for days afterwards, wrestling to come to a decision. Arthur is right; it is her money, and it should never have come to this, that she be forced into court with her own family to retrieve it. She is only too well aware of the position she is in; once again, she is damned if she does, and damned if she doesn't.

The consequences of going to court are only too obvious. Marlee, who doesn't speak to her anyway, will claim it is a further example of her betrayal of the family and Sara ... God, she hates to think what Sara will feel. However, Bonnie is angry, too: she should never have been put in this situation in the first place, to have to make such a tough decision. She knows if it goes to court, she will be used as a scapegoat for the family's problems and that it will be played out publicly. Her father, she knows, would fight for a principle, but he is no longer here to advise her. She has to work this one out herself.

'Okay, Arthur,' she finally decides. 'Let's go ahead with the court case, but I hope it's over quickly. I feel like I'm walking to my own execution.'

Bonnie's premonition that she would be made to bear the brunt publicly proves to be correct. It deals a fatal blow to her relationship with Sara. Bonnie doesn't believe she has to justify her decision to go ahead with the court case. Tired of defending her actions, she feels no guilt, just a sadness that a financial settlement has to be made through legal channels. She would have preferred it to be negotiated quietly, and the settlement offered graciously.

Instructing her lawyers to settle out of court on the proviso that she doesn't have to see either Bonnie or Arthur on the day, Sara agrees to settle for $30 000. For Bonnie, the settlement is simple proof that the money should have been paid to her.

Sara's claim in *From Strength to Strength* that, after signing the papers, 'on the 2nd of August, 1988, I lost a daughter', doesn't hold weight for Bonnie. The truth, she says, is that her mother had lost her long before that.

Danielle is on the phone to Bonnie, her voice breaking with emotion. 'Marlee's husband, Charlie, has been killed in a motorbike accident. His bike hit an ant hill and his neck was broken. Everyone, especially Marlee, is absolutely shattered.'

'I'll come straight down,' Bonnie says. She is shaking, desperately upset for her older sister despite the distance between them.

'Don't come down, please, Bon,' Danielle replies. It hurts her to say it, but she knows her sister's presence will only make things worse.

Piecing together what happened, Bonnie imagines this tall, strong man lying in the bush; Danielle frantically looking for him; Marlee, prostrate with grief; and Dick finally taking control and bringing them all back to the homestead. It is, Bonnie thinks, as if a curse has settled over Bullo: first Gill's shocking death, then her father's, Jane's car accident, and now Charlie. She recalls what Danielle has told her: that Marlee refused to leave her dead husband's side, lying next to him on their bed, sobbing and trying to recuscitate him, and Sara, unable to cope, falling apart in the next room. She has been out of Bullo long enough now, in a saner, calmer environment, to know things needn't be like that, that someone should have taken control earlier. She cries to think of Marlee laying there in her grief, holding in her arms the lifeless man she adores, willing him to come back to life; she cries to think of

Danielle trying to be strong for everyone and trying to keep Sara together; cries for herself.

Suddenly the isolation and desolation of Bullo scares her; even if she could go back, she could never cope with it the way she used to. Distanced from it, she now recognises what she never could before: that living in isolation goes hand in hand with chaos and mayhem.

CHAPTER TWENTY

Cyclone Tracy, which ripped through Darwin with ferocious intensity on Christmas Day of 1974, wiped out many of Gus and Nancy Trippe's documents, but it didn't wipe out their memory. Now living in a small town two hours north of Los Angeles, they are a world away from the frenetic lifestyle they once shared on cattle stations in Australia's north. Even so, at seventy-eight, Gus doubts he will live long enough to forget the bitterness and heartache which drove him into court with Sara eleven years ago.

It is a celebrated case which proves to have long-ranging repercussions; played out in the glare of the media spotlight, it casts Bonnie and Sara in opposing roles. At its heart is the promissory note signed between Gus, Charles and Sara, and for the media, it has all the elements of a sensational story: old friends slugging it out in a court battle, money, high emotion and a cliffhanger ending. The subplot is even more juicy: offstage, Bonnie is asked to make an agonising decision—to tell the truth as she sees it, or to protect her parents. For the first time, private differences are dragged into the public domain, and the fallout is savage.

Sara, practical, level-headed and in charge of the Bullo purse strings, was deeply concerned at the implications of the promissory note. In a lengthy meeting, she begged Charles, whose health was degenerating, and Gus to consider what else could be done.

'We simply do not have $500 000 to pay out,' she said. 'Can't we think about some other way, something that will satisfy the debt and not put us out of business? What we do have is cattle—healthy, fat beasts that will realise a good return. Could we come to some agreement over them instead?'

After many hours, a solution was found: the Hendersons would turn over eight hundred head of prime quality cattle over a period of three years, and the debt would be squared.

Sara, grateful that a working agreement had been reached, placed a hand on Gus' shoulder. 'Thank you. We will give you the best cattle we have.'

'It was, in my opinion, a very fair and equitable deal, for two reasons,' Gus recalls. 'The promissory note was in fact a substantial reduction on the amount of money owed to me, but I was happy to help out Charles and his family. In all our years of doing business together, Charles and I never fought over money. The value placed on the cattle worked out at six hundred and twenty-five dollars per head. At that figure, I stood to make a profit of two hundred dollars per head. I agreed to it because we dealt on the Maryland code: a man's word is his honour.'

In the first year, there was a substantial shortfall in the number, and quality, of cattle supplied. Nancy, Gus' wife, deeply concerned that the promissory note was changed, also had another major problem: their marriage, once so strong, was falling apart.

'I distrusted both Charles and Sara and couldn't hide it,' she admits. 'Gus believed totally in them, believed they would do as they said, but I was much more cynical. We would look over the cattle at Bullo and I'd end up in tears for the rest of the day because I could see Gus' generous spirit was being abused. We argued constantly over it, but in the end I made the decision that money was not going to wreck the best thing in my life—my marriage.'

With Charles now very ill and Bonnie in charge of the station, Gus says they were supplied with run-out cleanskins, not the branded, quiet, well-bred cattle they had been promised.

'Financially, I couldn't abide an on-going shortfall and at that time interest rates had sky-rocketed. Had Bullo supplied good cattle I would still have only got twenty cents on the dollar, but as it was, I got only a few cents on the dollar. These cattle can generously be described as derelict; some of the runty, bony rats were older than I was. Many were so poor in condition they died. Bonnie even threw in a heifer that was still sucking and called it a cow. But I didn't ever blame her. I figured she was just taking orders. I expressed disappointment and said I'd wait until the next year, but the same thing happened then.'

Unaware of the extent of Charles' illness, Gus did know that something in their gentlemanly code of ethics had gone wrong. 'For the first time in our life I felt like my old friend was cheating me,' he says. It is a wound that obviously still bleeds. 'Charles died before we ever had the chance to sort it out.'

Sara, in compliance with Charles' family's wishes, made the sad journey to Maryland to scatter half of his ashes. The remainder were scattered over Bullo and at sea. Murray-Lee, now running the station, called Gus to tell him she had some cattle to supply.

'We have only done one muster this season but we can offer you ten bulls,' she said.

'But the cattle around the yard are full of beautiful Brahman-cross, why can't we have some of those?'

'We're doing another muster shortly and you'll get your cattle then, Uncle Gus.'

As Gus was to learn, this conversation with Murray-Lee was to have bitter repercussions.

'I thought it was at least the beginning of a positive intent on their part to make good their contract,' he says. 'I wrote Murray-Lee a note, wishing her well on her second muster, but then I found out that she had put thousands of beasts through that yard already. It was far from their first muster.'

Furious at being duped, Gus says he made the tough decision to go to court.

The stranger at Bonnie's doorway, dressed in an ill-fitting suit and with an official air, is thrusting a piece of paper in her hand. 'Are you Sara Lloyd Henderson?'

'Yes, why?'

'Could you please sign receipt of these court documents?'

Closing the door, Bonnie rips open the envelope and reads the contents with a growing sense of dread. Pacing the floor, she waits impatiently for Arthur to come home.

'What am I supposed to do?' she asks him. 'If I tell the truth, all hell will break loose. If I don't, I will perjure myself.'

'Tell the truth, Bonnie,' Arthur advises. 'You're a hopeless liar and perjury is a serious offence. Tell the facts, the way you know them to be.'

The civil court is packed with lawyers and Bonnie is nervous. Unused to being the centre of attention, she is very uncomfortable with the ordeal she is about to face. Sara's defence team, huddled in last-minute discussions, looks grim. The subpoena served on their client's daughter from Gus Trippe could open a Pandora's box.

Bonnie takes the oath, clasps her hands in front of her to stop them shaking. Her voice is low, and the lawyer asks her to speak up. Her face is flushed, and she tries not to look out to the body of the court.

The questions came thick and fast.

'After you started work in 1980, did your duties on the property change at all through the years?'

'Yes. In 1983 I started running the stock camp myself.'

'When you started running the stock camp yourself, what were your duties then?'

'Overseeing all the work that was done, helping my father to make up mustering schedules, organising helicopters, where the cattle be put, how they'd generally be managed.'

'If any drafting of cattle needed to be done, who would do that?'

'I would.'

'In the course of your duties at that time, were you given directions by anyone?'

'Yes, my father.'

'Now, were you aware in early 1985 that there was an agreement between the interests of Mr Trippe and the interests of your father and mother about the delivery of some cattle?'

'Yes.'

'Were you involved in any of the negotiations before that agreement?'

'No.'

'How did you find out about the agreement?'

'I was told.'

'By whom?'

'By my mother and father, and Gus Trippe was present and lawyers, and whatever.'

'In the course of 1985, I think there were four deliveries of cattle to [Trippe's] station, do you recall that.'

'That may be correct, I can't remember.'

'At the time of any of those deliveries, were you aware of the precise details of the agreement between your parents and Mr Trippe's interest?'

'No.'

After several more questions, the lawyer asks: 'The first delivery was on 31 May 1985. By then, did you know anything about what sort of cattle and how many had to be delivered?'

'Not exactly, no.'

More questions, then, 'Were you present at Bullo River Station when each of the four deliveries was drafted to be sent off to Mr Trippe?'

'Yes.'

'Were you the person in charge of that?'

'Yes.'

'Who actually conducted the muster to get the cattle together for that purpose?'

'Most of the musters were helicopter musters.'

'Were you assisted in that drafting, or the general activities surrounding the drafting, by anyone?'

'No.'

Later, the judge offers the opinion that whatever instructions Bonnie received with regard to the cattle has no bearing on the ultimate decision. Only what she saw loaded, and how it corresponded with what Trippe received, was important. Trippe's lawyer then asks questions again.

'Can you describe the cattle you selected?'

'They were the Shorthorn types. They were the best of the lowest quality type cattle. Mainly only the younger stock.'

'Were any of the cattle you selected on this occasion Brahman or Brahman-cross?'

These are quality breeds.

'No.'

'Do you remember what the condition of those beasts were?'

'A bit poor.'

'What does the expression "strong forward condition" mean to you?'

'Strong means fit, forward condition generally referring to young cattle that could improve with good management.'

'To your observation were the cattle that you selected in strong forward condition?'

'No, they weren't strong, but could have picked up because they were young cattle and would need a fair spell and good feed.'

Admitting that much of the cattle drafted from different musters was not in strong forward condition, that they were 'probably poor again due to having been hassled around the yard', Bonnie goes on to say she could have delivered Shorthorn, Brahman-cross heifers and bulls, all in good condition, to Trippe. The cattle were available at Bullo Station for delivery.

'You've already indicated what the state of the herd was at the end of the 1985 season; when did you leave the station?'

'At the end of 1985.'

'Given that your knowledge of what was actually on the station at the end of 1985, in your view could that herd have supplied five hundred Shorthorn cows of the same sort in 1986?'

This is a crucial question, and Bonnie knows it. She wishes to God she didn't have to answer. She decides to keep her answer short.

'Yes.'

The lawyer attempts to show that Bonnie rewrote diary entries pertaining to the cattle—an accusation she strongly disputes—and the cross-examination which follows is tough and personal.

'Mrs Palmer, when were you last at the property?'

'In 1985.'

'You haven't been back since?'

'I went back once to pick my horse up.'

'When was that?'

'The end of 1986, I think.'

'Apart from picking up your horse, did you take anything else with you, any of your personal belongings?'

'No, I removed my personal belongings on one occasion when I left in 1985. I was in a very small aircraft and I had very few belongings anyway; they fit in one suitcase and there wasn't enough room in the aircraft to even take my personal books and things.'

'You didn't remove your father's diaries?'

'I had no interest in them whatsoever, and I didn't remove them, no.'

'Are you aware that you used to keep tally records, did you not?'

'At the end of each muster and draft, the tally sheets were taken in and given to my mother to be filed.'

'Did you remove any tally records?'

'I did not; when I returned in 1986 it was only to pick up my horse. I only went into the house to deliver a number of Christmas presents.'

'How long did you spend in the house?'

'About ten minutes; I had a glass of water and left.' Bonnie remembers this clearly; having given her family presents, she received none in return.

Southern gentleman, yachtsman, war
hero...Charles Henderson III.

Charles had a deep respect for the Aborigines he worked with. This shot
was taken in 1973 during an exercise to demonstrate Aboriginal tracking
skills.

Bonnie (on the horse), Danielle and Sara.

Bonnie and Danielle burying the dogs in the sandpit for fun.

Bonnie on Sara's horse, Blue; 1970. Gentle and reliable, Blue was a favourite with the girls.

Bonnie and a poddy calf.

Danielle on Blue, 1977.

Murray-Lee and Bonnie on Blue, 1978.

Out to camp, 1976.

Bullo homestead.

Neil Gourlay teaching Bonnie how to break in horses.

Ross and Lynette
Ainsworth on their
wedding day.

From left to right:
Hugh, Fraser and David.

Bonnie and Fraser on
Danielle's wedding
day. Fraser, smart and
elegant in his naval
uniform, gave
Danielle away.

Gus and Nancy
Trippe.

The comfortable way to view other competitors during their flight. Bonnie on the wing of the Extra 300S.

Bonnie and her aerobatic trophies.

Bonnie and the Pitts Special VH-SIS in which she won both the 1994 and 1995 National Open Championships.

Bonnie and Arthur on their wedding day; the picture was taken by Lynette Ainsworth.

'No conversation with your mother or sister?'

'No more than to give them the presents and depart.'

'You say you didn't remove the tally records for the years 82 through to 85?'

'Certainly not.'

'You say that you didn't remove your father's diaries?'

'I did not.'

'I suppose you didn't see any of those documents when you went back there at the end of 1986?'

'Absolutely not.'

'Apart from that occasion when you delivered some Christmas presents, you've seen your mother, I think—you've seen her in court in the last couple of days, but you've seen her also at the funeral of your father?'

'Yes, that's right, yes.'

'So you've seen her—apart from this week, you've only seen her on about two occasions since your father died?'

'That's correct.'

'And the same for Murray-Lee. You've only seen her once?'

'That's correct.'

'Relations between you and your mother and you and Murray-Lee have been very strained, have they not, ever since you left?'

'Yes.'

'And relations were also strained between you and your father before he died?'

'No.'

After further cross-examination, the prosecutor goes on to ask: 'In 1985 your personal relationships with your mother, father— your mother and father in particular—became worse than they'd ever been?'

'That's correct.'

'For a number of reasons, but there was certainly constant dispute concerning Arthur Palmer?'

'That's correct.'

'Your present husband. You had medical problems?'

'That's correct.'

'And you were sick and in hospital for some of the time, particularly in June of that year?'

'I think so, yes.'

'And you in fact left the station in August of 1985?'

'That was for medical reasons again.'

'Well, I suggest to you that the fact is that you walked off the job in August.'

'No, that's incorrect. I had a previous arrangement to go somewhere that was entirely discussed with my family and agreed on that I should go there, and for medical reasons I didn't return earlier despite many phone calls to return immediately to get back to work.'

'You left the job during the August muster, did you not?'

'I can't remember the exact time but I did leave for personal reasons and it was agreed that I should go.'

'You can't even remember whether it was during a muster that you left the job?'

'Musters were going on all the time. At one stage I was mustering every five days, so it's kind of hard to say whether it's during a muster or not. Cattle work goes on continuously throughout the year, every day of the year.'

'Well, the fact is that your dislike for your mother, and the dislike for your sister, is so strong that you are prepared to come to court and tell lies, aren't you?'

The question, issued in a cold, clear tone, startles Bonnie. She shifts in her seat, stares back at the lawyer. 'That's not true.'

'And that's what you've been doing?'

'That's not true.'

'And that you would do anything you could to cause financial trouble for your mother?'

'That's not true.'

Shortly after this exchange, Bonnie is asked to stand down as a witness. Leaving the courtroom, she feels the intense gaze of her mother and sister. She has told the truth as she saw it, and spared more elaborate details that could have damaged them further. But her conscience remains clear: when she left the station, all responsibility for the supply of cattle to Gus Trippe fell on Murray-Lee and Sara's shoulders. It wasn't until after she left that he decided to sue.

After days of cross-examination on both sides, the judge informs the court that he will not take into consideration the origin of the debt owed to the Trippes. The ruling would only be based on whether or not the debt had been paid.

The decision, which takes an interminably long time to come in, goes to Sara. But her elation at the victory doesn't last long: the Trippes lodge an appeal.

'I appealed on many grounds, but mostly on principle,' Gus says. 'Three supreme court judges reviewed the case and the testimony, which took a very long time. They ruled in my favour. Years after I had started the action, I finally had my day in court.'

In a letter to Bonnie and Arthur, he writes: 'I would still go to hell for Charlie as I have done over the years. But I would not cross the street for Sara.'

CHAPTER TWENTY-ONE

B y mid 1990, Bonnie realises with joy that she is pregnant again. Amelia, now two, is proving to be a lovely companion, trotting around after her mother to help feed the horses on their twenty acre property, an hour south of Darwin at Tumbling Waters, on the edge of a national park. Amelia chats incessantly to Bonnie in her childhood language. She relishes the idea of having a baby brother or sister to play with, and is glad when Bonnie gets over the morning sickness that plagues her mercilessly in the early stages of the pregnancy. Arthur is away more often than he is home, doing Aboriginal field work with an attractive female doctor. Bonnie doesn't ask if his relationship with the doctor is more than just platonic, but she wouldn't be surprised if it was. Having grown up with men, she knows their weaknesses for a pretty woman, particularly in the middle of the scrub. She chooses to ignore her doubts, instead bends like a willow to make their marriage work. From hard experience, she knows she will always come off second best in a verbal disagreement with Arthur, who baffles her with inverted logic and long words.

'Why don't you speak to me in English?' Bonnie complains.

'I do, Bonnie,' he replies. 'Why don't you use a dictionary to understand what I am saying?'

Quick to learn, Bonnie keeps a dictionary close by from now on so that next time she won't be so easy to tie up in verbal knots.

Sitting outside one day and playfully throwing grass at Amelia from the lawn she has just mown, Bonnie realises with a start that she is bleeding. At fourteen weeks, she knows this is an ominous sign, and she hurries inside to phone the hospital.

'Put your feet up and rest, Mrs Palmer,' they advise. 'You must try and stem the blood flow.'

Alone in the house with Amelia, Bonnie can only manage to lie down for an hour. Her daughter needs lunch and the horses have to be fed; Arthur will be home by dinnertime, and she can rest then. By nightfall, Bonnie is fearful and panicky. The low, dull ache at the base of her stomach has intensified with the bleeding, even though she is in bed with her feet up. She has to get to hospital, fast. From their bedroom, she can hear Arthur talking on the telephone, a protracted business call that she needs to interrupt. Now too frightened to leave the bed, she repeatedly calls out to him, but it seems to take an interminably long time for him to appear.

'Arthur, I need to get to the hospital. I'm scared I'm losing the baby.'

When they finally reach the hospital the doctor tries to break the news gently to Bonnie, but she is inconsolable. 'I'm sorry, Mrs Palmer. It's too late.'

Bonnie could die of heartache. Memories of her termination come back to her, and she turns away from the doctor, immersed in grief and private pain.

* * *

Tired out from the miscarriage, saddle work and looking after Amelia, Bonnie becomes increasingly weaker. With her immune system low, she gets a head cold that won't go away, and progresses to bronchitis. Within a week, unable to eat and with no energy left, she asks a friend to come over and take Amelia for the night. The friend takes one look at Bonnie and expresses her concern.

'You look bloody dreadful. You should be in hospital.'

'I'll be right,' Bonnie says. 'Arthur is coming home later in the evening and I'll see how I feel then.'

By nightfall, coughing, retching and in shocking pain, Bonnie is too ill to get out of bed. Conceding to Arthur that she needs some urgent medical attention, he drives her to hospital, but by the time they arrive, she is too weak to hold herself up for the chest X-rays.

The doctor is blunt with her. 'You could have died,' he says. 'You have double pneumonia and will need to spend ten days in here on a drip.'

Despite massive doses of antibiotics, Bonnie is still very weak three weeks after leaving hospital and can't walk from one side of her house to the other. During the relapse she suffers, she coughs so severely she breaks a rib.

Sometime later Bonnie begins to feel nauseous, her breasts are tingling and her jeans, usually loose, are suddenly a tight fit. She is thrilled to find she is pregnant again, but is still bone tired from the double pneumonia and miscarriage. She has just started fencing the new airstrip block, where they intend to move when their donga—a colourful colloquialism for a house that essentially is no more than a shed—is built, and there are still seven and a half kilometres of pickets and wire to erect. She will have to try and finish it before the baby is born.

At the beginning of the wet season, a lightning strike hits the fence where Bonnie is working. Knocked over with its force and now three months pregnant, she is desperately worried that it might have affected the baby. She phones Danielle, now living in Cloncurry; angry and concerned that Bonnie is trying to do too much on her own, Danielle promises to come over. It is important that they get as much fencing done together as possible before Bonnie reaches the later stages of pregnancy. She knows how determined her sister is: once Danielle leaves, she will tackle the job alone.

Arthur's time has come to fulfil his dream of entering politics. His grandfather, Sir Arthur Palmer, was the premier of Queensland and the calling is in his blood. Arthur is well aware of the risks. A new candidate with the Country Liberal Party, he is running against a popular candidate, a strong Labor seat. Snowden, the Labor candidate, has romped it in in the past, but Arthur intends to give him a run for his money. His eyes are firmly set on Canberra, and he intends to become the new Minister for Aboriginal Affairs. He has two years campaigning ahead of him to get there.

His supporters believe in him totally: young, idealistic, bright and outspoken, he has the street savvy to fight a tough battle, feet in both black and white camps, a smooth tongue to woo swinging voters, and a politician's ability to keep smiling. Most importantly, he believes in the promises he makes the electorate.

Preselected for the federal seat, his campaign is a long, hard road: two years travelling the Territory, knocking on doors, smiling, shaking hands, listening carefully to the problems faced by people in his electorate. Bonnie, popular and well known, could prove to be one of his greatest assets, but she feels like a fish out of water at the rare flash functions she attends. Mostly, she stays home, busy breeding Waler horses—Australia's most famous breed, used for stock and army horses, well known for their role in battle during World War I—and with her saddle-making business. Word has spread that Bonnie's saddle work is superb, and the business has taken off. On the rare occasions when she does accompany her husband, her behaviour is usually criticised.

Never one to be a wallflower, Bonnie happily chats to people whilst Arthur works the room. As a Henderson, she is well known, and she attracts strangers to her like magnets. Arthur finds her popularity an embarrassment and an annoyance.

'Must you continually draw attention to yourself and be so outspoken?' he chastises.

'But I'm not, Arthur. I was just standing there and people started talking to me.'

'Yes, well, it's probably best in future that you stay home, then,' he decides.

That suits Bonnie admirably: the baby is due soon, and she senses there will be problems. In her last four months of the pregnancy, neither mother nor child has gained much weight at all. Normally sixty kilos, Bonnie still weighs only sixty-eight in her third trimester. She tries to remain cheerful and positive, tells herself Amelia was a perfectly healthy child, but her doubts persist.

Her final check with the doctor proves that the blood levels going through to the placenta are falling dramatically. Induced, their daughter Georgina is born while the placenta is failing. Seriously underweight, she is a tiny scrap who sleeps fitfully and needs extra love.

'Your baby needs to be in a humidicrib in the intensive care unit,' the nurses tell Bonnie.

Refusing to accept this, Bonnie tucks Georgina inside her gown and sits day and night in the ward with her. By the fifth day, the nurses give up trying to chase Bonnie out of the room or to take Georgina from her.

'You can take your daughter to your room, but it is highly irregular,' they say.

Bonnie cuddles Georgina close, holding her next to her breast and begging her to feed. Ignoring doctor's orders that the baby must have formula by tube every three hours, Bonnie persists in her attempts to feed naturally. On the fourth day, her patience pays off, and she looks hopefully at the doctor for confirmation that her baby is in perfect health. Her hopes are dashed.

'I'm concerned about Georgina's eyes. May I have the specialist look?'

The diagnosis is shattering.

'She has glaucoma, which causes postnatal blindness,' the doctor says. 'She will need to go to Brisbane for an operation.'

Bonnie's heart sinks. She cradles her daughter in her arms, promises her everything will be okay. 'We'll be right, Georgie. We'll be right.'

The operation to cure the glaucoma is a success, but the haemorrhaging that follows is so severe Georgina remains blind for months after. Bonnie takes her back and forth to Brisbane for check-ups, which are harrowing for both mother and child. Still tiny and frail, at seven months she finally regains vision in her right eye, but her left is slower to catch up, and never regains full sight.

Arthur is often away, campaigning. Bonnie stands with Amelia and Georgina, tearfully watching as his aircraft rumbles down the airstrip, the undercarriage wheels fold up and the wings dip over the trees before disappearing into the blue yonder. She remembers her mother doing the same thing when they lived in America, standing on the steps crying as Charles drove up the laneway; she remembers, too, that after a while Sara didn't cry when he left.

Despite its problems, Bonnie desperately wants her marriage to work. Sometimes she feels as if she must walk on eggshells to keep the peace, tiptoeing around Arthur's eccentricities and volatility, and continually working to please him emotionally. She still adores Arthur, even though they are so very different in many ways. They handle their problems differently too. He prefers a confrontationist approach; Bonnie takes the line of least resistance. To avoid a fight, she often backs down, capitulating to him; this is how Sara handled Charles, and it is how Bonnie has been conditioned to cope. Now that Arthur has instilled in her the idea that she has the right to be happy, Bonnie clings to the concept tenaciously. He has given her a feeling of self-worth, and she likes it. If Bonnie is disquieted by some people's observations—he is Henry Higgins and she is his Eliza Doolittle—she doesn't show it. Their relationship is intense and passionate, and often their arguments are dissolved with laughter. When they work well together, they light up the room. But Susan Seppelt, who knows Bonnie as well as anyone, doesn't pull any punches with her analysis of their marriage. Consciously or subconsciously, she says, Bonnie married her father.

CHAPTER TWENTY-TWO

Georgina has a distinct lack of interest in food. It has become a major issue; still being breast-fed at ten months, she has reached the stage where she now needs supplementary iron. She is ghostly pale, and the pediatrician suspects she is anaemic. Her next glaucoma test, performed under general anaesthetic, will prove whether or not their fears are warranted.

The family has gone to Melville Island, an Aboriginal community thirty minutes from Darwin, for a break. They return home late in the afternoon, and Georgina is obviously not well. It is a hot January evening, and Bonnie tries to settle her daughter, giving her Panadol to abate the fever, hoping she is just teething. Fretful and restless, Georgina finally settles into a fitful sleep. Sitting next to her bed, Bonnie constantly checks her temperature, which doesn't go down, and brings a fan into the room to blow directly onto her. By early morning her fever has risen and Bonnie calls the hospital in panic.

'I live an hour's drive from Darwin, and she hasn't improved during the night. I want to see her pediatrician,' she tells the nursing sister.

'Bring her straight in,' the sister replies. 'The doctor will be waiting.'

Hitting the pedal to the metal, Bonnie screams at full speed toward the hospital. Arthur is away campaigning and her girlfriend is nursing Georgina in the passenger seat. Suddenly she lets out a desperate cry.

'Oh God, Bonnie, drive faster! Georgie is having a convulsion!' Georgina's little body, tired of trying to fight the fever, has gone into spasm, jerking uncontrollably.

Bonnie is tailing traffic on the road, pushing the horn in frantic desperation for them to let her pass. The air-conditioner in the car is on full power, and they cool Georgina with a wet washer until the convulsion passes.

'We're nearly there, Georgie, nearly there, darling,' Bonnie repeats over and over as the car swallows up the miles.

Dashing through the emergency entrance, she runs into the pediatrician's room. Now fifteen hours into the onset of her fever, the doctor takes a cursory glance at the raised fontanelle on Georgina's head and makes an immediate decision. 'We need to do a lumbar puncture straight away.'

The nursing sister has already described the severity of the child's symptoms to him after speaking with Bonnie and, certain of his diagnosis, he has obtained special clearance from Canberra to begin administering the three hundred dollar per day drug necessary to combat the virus. He can only pray that his diagnosis is wrong.

Georgina is now so distressed she needs three doctors to hold her still while they take the lumbar puncture. Afterwards, she is placed in isolation in the intensive care unit. Bonnie doesn't leave her side, waiting for the doctor to come in with the results.

'I had feared it was meningitis, but the tests have come back clear,' he tells her. He is looking tired and strained, gazing down at the tiny child as he speaks. 'I don't know exactly what it is, but I must warn you, Georgina is gravely ill. I have ordered another test to be done on the spinal fluid to make doubly sure and I will personally supervise that test.'

Bonnie looks at her daughter, at the burst blood vessels in her face from screaming in pain from the last test, and starts to cry.

'If it's not meningitis, what can it be? Please, don't hurt her again. She's so very little.'

The new test results are devastating.

'The test has come back positive,' the doctor says. 'She has meningitis. It initially didn't show in her system because it was caught at such an early stage. She would have picked up the infection at Melville Island. She is critically ill, and had you not brought her in when you did, she would not have survived another day.'

Bonnie refuses the offer to sleep on a roll-out bed in the isolation ward, instead asking that her swag be brought into the hospital. When the nurses find her stash—a six-pack of stout—they only smile at the antics of this wild woman from the bush.

'I suppose that's doctor's orders, is it?' they ask.

Overhearing the conversation, Georgie's paediatrician walks into the ward. 'Actually, it is,' he says with a smile.

In the midst of Georgina's crisis, Bonnie rings her half-brother, Fraser, in London. Now Director of Neurosurgery at Georgetown University and one of the most highly-decorated neurosurgeons in the American navy, Bonnie trusts him implicitly. It is as if he was born to do medicine. While he was living at Bullo, Dick had advised him to go to university and return to the station after that if he still wanted to. Missing all the deadlines for admittance to the University of Virginia, Fraser sent a telegram which was not acknowledged. Charles advised him to fly the 12 000 miles to meet the dean, who initially told him he was too late. Finally, having talked to him for a while, the dean offered Fraser a compromise. If he could pass the tough admittance test, he would allow him into the university. Fraser not only passed, he passed with the highest marks.

Fraser has seen a number of paediatric patients with similar symptoms to Georgina's, and his advice to Bonnie is sage. 'We can only hope that the infection leaves her system with no side effects,' he says. 'But keep a very, very close watch on her.' When he hangs up the telephone, he prays that Georgina will survive. Meningitis can be deadly in any child, but it is particularly so for one as frail as Georgie.

For ten days, Georgina remains on a drip, lying next to her mother on the swag. It is their last night in hospital; finally, the doctor has given them clearance to go home the next morning.

Sometime after midnight, a sixth sense wakes Bonnie up. She bolts upright in her swag and gropes in the darkness for the light. Georgina has rolled onto her side and is drowning in her own vomit. Bonnie picks her up, scrambles out of their isolation room into the intensive care ward.

'Please, get a doctor, quickly!' she yells.

The sister, stony-faced, is from the old school: doctors are like gods, and she has no time for hysterical parents.

'That won't be at all necessary, Mrs Palmer,' she rebukes. 'Just calm down. The doctor will be here in the morning on his rounds.'

'Bugger the bloody morning rounds! I'm asking you to call our doctor, and to call him now!' They are glaring at each other with mutual contempt, Georgina crying between them.

'If you insist, Mrs Palmer,' the sister sniffs. 'But I'm warning you, this call will not be appreciated at one o'clock in the morning!'

Within fifteen minutes, the doctor, still pulling on his coat, dashes into the ward. He touches the top of Georgina's head, now soft like rising dough, and passes instructions to the sister standing behind his shoulder.

'The fontanelle is swelling again; order an immediate CAT scan. Suspected hydrocephalitis.'

The tests confirm water on the brain, and the next three days are a nightmare of repeated emergency surgery. Bonnie has no sleep, waiting until the fluid builds up again; the only way to save Georgina's life is to draw the water from her brain under anaesthetic. On the fifth day, the doctors admit they can do no more for her. She must be evacuated to Brisbane to stop massive brain damage.

Bonnie remembers a nightmarish scene from her childhood: a horse, looking for feed, wandered into their small bedroom in the night; mad with claustrophobia, it bucked and thrashed to be let out. She and Marlee woke up screaming, and Sara threw a mattress over them to protect them from the wild animal. She tried to buffet herself from the horse's mania, but it kicked her repeatedly in the head and body. It seemed to take an eternity for the air ambulance to arrive and take Sara to hospital to be treated for concussion. Bonnie realises her mother saved their life that night.

Bonnie hasn't seen Sara since a chance meeting at the airport when Bonnie was farewelling Danielle, but she knows her mother has been told that Georgina is desperately ill. Danielle rings her and relays Sara's offer to look after Amelia at the station.

'Tell Mum thanks anyway and that I really appreciate her offer. But Amelia's okay for the moment.'

Sara and Georgina are strangers, but Bonnie knows her mother should hear first-hand just how critical her granddaughter is. She uses the hospital phone, her despair obvious in her voice.

'Mummy, it's Bonnie. I know Danielle has rung you, but Georgie has taken a turn for the worse. She's critically ill. The doctors don't know if she will pull through.'

'You must be worried out of your mind. I will do anything I can to help you,' Sara says. She doesn't offer to come into the hospital, and Bonnie doesn't ask.

'We've had a terrible time down here,' Sara adds. 'There was a terrible storm that blew the roof off the house.'

They chat idly for another minute, and Bonnie is now anxious to get back in to see Georgina. 'I've got to go now, Mum. I'll let you know how we get on.'

Her mother's closing comment strikes her like a slap in the face.

'You really must understand, Bonnie, that it is not good enough to ring someone just when you need something.'

Stunned and mortified, Bonnie's hands clench around the telephone. She inhales sharply, wonders how her mother could say something like this when her granddaughter is hovering between life and death.

'You're right, Mum. I'm sorry,' Bonnie replies, and quietly puts down the receiver. She will never ring her again.

With the fifth general anaesthetic in as many days, the neuro-surgeon, standing-by for the air ambulance, drains double the amount of fluid from Georgina's brain. When she leaves surgery she sports a tiny turban and is afraid to move or sit up. She has also become extremely timid of being touched; it appears to the tiny child that, apart from her mother, everyone who goes near her, hurts her.

'We have to pray she doesn't need any more surgery,' the specialist tells Bonnie. 'We've run out of veins in which to put the drips.'

Now living entirely on nervous energy, Bonnie is in no mood to face the nursing sister who bluntly informs her on her arrival at the Mater children's hospital in Brisbane that she can't sleep in Georgina's room.

'There are parents' quarters down the hall and across the walkway. You have to sleep in there.'

This statement evokes a bitter laugh. 'You have got to be joking! I'm not leaving my daughter for anyone or anything. I'll sleep on the floor, in my swag.'

'That is not allowed!' the sister insists.

'Look, I'm not concerned with what's allowed, mate. If you force me to leave, you'll have to drag me out!'

'There are no meals served here for parents,' the sister continues. She is alarmed at this bushwhacker from the Northern Territory who refuses to abide by hospital rules.

'Well, I'll starve then!' Bonnie bites back.

Heading back to Georgina's room with a cup of coffee in her hand the next morning, the matron confronts Bonnie with a steely gaze. 'You are not allowed to take coffee out of the breakfast room!'

Bonnie snaps. Weeks of desperate concern about Georgina have finally taken their toll, and she can take no more. She stares open mouthed at the matron, tears rolling down her cheeks. Any second, the coffee is going to slip out of her hand.

The matron softens, puts an arm on her shoulder. 'All right, dear, just this once,' she says.

A week later, to the doctor's astonishment, Georgina is finally well enough to go home. 'You have willed her to live,' he tells Bonnie. 'But for you, I'm sure Georgina would never have made it.'

The traumatic episode over, Arthur is later furious that Sara misrepresents her role in rushing to Bonnie's assistance during Georgina's illness. He is scathing in his criticism.

'[Sara] claims that when our daughter Georgina almost died ... she was a caring grandmother ... a leading luminary on children ... She has never, ever played with her grandchildren. When Georgie was born with neo-natal blindness, Sara did not call. Nor did she visit when Georgie later developed meningitis. All we got was a second-hand message offering help.'

At the age of two, Georgina still can't walk, talk or hold a pencil; but slowly and painstakingly she makes progress. At four, Bonnie teaches her to swim; at five, she starts to understand and repeat concepts she has previously been unable to grasp. At six, she shows obvious intelligence, a fiery determination and an increasing use of language. But her tiny frame and inability to respond to the world in the same way as her peers still reflects this shocking ordeal she suffered in infancy.

CHAPTER TWENTY-THREE

The 1993 election is six weeks away, and Arthur's campaign has reached fever pitch. The pundits are predicting a huge Liberal swing, which would put Arthur in Snowden's office. But the question remains: is the Territory ready for a change, and particularly for the baton to be passed to a newcomer?

Arthur is tired of knocking on doors, tired of flashing the press-button smile, but he wills himself to continue. There is not long to go now.

He bounces up the driveway to yet another house, ready to launch into his patter. Out of the corner of his eye, he can see the mongrel dog that had barked ferociously at him when he got out of his car. But he can't miss a house; every place is a potential vote. The dog slinks nearer, baring his fangs, launches into a furious attack just as Arthur rings the doorbell. He plasters the smile on his face as he kicks the dog away and hisses out of the side of his mouth. 'Get off me, you mongrel bastard!'

The dog won't be defeated, sinks his teeth into Arthur's bum and tears away the seat of his pants. No-one has answered the doorbell and he takes the opportunity to hightail it back down the driveway, clutching at his torn clothing to try and cover his naked buttocks. Oh God, he hopes no-one is watching.

Just then the front door swings open. There stands a suburban picture: cigarette hanging out her mouth, her hair ruffled, her feet encased in fluffy slippers. 'Eh, did you want me?' she calls out to Arthur.

He has no choice but to turn back, but right now, he could die of humiliation. The smile returns in an instant, and he holds the back of his trousers with one hand as he shakes hers with the other.

'Hello, I'm Arthur Palmer, your CLP candidate.' He doesn't know what she has seen, thinks it better to own up to his sin. 'I'm afraid I had a small problem with your dog. He doesn't appear to like me. I must apologise.'

The woman looks at him, baffled. 'I don't have a dog.'

'Well, who owns the one that just bit me?' The cur is waiting at the bottom of the driveway, and Arthur is not keen to take him on again.

'Oh, that one,' she says, taking a drag on her cigarette. 'That's the neighbour's dog. I've been trying to get rid of the bastard for years.'

After two years of campaigning, the CLP hope that their candidate is by now easily recognisable, but they reckon badly. Just a week before the election, a sign on the Stuart Highway proclaiming 'Send Arthur to Canberra!' is given a touch of graffiti. Underneath, a wag has written, 'Who the hell is Arthur?' Worse is to follow. When bumper stickers with the 'Send Arthur To Canberra' message appear on cars, some have the word 'Please' scribbled underneath. The idea of failure is anathema to Arthur. He pushes on, talking, shaking hands, repeating over and over his party's promises. Exhausted, he sits like a broken man amongst the brightly coloured streamers which festoon the tally room on election night, watches as the forlorn figures tell their story and the balloons deflate with his dreams. His world has fallen apart; Snowden has again romped home.

Having fought so hard for victory, the humiliating defeat takes a heavy toll. For the next twelve months, Arthur loses the will to return to his consultancy work, preferring to stay close to home.

Bonnie is due to have her third child, but that doesn't stop her flying south to coach for the 1993 national aerobatic titles. With so few people competing at the unlimited level, it's a team effort to keep each other going. At great personal expense, some of the pilots have imported the very best machines available to bring Australian aerobatics into the international arena. Bonnie knows that as the pilot skills increase, Australia will eventually stand up and be counted with the world's best.

Shortly after she returns home, her doctor tells her he wants to induce the baby. With vivid memories of her last births, Bonnie readily agrees. But getting out of the house on time, with two children and a property that needs looking after, is not easy.

'Trust you, Bonnie,' the nursing sister laughs when she finally sways through the hospital doors and into the maternity section. 'You're late for your own labour!'

Within a few short hours, Bonnie reaches out her arms to hold her beautiful baby girl for the first time. She smiles up at Arthur, realises the irony.

Now she has three daughters, just like her mother.

* * *

Bonnie has made a firm promise to Danielle that she will behave at her wedding. Danielle desperately wants her wedding day to be a happy occasion and not marred by family disputes.

'The less you say to Marlee the better,' she advises Bonnie, 'and God, please be tactful and considerate with Mummy.'

Bonnie responds tongue-in-cheek, leaving Danielle unsure about how she will behave. 'Of course, my dear, I will, naturally, be on my best behaviour,' she says with exaggerated pomposity. 'I always am. Nothing but.' Then she adds with a cheeky grin, 'And how much rum have you ordered for the reception?'

Bonnie is so proud of her younger sister. Through all the family turmoil, she has kept her own counsel and her generous spirit. For a long time, she and Bonnie had to meet secretly, but Danielle finally jacked up, said she wouldn't do that any more. 'Bonnie is my sister,' she told Sara and Marlee, 'and I won't sneak around to see her.'

Blunt, smart and sensible, Danielle has shown extremely good judgement in her choice of man. Quiet and humble, Martin is the ultimate bushman: as tough as nails and a gentleman of integrity.

The night before the wedding, Danielle organises a large dinner for her family and close friends. There is method in her seeming madness in having them all together in one small room the night before her big day. She wants to test the water, to ensure that if there is to be any tension, it is over and done with early.

Bonnie hasn't seen Sara for several years. Amelia, half hiding behind her mother's skirt, peeks out with shy interest to see her grandmother from Bullo. The last time they met, when Bonnie and Sara had shared an icy meeting in the corridor of the court house during the Gus Trippe hearing, Amelia was only 6 months old. The lack of bonding is painfully evident: like the strangers they are, Sara and Amelia exchange cursory, polite greetings and then go their separate ways. At two and a half, Georgina, only just walking, has no idea who Sara is and clings to Bonnie. Harriet, still a babe in arms, is happy and cheerful on anyone's bouncing knee.

Bonnie tries to engage Marlee in conversation, but she is studiously ignored. Uncomfortable and angry at her younger sister's presence—particularly after Bonnie asks her second husband, Franz, to dance—Marlee leaves before the bride and groom. Bonnie fares better with Sara; if there are tensions between them, they are overlooked on Danielle's special night.

Old Dick, the man who perfected the art of making ingenious bush cocktails, and who, when sober, worked like a dog at Bullo for little more than his board and keep, has died. Over the years, he often stayed with Bonnie when he was in town. He missed her and Charles; Bullo, he said, just wasn't the same without them there. Always thin, the cancer which slowly ate away at him rendered him painfully so. He was too weak to work; his cheeks were sunken and his legs like sticks. Peter Williams, Bonnie's former fiance, noted his deteriorating condition with alarm, and arranged a place for Dick to live at Barcaldine in Queensland. Only Dick's eyes, bloodshot and yellow from years of belting the grog and smoking rollies, betrayed the man he had once been. On a good day, when his pain let up for a while, his eyes shone with reminiscences about his wild youth—or what he could remember of it. Worn out before his time, he finally slipped away quietly.

Bonnie takes the news of his death hard. She remembers his craggy face, drawn with character lines, the grizzled look he would get just before he went on another of his legendary benders, the delight he radiated when she would knock with her elbows on his donga door and they would share a few unscheduled beers. Dick had his own code which he would send to the station manager, Les Wright, via the station requisition list. The order would end: 'one tub of ice cream', and Les would smuggle him back a bottle of brandy. An utter reprobate, the bum was always out of the seat of his pants, and after a session on bush champagne, he looked like 'six-penneth of God help us'. But he had a great heart, and was always very kind to Bonnie, happily imparting his knowledge to her. They were good mates.

She remembers listening to him tell stories to Danielle when she was little, changing and embellishing them to add an Australian flavour. Bonnie tells those stories to her children now, and they sit and listen in childish rapture.

'Little Red Riding Hood's grandma is crook, and she thinks she had better go and have a cuppa with her to cheer her up. She packs her billy can with damper and treacle, high tails it across the flat, into the scrub and past the river. A dingo stops her and wants a chinwag, asks her where she's off to, and Little Red Riding Hood tells him she's going to see her grandma who's crook ...'

Poor Uncle Dick. She'll miss him a lot.

They have decided to go ahead with the building of the donga up at their airstrip and to move there when it is finished. Bonnie's pleas that Arthur return to work to regain his confidence fall on deaf ears. Arthur is also adamant that he will not use skilled labourers to build the shed—he and Bonnie will do it themselves. Bonnie admires him for his intelligence and charm, but she is less enthusiastic about his building skills. From experience, she knows she is the one who can wield a mean crowbar and shovel, but she hopes he can use a power-saw and drill. To her horror, she finds out his bush carpentry skills are even more rudimentary than she feared. She begs him to recon-sider using skilled tradesmen, but the request creates further conflict.

'That idea is a waste of time, a waste of money and just plain silly!' he retorts.

Now getting her old energy back following the physical strain of her illness, the miscarriage and Georgina's sickness, Bonnie reluctantly recognises that nothing she does or says is of any interest to her husband any more and that they are moving inexorably apart.

With Georgina and Harriet in tow, Bonnie goes to Griffith, New South Wales, to compete in the Australian aerobatics titles. She hasn't flown in competition for two years and Arthur, convinced that it is a fruitless and expensive exercise, does not want her to compete. However, from her saddle-making, Bonnie puts aside one hundred dollars a week to finance the trip. She badly wants to do well, and this time she takes her father's advice to play mind games and psych out the competition.

'May the best woman win!' she says, shaking the other competitors' hands before she climbs into the cockpit.

'Be prepared, poor old body, for another beating,' she says to herself as she straps in. She climbs, looks at the centre marker as she pushes the nose down into a steep dive and executes three ninety degree wing-wags to signal the judges she has started. Over the roar of the engines, she remembers her flying instructor, Guido's, comment. 'You can do this, Bonnie! Just push harder!'

Hanging in the straps, the world upside down, she approaches the end marker, pushing to vertical. The world is now sideways; she executes a half roll, then a full one; steadies back to half, and stops. The aircraft slows before she gives it full rudder and the nose cartwheels around the tail. She must watch the wind, mustn't drift too far from the judges, has to keep an eye on the end marker. The needle on the G-force meter is flicking wildly, peaking at plus ten and falling to minus eight. She has to be careful here after the negative brace, pulls into a half downward loop. Her eyes are greying over in tunnel vision, the roar of the motor pounding in her ears. She feels the stick and throttle between her fingers but the positive G is taking hold. Think, think! She must fight the blackout, but her thoughts are hazy; what is she supposed to do after she pulls back? She can't see her card through her blurred vision, suddenly remembers she has to do a roll. There is no time left to wait; she slams the stick over and then stops as her vision clears, the wings just short of the mark. Now there are only three seconds to go before she reaches the end marker. Three manoeuvres down, and only twelve more to go.

At the end of the competition, she proudly walks away with the open national title. She has won it in the toughest category of all—unlimited.

Her practice mate, David Lowy, comes over to congratulate her. He peers into the cockpit of her bedraggled, borrowed Pitts and shakes his head.

'How did you manage to win? You don't even have the advantage of a perspex window to look down at the ground.'

Bonnie grins. 'I just pushed harder, David.'

Again selected for the World Aerobatics Championships in Hungary, Bonnie has twenty-four hours practice in the German-built aircraft in which she will compete. Her expectations for this contest are realistic: the international competitors have government sponsorship for their training, and their extra practice hours show in their performances. It's frustrating to know that while she has the ability to compete with the best, she doesn't have the monetary backing vital to success.

She wants to get through without a zero score for any manoeuvre and no boundary penalties—'outs'—for flying out of the contest zone—the 1000 square metre box. Flying through high winds and on a hazy horizon, she almost achieves her wish, scoring no more outs than the top ten pilots. In her second program, she takes it good and steady, wanting to average a score of seven point five. She knows she has no outs this time.

The scores come through, and she is devastated. Her first manoeuvre has scored zero, and her mind races to think why. What could have gone wrong? It felt so good, and the first manoeuvre in a competition flight is always the one remembered best. She figures it should have averaged at least the eight point five score that three of the ten judges have given her. Instead of crying, which is what she feels like doing, she decides to find out why she scored so badly.

Lodging a protest, she tramps up to the contest office and asks to check the judges' sheets. In dismay, she realises she has drawn the manoeuvres she would perform, and which the judges use as a reference, incorrectly. She had flown correctly and with style, but can only be judged on what is on the paper. Three of the judges, realising she has made a simple error, scored her manoeuvre according to what it was worth. But majority rules. Another lesson learned.

'I think we need to see a marriage guidance counsellor, Arthur. We've tried to sort things out ourselves, but it isn't working. Would you come with me?'

Many of their arguments centre on Bonnie's popularity: her ability to draw a crowd and engender respect. Arthur tries to civilise her, but she is growing tired of it. At the Katherine Show, Bonnie accepts the challenge to buck out on a saddle bronc; she loves the danger, the excitement, and the crowd love her, but Arthur is furious.

'You are setting a bad example! What will people think of me?'

Bonnie recalls another event at the Darwin Show when she enters the chainsaw competition, working in the heat alongside strong, strapping men.

'Must you always have a go at these masculine events?' Arthur seethes. 'You are just an embarrassment!'

'What do you want from me?' she storms at him. 'Everything I do is wrong! Why can't you accept me for what I am?'

She has accepted what Arthur has always told her—that she has the right to be happy—and she now fights for that right. Increasingly, their home has become a battleground: they rage at each other and then retreat into a silent, shaky truce until the tensions build up again. Bonnie recognises that if they are to save their marriage, they have to do something about it, and fast.

'All counsellors do is dig around and try to get people to accept responsibility for their actions,' Arthur says. 'We can work that out for ourselves. Counselling is for uneducated people.'

This last statement, Bonnie knows, is directed at her, but she ignores it. 'Okay, if you're not prepared to compromise, then I'll go on my own.'

The sessions help a little, but the counsellor is concerned. 'Marriage guidance is a two-way street,' she tells Bonnie. 'It would be beneficial if your husband came as well.'

When Arthur finally capitulates, a year later, it is too late. He goes once, but doesn't return for another session.

CHAPTER TWENTY-FOUR

Bonnie is in practice for the 1995 national aerobatics titles and for a place on the Australian team. With just five days to go before the competition, the pressure is on, but the atmosphere is electric. All friends, the competitors offer each other support and encouragment.

Bonnie walks out towards her Pitts for her last practice flight of the day. The Pitts has no starter motor or electrics, and requires skill to hand-swing the propeller. David Boughen, a friend and team-mate, is busy refuelling his aircraft.

'Can you give me a start?' Bonnie asks. 'I'll be up and down before you even strap in!'

They share an easy banter, and as the machine leaps into life with a roar, David steps back, smiles and gives her a thumbs-up. Bonnie taxies out to the strip, takes off and climbs into the late afternoon sun. She hurls through her routines and comes in to land as the wind drops and the sun is a red disc just above the horizon.

These are superb flying conditions, and there is still twenty minutes of daylight left. She passes David on the taxi way, gives him a wave as he prepares to take off.

Beer in hand, Bonnie steps out of the hangar to watch David's routine. He is a fine pilot, only a newcomer to the aerobatic club but showing lots of potential under the instruction of long-time friend Mal Beard. She turns for in instant to look at David's brother, Peter, standing next to her, notices his face has gone grey and ashen. She cranes her head back up to the sky, whimpers, 'Oh my God, oh God, no!' as the Pitts, silhouetted by the sun, plummets at sickening speed toward the ground. In less than five seconds, the splintered aircraft lies like a broken bird, its wings misshapen and its pilot dead. Half a minute into his routine, David suffered a cardiac arrest; he died before impact.

The silence outside the hangar is shattering as David's teammates bow their heads in shock. Bonnie's beer has fallen out of her hand, and puddles of foam lie at her feet. The silence is broken by sudden pandemonium: the squeal of ambulance sirens, firemen dousing the aircraft and over it all, Peter's grief, which is palpable.

Out of respect, many pilots withdraw from the contest, and Bonnie plans to do the same. Peter approaches her as she quietly packs up her swag.

'Don't give up, Bon. David would want you to fly. He'd want you to win.'

Bonnie has no inclination to fly, to get back into the little Pitts. She hasn't stopped crying since the accident, and is still in shock. Peter's haunted eyes stare back at her, and she gently takes his hand.

'Okay, Peter. I'll do it for David.'

She slides deep into the seat and straps on her harness. The airstrip is now virtually deserted and is ghostly silent, and her hands are shaking as she climbs high into the air. She can't concentrate on her sequence, her timing or her positions; all she can see are the box markers looming up and David's aircraft falling out of the sky. By the time she limps in to land, she is in a cold sweat, pale and tremulous, and she bursts into tears.

'I can't do it, Mal,' she says to a team-mate. 'I can't do it!'

'You mustn't let this get to you, Bonnie. Try and put it behind you; David would have wanted that.'

She remembers this advice as she prepares for takeoff at the championships, remembers David giving her the thumbs-up sign just before he died, and his encouraging smile. Summoning all her courage, she takes a deep breath, taxies fast, gives the judges a wing-wag and is away, rolling, spinning, making the plane dance in midair. At the end of the contest, with her second national title win under her belt, she holds the trophy high, for David.

Her flying instructor, Guido, chuckles when she rings with the results. 'Two times, eh! Two times! That's really showing them!'

But if she expects the same encouragment from Arthur, she is badly disappointed.

'You are becoming unbearably cocky, Bonnie,' he says. 'You need someone to knock you off your perch!'

They had always shared an interest in aerobatics, and his comment saddens and angers Bonnie. There is now a great divide between them, and she doubts they can continue their marriage much longer. When they move up to the donga to live, she quietly gets on the roof when Arthur's back is turned and patches up the holes where the rain leaks through, but she can no longer patch up the holes in their marriage.

When Fraser hears that Bonnie has won the national aerobatics championship for the second time, he is not at all surprised.

273

'Bonnie is extremely hardworking, like Father. Everything she does, she does well. She is a great equestrian and rides beautifully. She is one of Australia's finest saddlemakers, because she understands the nuances of horses. I have no doubt that if she had the finances to practise aerobatics for a month, rather than a week, she could be world champion in that too.'

He grins, recalling an incident from their childhood. 'I had a difficult math problem to solve, and even though I gained maximum score in math, I didn't ever regard it as my strongest subject. Bonnie was eight at the time, and I was eighteen. She solved the problem for me, and I realised then that she was probably a genius.'

For a moment, his mask slips.

'Bonnie is painted as the black sheep of the family,' he says. 'But she is far from that. A long, long way from that. There is no doubt that she is an incredible woman, in many ways.'

The kids, wild and untamed like the bush around their property, wander barefoot on the dust and grass. Tougher than their city friends, the girls know the horses by name and can ride bareback. Clothes are to be worn only on trips to town; often the two little ones tear around in only their knickers, happy as larks. They all have more pairs of underpants than they know what to do with: Bonnie is determined her kids won't share knickers like she had to.

Bonnie is open and friendly with the children and doesn't adhere to the theory that they should be seen and not heard. She is determined her children will be her friends and that history won't repeat itself in her family. But she is tough with them.

'You have a right to your opinion,' she tells them, 'but you do not have the right to hurt other people's feelings.' Arguments are negotiated and compromises achieved, and Bonnie uses adult power only as a last resort. The girls' arguments, often loud and protracted, are a battle of wills to see who will come out on top. They have all inherited a fiery temperament, and sometimes their fights are physical.

Working in the saddle room, Bonnie hears a pitched battle being played out on the verandah. She puts the saddle down, goes out to intercept. Georgie is screaming, her ego as bruised as her bitten arm.

'Hattie, let Georgie go!' Bonnie shouts, grabbing hold of her middle daughter and pulling her away. 'What the hell do you think you're up to?'

Hattie is unrepentant, flailing around and wanting to sink her teeth into her sister's arm again. This is becoming a habit, and Bonnie has to stop it now. She picks Hattie up, takes her into the workroom and shows her a massive pair of pliers.

'Right, next time you bite Georgina, I'm going to pull one of your teeth out,' she warns. It is a scare tactic, of course, and Bonnie will never follow through with the threat. But Hattie doesn't know that: when Mummy threatens punishment, she means it. 'Now, please go and tell Georgie you're sorry, and give her a cuddle,' Bonnie adds. This is the tough part: apology and a hug has to follow an argument before it can be buried.

Hattie totters up to her sister, wraps her arms around her neck. 'Sowwy, Georgie,' she says. 'I won't bite you again.' As an after-thought, she adds, 'Because Mummy says she will pull my teef out if I do!'

Bonnie is looking for an escape route, and she finds it. Emotionally broken, her marriage in tatters, she starts drinking, using alcohol as a serious drug. A seasoned drinker, she knows that while she is not necessarily drinking any more than she has ever done, she is using it for different reasons. She wants to create conflict rather than avoid it, wants to bring the problems in her marriage to a head, to drive Arthur to distraction. She reasons if her behaviour is bad enough, he will finally start to notice her, to try and work out some solutions.

While she is working, a pannikin of rum is always close by, as if chained to her wrist. When the fancy takes her, she heads to the local pub, arriving home late and usually plastered. Often she brings some drinking mates home with her, partying until the small hours and listening to loud rock and roll. Arthur's suggestions that they go home so that he can sleep in peace are met with a silent rebuke from Bonnie. She will not be told what to do any more, nor told whom she can spend her time with. Infuriated at her reckless behaviour, Arthur could shake her, and sometimes does. Increasingly inconsiderate and selfish, her antics do no more than cause conflicts that cannot be resolved.

There is now little pretence left at a marriage. Months of living on the edge and studiously ignoring Arthur's cold fury have achieved the desired result. It has brought their problems to the surface, but Bonnie also now recognises they go too deep to heal.

It is time for her to get her life in order again, time to stop seeking escape in alcohol's oblivion. To sort out where she will go from here, she needs a clear, sober head. She can give the grog away, and will—at least for a while. Years of living around seasoned drinkers at Bullo have taught her that while she likes a drink, she doesn't need one.

Bonnie makes a firm decision to put the rum back in the cupboard, leave the beer in the fridge and stop going to the pub. She doesn't touch alcohol again for six months.

* * *

The 1996 airshow is on at Norfolk Island, and Bonnie badly wants to be part of it. A flying mate, Barry, has offered her the chance to ferry over the Sukhoi 29 two-seater—a savvy little aircraft with a personality all its own—and she is only too happy to oblige. It's also an opportunity for her to increase her hours in the plane ahead of the world championships in Oklahoma.

'Sure, sounds like fun,' she says. 'But where exactly is Norfolk Island?'

Barry twirls his moustache, points vaguely to the east, mumbles an incoherent answer about a stretch of water, and tells her to turn up for the briefing. Bonnie knows that her father, if he were alive, would definitely advise her against the trip, knowing the risks of flying over oceans as he did. That clinches it: this is one challenge she won't pass up.

After the briefing, Bonnie and the pilots of the other five aircraft stage a staggered departure, overlapping in order to make VHF radio contact with each other for the entire flight. Bonnie climbs to 10 000 feet, sees Australia's eastern coastline spread out beneath her. The Sukhoi has little forward vision; peering over the leading edge of the wing, she stares down at the black ocean, which appears close enough to touch. What little room there is in the aircraft is taken up with emergency equipment and the long-range fuel tank; there is only space for her to rest the paperwork on her knee.

The shoreline is a haze over her shoulder as the morning sun flashes on the wing tips and her GPS—Global Positioning System —starts flashing 'no signal'. Great. She needs a plan, and needs one fast. Fuel doesn't appear to be the problem: she could get to Lord Howe Island, her first stop, and return with what she has in the custom-built long-range tank. Last night's test run proved that the system is working perfectly. She looks again at the GPS; now it is flashing 'off track'. Her direction is out by thirty nautical miles. She banks steeply to the left to correct the problem and notices that something is wrong with the fuel system. The needle on the wing-tank gauge is slowly but surely going down, but with the wing tank selected and auxiliary valve open, the fuel should gravity feed from auxiliary tanks. The engine is clearly draining fuel from both tanks.

'Damn this bloody system!' Bonnie thinks aloud. 'It worked perfectly well last night; it would have to play up in the middle of the ocean!'

She can't look down at the white caps, forces herself to think about emergency procedures and fuel systems. Years of flying around Bullo have given her no experience of flying over water, and this is scary. Even at 10 000 feet, the white caps on the ocean look as if they will splash in her face. Bonnie is terrified. She remembers that when her father taught her to fly, he made her learn his special game.

'You have to convince yourself you can land a plane any-where,' he said. 'Always be prepared for potential engine failure. Where would you land now if you had to put her down quickly?' The game was easy in the bush; if you looked hard enough, there was always somewhere to land.

'If you can't play that game, Bonnie,' Charles always said, 'you shouldn't be flying.'

But out here, surrounded by a vast sea, the game doesn't work. If something goes wrong, there are no hills to look out for, no trees to dodge. If she goes down, it is into a watery grave. She can feel her heart pounding, and checks her watch. There is still another hour to go before she reaches Lord Howe Island, and there isn't a skerrick of land in between. She thinks about tiny Lord Howe, out there in the middle of all this water, and wonders how the hell

Charles ever found his aircraft carrier, the USS *Enterprise*, on return from missions.

Above her head she jiggles the hose which passes out through the cabin vent into the slipstream, pressurising the auxiliary tank to aid the gravity feed. Everything appears to be in order; an aircraft technician had taped around the hose to prevent freezing air entering the cabin during flight.The tape blocks her seeing the end of the hose. Bonnie is becoming increasingly nervous. What the hell could be wrong with the fuel system?

The fuel problem remains until she lands at Lord Howe, where she checks with Barry about what could be causing the blockage. It is critical that the auxiliary tank be working for the second leg.

Barry is bemused. 'I flew this Sukhoi yesterday and everything was fine.'

'Yeah, so did I,' Bonnie replies. 'But it's not fine now!' Together, they try every combination possible to get the system up and running.

Bonnie looks up at the plane, at the open canopy with the vent, and suddenly spots the problem. The piece of tape, used to stop the wind from blowing into the cabin, is covering the end of the vent. She smiles, removes the tape. 'I'm ready for take-off now.'

A front is passing through between the islands; the stronger the tail winds now, the longer it will take to get back if she has to abandon the flight. She looks at the GPS, prays that nothing else will go wrong.

'Stay with me, you bastard,' she mutters. 'Please, stay with me!' Beneath her, the ocean is an inky black and clouds are slowly joining together to block her view of it. It is evident that Bonnie will have to fly through the front, for it is not going to dissipate. Advancing the throttle, the aircraft jumps like a race horse out of the starting gate, and she flies up through the cloud until she is skimming over the fluffy tops. Twenty-five nautical miles out from Norfolk, the front still hasn't moved; she will have to fly down through it. She hasn't wanted to think about that possibility; down, down, down she takes it, levelling eight nautical miles from Norfolk, at seven hundred feet. The horizon is dark here and occasional rain showers drop out of the swirling clouds. Five nautical miles out, she kicks the nose around, expecting to be greeted by an enchanting piece of land, but there is nothing— just sea and clouds and rain. Oh God, what could be wrong this time?

Bonnie checks heading and compass direction, crosschecks with flight plan times and track, crosschecks the GPS. Everything's functioning, but where is the bloody island? Two nautical miles out now; she kicks the nose round again, and the GPS finally flashes 'approaching'. The island is covered in cloud and only parts of the shore line are visible with waves crashing on the rocks. Bonnie heaves a sigh of relief; this has been a trying trip and the land looks like heaven to her.

Not wanting to overfly the runway and disappear into the cloud, she aims to land short. Straightening the nose and flaring to land, she glances out over the wing tip and realises with horror that there is a steep slope rising up to the runway. The down draft hits the aircraft with full force; she hauls back hard on the stick and the machine rears up like a snake about to strike. Bang! They hit the slope just short of the runway, the undercarriage spreading to absorb the impact and the prop biting into the soft dirt. Bonnie recalls all the stories she has read about the pioneer aviators who flew miles and miles over oceans just to crash on landing. Now she finally understands how that could happen.

'By Christ, that was hairy!' she says, falling out of the cockpit. She pushes the thought from the back of her mind that now she is here, she has to get back.

She heads up to the airport pub with the other members of their entourage. It's a quaint little island, and the sheep and cows have right of way on the road. With all their stops and starts, it takes quite a while to get to the cafe, but Bonnie doesn't care.

Chatting about the flight later to a navy chopper pilot, Bonnie voices her fear of the ocean.

The chopper pilot smiles. 'The sea is beautiful, and when you learn to love it, it will be good to you. Besides,' he adds, 'you've got to get that plane back yet.'

After a successful air show, Bonnie heads the Sukhoi back to Australia. It is a glorious flight: when the mainland appears out of the haze it seems to clutter the horizon. She remembers the pilot's advice on the way home and pretends the sea's white caps are clouds and the blue water just a giant billabong.

The world championships in Oklahoma are the perfect opportunity for Bonnie and Georgina to visit the family, particularly Bomma, who is now one hundred and five. Arthur no longer pretends to support her aerobatics, and Bonnie has made a tough decision. When she gets home from the States, they must separate.

In the middle of the contest, Hugh rings Bonnie to tell her that Bomma died overnight in her sleep. The news devastates her; although Bonnie's glad she saw her only two years before she died, she wishes she had had the chance to say goodbye to her beloved grandmother who nurtured and protected her during her childhood. She had thought Bomma—proud, regal, and strong who had loved her so unconditionally—would live forever. Crying, Bonnie stumbles to a corner of the aircraft hangar and crumples to the floor, her grief washing over her in waves.

She wills herself to keep going, though, knows that Bomma

would have wanted that. Finally she will be flying the treasured Sukhoi in competition, a machine which is so alive it dances under her touch. Again, she is not under any illusions: she would need fifty hours training time even to get through a competition sequence. It has been a nightmare just getting the aircraft. First, she tried to hire one in Russia, which needed somehow to get to America; when that fell through, it was arranged that she would use a British team plane. Tragically, the team lost a member during training shortly before Bonnie joined them. Just four days before the competition started, she finally organised to share an aircraft with the Ukraine team.

She now has only limited practice time in a Sukhoi she has never flown before, and knows that she has no chance of making the top percentage of competitors.

Determined to do the best she can, she realises too late that the aircraft has incredibly heavy controls. When she tries to bank, the resistance on the stick proves so great she thinks the controls are locked. For the rest of her time in the air, she uses two hands, putting the friction lock on the throttle and giving it all she's got.

Her scores prove what she already knows, but she is still bitterly disappointed. With training and practice in the expensive Sukhoi, she knows she can give the world titles a good shake and fly the flag for Australia.

CHAPTER TWENTY-FIVE

A chorus of little voices goes up from the lounge room. 'Mummy, Mummy, your mummy is on television!'

The program, "This Is Your Life", honours Australian achievers and flies surprise guests to compliment the star. Bonnie is confused at how her mother can take credit for turning around a million-dollar debt at Bullo when most of the debt was paid out by Charles from the sale of Montejinni Station. Much of the work which Sara claims to have done at Bullo was in fact done by Bonnie when she was at the station, and Bonnie wishes Sara would stop painting her father as just a philanderer. In truth, he was far more than that. She admires her mother for her success, and if she has any resentment, it is that her mother is known to millions of Australians, but has no interest in her own grandchildren.

Bonnie keeps turning the omelette she is cooking, half watching the show at the same time. No-one has told her Sara is to be on this program, and she hasn't been invited by the producers to have any input. She wonders how they will get over that one, braces herself for what she is sure will follow. This, she thinks, is like a soap opera, and she is fed up with being cast publicly in a role for which she didn't audition.

The children are intrigued: they haven't seen Sara for years and have had nothing at all to do with Marlee. Bonnie notices other people who aren't there too: Ross and Lynette, still good friends of Bonnie and Arthur, struck off the friendship list for having drifted into their camp by default. Bluey Lewis: all those years at Bullo and not even mentioned. Charles' sons, non-existent; and no other representative from Bullo apart from Marlee and Danielle. People from Sara's past are speaking: her brothers, her tennis doubles partner, the ex-Governor of Hong Kong who married her and Charles. Now Sara is defending her own extra-marital affairs, with that martyred air that Bonnie knows so well. 'Oh yes, I did have affairs to get even, but it didn't do me any good.'

Bonnie wonders how soon it will be before her name is dragged in. She doesn't have long to wait.

'In the next year,' the compere says, 'Bonnie leaves Bullo, and only Murray-Lee and Danielle are there to help. There is no way you could have got through without them, is there?'

'No, no way at all.'

Marlee walks on stage, her eyes dewy as she speaks. Bonnie groans: bringing her sister on next is a clever ploy to win the audience's sympathy. Death by association. 'She's more than my mum, she's my rock of Gibraltar,' she says. 'She's always been there for me.'

The compere is talking again, rolling Charles' operations and subsequent death together. 'How did you feel about that, Sara?'

'I was in shock.'

Bonnie is in shock, too, and her telephone is ringing. She ignores it.

'You wrote: "Our lawyer called to say my daughter Bonnie was suing me for $30 000. No, not me personally, but Bullo River Station Pty Ltd. That was different?"' There is a dramatic pause, before he asks the million-dollar question. 'Why?'

'For wages,' Sara replies. 'Apparently for wages.'

'Apparently!' Bonnie splutters to the television. 'What do you mean, apparently?'

'There was a cheque from Charlie apparently, which bounced. There was nothing in the bank.'

'Your mother and Charles died, and you decided to settle out of court. You wrote, "On that day, I lost my daughter."'

'Yes, I decided to settle out of court. On top of Mum and Charles I couldn't handle a court case.'

'What is happening with Bonnie?'

'We've had a few meetings. It's a slow process, it has to work its way through.'

Bonnie splutters, 'What meetings? When?'

Sara continues, 'The time will come, though, and when it comes, I'll know it.'

'You'll grab it?' the compere asks.

Sara's eyes are misty; she nods her head. The compere closes the book, hands it to her with a grandiose gesture.

'Sara Henderson—this is your life.'

Bonnie is numb.

'This is your life, Mummy,' she says out loud. 'But what about mine?'

The omelette is cooked, but she has lost her appetite. It is laughable that her mother would go on national television and talk about their reconciliation when there has been no contact between them at all. She supposes that the truth would be hard to acknowledge, that to admit publicly that she speaks to her daughter

285

once in a blue moon, and only then when she has to, would raise more questions than it answered.

The children sometimes ask why they don't see Sara, and working from their sketchy questions, Bonnie colours in the details. She describes Bullo to them, working from memory, tells them about the river pulsing with barramundi, the ferocious crocodiles, the dust that paints the landscape ochre. It has been eleven years since Bonnie has been back, but she still misses it terribly. She is sad for Sara that she had nothing to do with the children when they were babies, sad that Sara's own flesh and blood are mere strangers to her, and that she has missed out on their childhood. At ten, Amelia has met her grandmother twice. Georgina has met her once, and Harriet doesn't remember her at all.

'Grandma's busy,' Bonnie tells them when they ask, hoping that will stop their questions. She doesn't know what else she can say, doesn't want to hurt their feelings.

For years after she left Bullo, Bonnie faithfully sent Sara Christmas and birthday cards, but none was ever reciprocated, and none ever sent to the children. Finally, she stopped sending them.

When the children go to bed, Bonnie sits quietly and reflects on her broken relationship with Sara. She can't define when it really started; as far back as she can remember, they have never been close. Was it because Bonnie was, as her mother told her, 'an accident of contraception'; and therefore not wanted? Was it because Sara didn't bond with her immediately following her rushed birth in that darkened Manila maternity ward? Did her close relationship with her father drive a wedge between her mother and herself; did Sara resent that Bonnie was so obviously the inheriting daughter? Bonnie knows that through her years of pain with migraine she could be difficult and unruly; did Sara find her too hard to cope with? She wonders whether, if it hadn't all become so public, their estrangement might have been patched up by now; she wonders, too, how she would feel if a rift ever developed between her and one of her daughters. Her children are her friends, and she intends it to stay that way. Bonnie thinks of the ironic similarities between her and her mother's lives. Both women have three daughters raised wild and free in the bush; both married arrogant, strong men with complex personalities and an eye for a pretty woman; and both paid a high emotional price for their love. Bonnie hopes that one day she and Sara will become better friends, that they can resolve the bad chemistry between them. But she won't hold out the olive branch just to have it slapped out of her hand again.

'Where are we going, Mummy?'

'I'm not sure yet, Amelia, but we're going away from the fighting. I don't want you or Georgie or Hattie to watch Daddy and me fight any more, and we have decided we can't live together. Don't worry, everything will be okay, you'll see.' The last sentence is spoken with more conviction than Bonnie feels, but she is determined not to let the children know that. God knows, they have seen too much already. She no longer has any desire to resolve her marital problems; this time, she just wants out.

Lately, Amelia has taken to sitting between her parents when their voices are raised, begging them not to argue, to stop shouting. Bonnie remembers her own childhood, when she hunkered under the eiderdown at their cottage near Lloyds Landing, trying to block out the sound of angry voices, wishing her parents would stop fighting. She is resolute that she won't put her own children through that, but she doesn't know where the hell they're going to go to. She can't go to a friend's place, doesn't want to drag her domestic disputes into someone else's home; but she can't just drive around aimlessly all day. The kids are tired and need to be settled somewhere. The last time Bonnie said she was leaving, Arthur threw all their clothes in a heap on the floor. This time, she doesn't bother trying to pack; they have walked out with only the clothes on their back.

Bonnie has already sought legal help, but the answer is always the same: unless a man threatens physical harm, there are no grounds for an injunction against him.

Clearly things are not going to get any better. While Arthur refuses to accept their marriage is over, Bonnie is resolute.

'I don't want to compromise any more. We're not getting on, haven't got on well for a long time, and it is damaging for the children as well as us.'

'You can't make a decision like that, that our marriage is finished!' he thunders. 'It takes two to make a decision to divorce, and I won't countenance it.'

'It takes two to make a decision to stay together,' Bonnie replies quietly. 'It takes one person to leave, and I'm leaving. You can take full credit for civilising me, but I don't want to be civilised any more. You've made me, Arthur, now go and find someone else to make.'

Bonnie drives past the women's shelter a few times before summoning the courage to get out of the truck.

'Here we go,' she mutters under her breath as she walks hand in hand with the children to the front door. She is suddenly overwhelmed with fatigue, wants to crawl into bed and stay there. Georgie and Hattie think this is a grand adventure, but Amelia, sensitive to her mother's despair, is less enthusiastic.

'What is this place, Mummy?' she asks. 'Is this where we are going to stay?'

The woman's shelter is stifling and overcrowded. Mothers with bleak, bleary eyes sit in groups on the verandah, monitoring their children's heat rashes and squabbles, willing some rain to break the oppressive build-up. They smoke furiously, their language black as they recount the bitter details that led them here.

Bonnie watches them from the shadow of the doorway, leaning her head sideways onto its frame and thrusting her calloused hands deep into the pockets of her Levis. She spoke to a couple of the women last night when she arrived, heard their stories; somehow, she senses, they will be endlessly repetitious. Snatches of their conversation drift to where she stands.

'Bastard come home pissed again, started in on me and the kids ...'

'We haven't got any family or friends up here, and I had nowhere else to go. Nowhere else ...'

Bonnie sighs, feels a sadness for these women and the circumstances they are in. She turns sharply as Harriet tugs at her jeans. 'I'm thirsty, Mummy, and Georgie won't share her drink!'

Suddenly Bonnie realises how tired she is, tired of the pressure and heartache. She tries to hold back the torrent of tears built up like a dam behind her eyes; she mustn't cry, has to keep a cool head and a calm heart. Somehow she has to work out how to get out of this mess.

She badly wants to take the children home; home to their property where the mares nuzzle their silky heads into her waist, and the children run barefoot through the bush. Georgina is sitting on the floor, hunched silent and pale. Bonnie sits on her haunches next to her, wraps her arms around the child's tiny chest.

'Georgie, you must share your drink with Harriet. Amelia, could you get the girls a drink.'

The oldest girl, tired of her younger sisters, glares back at

Bonnie with cat-green eyes. Short, sharp and abrupt, Amelia has her mother's independent spirit and her father's street smarts. But lately, her wounded heart is showing; like Bonnie, she shuts down from emotional crises.

'They've been fighting all afternoon, Mummy, and I'm hot,' she snaps. 'When are we getting out of here? I want to go home!'

Bonnie inhales a deep breath and returns her daughter's stare. 'Just try and be patient, will you, Amelia? I'll sort this out as quickly as I can. In the meantime, could you please do as I have asked.'

In the sanctuary of the shelter, Bonnie reflects on her marriage. They were happy together for a long time, despite their differences; but, increasingly, that happiness came at a price. For a long time she put their problems on the back burner, happier to capitulate than fight, but she can no longer tolerate emotional subjugation. Arthur has civilised her, made her a woman, fathered their three children, but it's no longer enough. Now in her early thirties, she has learned to flail against the restraints he imposed upon her. She has changed, doesn't want to continue to grow in someone else's shadow, to bend even when he is the one in the wrong. Their interests have changed. She recalls a recent time when Arthur came into her workroom and said, 'After all these years it just looks like you're still working on the same saddle.'

'It's a different saddle, Arthur,' she replies. 'It's just that you and I are on a different plane.'

She is angry with herself too. She always wanted a man who was strong, not someone who needed to twist her into shape. Bonnie has discovered Arthur's insecurities and need to dominate; but, over the years, she has also discovered something else. She is stronger than him, and she can't abide weakness.

Gradually, she has fallen out of love with Arthur, and it is time for her to stand alone. Part of the words of Rudyard Kipling's poem 'If', which she learned at her father's knee, resound in her head as she sits by the children's bed, watching them sleep.

> *If you can force your heart and nerve and sinew*
> *To serve your turn long after they are gone,*
> *And so hold on when there is nothing in you*
> *Except the Will which says to them: 'Hold on!'*
> *If you can talk with crowds and keep your virtue,*
> *Or walk with Kings—nor lose the common touch,*
> *If neither foes nor loving friends can hurt you,*
> *If all men count with you, but none too much;*
> *If you can fill the unforgiving minute*
> *With sixty seconds worth of distance run,*
> *Yours is the Earth and everything that's in it,*
> *And—which is more—you'll be a Man, my son!*

Bonnie watches as dawn's light struggles through the dense, grey clouds. She feels haggard and tired; the strains of the past twelve months show in her face, which is drawn tight. But she also feels strangely calm: during the long night, she has never once wavered from her decision that she wants a divorce.

An hour before they are to go to court for an interim hearing, Bonnie and Arthur reach a short-term resolution. Pending the custody and residential battle, he will find alternative accommodation and she will return to their property with the children.

Bonnie and the girls are elated to be home, piling out of the truck and running over to the stables to see Julia, their mare who is in foal, and the calves.

Bonnie rises an hour before dawn, the quietest time in the

day when she can gather her thoughts and work on a saddle before the morning rush starts to get the lunches cut and the children to school.

After giving the grog a serious beating leading up to Christmas the year before, Bonnie makes a bet with Danielle that she will give it away for at least six months. She doesn't find it difficult: she no longer has an excuse to drown her problems and can happily live without alcohol. While she misses the social part of drinking, she proves to have an iron will, even when her favourite rum is put in front of her.

'Come on, Bon, have a drink. Your sister is in Cloncurry. She won't know if you break.'

'No, she won't, but I will. I've given her my word.'

Looking across the paddock from the window of her workroom one morning, Bonnie notices a movement in the grass at Julia's feet. She is not due to foal for another six weeks, and instinctively Bonnie knows there is a problem. With trepidation, she crosses the paddock, quietly calling to the mare who is standing over her newborn, nervously nuzzling into the foal's neck in a protective gesture. Sprawled on the grass, the foal's head is weak and her body frail. Her ribs protrude and are no bigger than hands; her unformed hooves no more than long sinews of coarsened hair; and her breath is shallow and heaving. Bonnie does a quick mental calculation; there is a spark of life in the foal's eyes, and if she can get her out of the morning sun and coax her to feed, she might pull through.

She lifts the foal gently into her arms. Her tiny legs flap and the mare nickers close to her shoulder as she walks across to the stables. The new mother trusts Bonnie, but needs reassurance.

'You're a clever girl, Julia, a very clever girl. Your foal will be fine, don't worry.' Bonnie perseveres to express the mare's colostrum. She is fretful and uncomfortable with milk fever, but it is imperative the foal starts to feed. She is too weak to stand herself, so Amelia holds her back legs whilst Bonnie feeds her through a baby's bottle. The colostrum dribbles down the foal's face and the mare watches intently. Bonnie remembers Georgina, how desperately she tried to feed her in the first few days of her life, how little it actually takes to build nourishment in a newborn. She remembers, too, her own pain and despair, and keeps comforting the mare.

For two days Bonnie expresses from the mare and feeds Willo by the bottle until, finally, she has enough strength to feed herself. With her long, spindly legs splayed, she tucks up under her mother for a drink, and by the end of the week is friskily following her around the paddock, wheeling and bucking. A memory of Arthur telling her she poisons everything she touches, that she has the touch of death, flashes through Bonnie's mind. She suddenly feels liberated, saved, like the foal.

'She's happy now,' she tells the girls who are sitting next to her on the fence, watching the horses at play. 'She will grow big and strong.'

Guido is dead. Her great friend and mentor, who inspired and encouraged her and fine-tuned her for competition, killed in a plane crash on takeoff out of Katherine. Bonnie is disconsolate when she hears the news. At his funeral service in Brisbane, she clutches the prayer book, remembers how his words, 'You can do this, just push harder!' drove her to win. There is something sad but special in his dying whilst he was doing what he loved best; but it is frightening too. How mortal we are, she thinks.

In his memory, Bonnie writes: 'Guido took over from my dad in instilling in me a love of flying. His humour, enthusiasm and accomplishments will stay with us all and give us encouragement to succeed. May we, who have benefited from knowing him, have the courage to teach and share with others as he did with us.'

In a poignant reminder of his life, the eulogy reads: 'The landing lights of heaven shone softly to welcome him home.'

CHAPTER TWENTY-SIX

Bonnie has slowly improved the pasture on the property, and has increased the number of stock. It is a small start, but she has big dreams for it. Most of twelve cows are in calf, and some have calves at their feet. By the end of the year she hopes to have some poddies for the children to ride. She can count the steers and bulls on one hand, but they are strong and in good condition. There is no difference in what she does here than in what she did at Bullo—only a few less zeroes on the tally.

Her breeding program is coming on well. She has always wanted to breed horses, and what better choice than Australia's own Walers, which she handpicks from the Alice Springs region. Now she has eight brood mares, three ready for breaking in, and a number of yearlings, weaners and a stallion.

The old ways she learned at Bullo have stayed with her and she won't trade them for modern technology. She is going to build a bronco yard and build it in the old-fashioned way. She doesn't want the electronic pulses that render the beasts immobile and make for quick work. It will be the old way of branding: roping the calves out of the mob on horseback and dragging them to the bronco panel to throw and brand. She needs good horses and good men for the job, but there is a method in her madness. She wants to keep some Aussie spirit alive.

That spirit will be passed to her kids, and maybe one day to others in need of some help. She watches young people when she goes into town, notices with sadness how they drag their feet around aimlessly in search of something to do. They drift into trouble, drift through the children's court and out again, like human flotsam and jetsam.

If they had something to keep them occupied, she argues, they would expend their energy in a more useful manner. There is nothing like raising your own stock, mustering them on a horse you bred and broke yourself, sitting a saddle you made with your own hands, putting them in a yard you built, and finally butchering and boning out the meat to be cooked up on a barbie with friends.

Bonnie has a saddle to make, and she is behind schedule. To get it finished in time she will have to do what she does so often lately: get up at three in the morning, before the household wakes. The bush theory of mañana doesn't hold weight for her. If she lets her work pile up, she will never catch up. The last twenty-four hours have been a nightmare, and she sends a fax to the person waiting on the saddle to explain.

Don't give up hope! I am working on it. Cattle escaped, two in yard, one in truck, killer in chiller waiting to be boned out, three poddy calves to deliver, Amelia sick, friend with broken collarbone, but otherwise, everything fine. Saddle ready tomorrow!

Her reputation as a fine saddle-maker has spread through the Territory, and she has plenty of work. Encouraged to have a saddle judged at Darwin's rural show, she submits one of which she is particularly proud. The interstate judges look at it and sniff.

'We can't allow this saddle to be put in for judging!'

'Why not?'

'Well, it's quite obviously been bought from a shop. The stitching is perfect—it's a superb saddle.'

'But I made it!'

They look at the business card she offers them, look back at the saddle. It takes first prize.

Bonnie's workroom is her sanctuary. The rough hewn wooden bench houses dyes and paints, and bits of paper are stuck to the wall to remind her of the jobs she has to do next. The concrete floor is piled high with the tools of her trade: saddles, leather, hammers, nails. Visitors are heralded by flying gravel and dust; often, the place is so busy it resembles an airport, but Bonnie doesn't knock off to talk. If she did that, she'd never get a thing done. Friends plonk down behind her on the cement floor, give her snippets of news from the bush telegraph, examine the latest saddle she is working on. Cheerful and friendly, Bonnie doesn't mind the interruptions, tells them to grab a beer from the fridge as she keeps stitching.

She loves living here, far from the chaos of the city, surrounded by lush sand palms and native wildflowers. Wallabies and bandicoots call to say hello at dusk and frogs play in the puddles left behind after a big rain. Magnificent native birds squeal overhead and dive-bomb to catch a bush rat scurrying for shelter. Centipedes, scorpions and snakes crawl through the scrub; occasionally Bonnie hauls out her shotgun and shoots a king brown if he gets too close to the house, but she prefers to leave them in peace.

A whizz in the kitchen—a throwback from her years of cooking for the multitude at Bullo—she is a welcoming hostess. Some habits die hard: after a few rums, she sometimes offers an impromptu recitation of a bush poem. At other times she cracks the stockwhip, dares her guests to stand still while she whistles the hat off their head.

The feeling starts slowly, and at first she tries to bury it, to push it away. There are enough complications in her life right now without falling in love again as well. She has known Paul for years, as a neighbour and a friend. She knows his wife, and children, knows they were childhood sweethearts, knows, too, that his marriage is over in all but name. She circles around him, wanting to get closer but frightened to. There is so much at stake. For the first time since her friendship with David at Bullo, she knows she doesn't have to pretend with this man. He accepts her for what she is and loves her for it.

He is the complete antithesis to Arthur: quiet, rough in the way that Australian bushmen are rough, but gentle too. When he listens to people talk, he dips his head to one side, sizing up their character as much as their conversation. Tall and slim, black Levis, dusty work boots and Akubra are his uniform. This is not a man comfortable in a fancy suit and tie. There are no fancy words with him, either, to tie her up in knots, no mind games that she has to play. He is a simple man, a worker, with honest, simple dreams.

Bonnie watches him crack a stockwhip, watches as he hammers in fence pickets in the rain, watches him through the end of one season and the beginning of another. He never changes, and she is glad of that. They sizzle together, like kerosene thrown on fire; they work as hard as they play, and share trust. When both their marriages end, they come together, not only as lovers, but as great friends. It is then Bonnie can admit what she has known for a long while: she is in love again and the love is good.

Danielle has rescued some of Bonnie's old school papers, sketches and poetry from Bullo, and hands them on to her sister.

'I thought you might appreciate having them back, Bon. It would be awful it they were thrown out.'

Bonnie doesn't smoke very often, but she feels like having a cigar tonight with her rum. She holds it between her thumb and middle finger, inhales deep and screws up her eyes to ward off the invading smoke. Her hands, arthritic from years of fencing, are often swollen and sore, and she can't stretch out her index finger to hold a cigarette. She feels mellow tonight, relaxed and comfortable, with her feet stretched out on the verandah table. Leafing through the pages, she marks the passages of years, recalls Bullo, that country she loves so much, and the characters who floated through it. She is no longer as innocent as she was as a girl, no longer willing to put up with torments beyond endurance. But she still believes in friendship and love, still believes that life is precious. She smiles as she reads a poem she wrote when she was fifteen, realises she could still write it now—and believe in it.

Time passes as a river flows,
Time passes as the soft wind blows,

Live for today, before it goes.
  Do the things that must be done,
  Do not tarry, for everyone
  Has their race of life to run.
None can say for how long,
None can say what's right or wrong.
So run it fast and run it strong.
  Set your mind and onward drive,
  Set your goals, and for them strive.
  Bear all let-downs and survive.
Take your chances to be first,
Take your road and be diverse,
Make the best out of the worst.
  Hope and cherish, laugh and cry.
  Seek excitement, do not shy
  The fear of death, for all must die;
Yes, meet the challenges you face.
Love, be loved and set the pace,
For only once you'll run this race.

She thinks about the fun she had at Bullo, despite the pressures, and misses the rough and tumble of working huge mobs of cattle and horses. She belongs out there. Like Charles, whose ashes were scattered over the flat and lifted in a strong wind over the escarpment and billabongs and rivers, she belongs there. Some days, her spirit cries out to return.

Bonnie is about to ride a bull for the first time, and Harriet's small fingers grip around her own. 'I 'fraid for you, Mummy. Don't det hurt widing dat bugging bull.'

'No, I'll try not to, Hattie. I'm a bit 'fraid for me too. You climb up on that rail and cheer for me, even when I fall off. Don't worry, Mummy will be fine.'

Bonnie has always jumped on the calves as they come out of the chute after branding, but this is an altogether different challenge. At the rodeos she has often asked if she can have a ride, but the boys' club closes ranks. 'No, you can't get up. You're only a girl. Girls can't ride bulls!'

Janette, a good friend of Bonnie's and well known as the Northern Territory's only female competitive bull rider, has spotted a pair of bull spurs hanging in Bonnie's workroom.

'Who blong dis one?' she grins.

'I do,' Bon replies.

'Well, girl, if you've got the equipment, you may as well take the ride!'

Janette has thrown down the gauntlet, and Bonnie picks it up. 'Okay, let's organise it.'

On a quiet Sunday afternoon, in teeming rain, they truck a huge black Angus bull, as well as spurs, gloves, bells, bull-ropes, chaps, boots, hats, and of course the obligatory carton of beer and cheer squad of children, to the rodeo ground. After lengthy preparations and dire warnings not to get her gloves wet and not to dirty the rope tail, Bonnie is standing over George, the bull in the chute. George is settled and quiet, and rolls a beady eye back to look at his rider. But looks are deceptive, and no-one can predict how he will react when the chute gate clangs open.

'Keep your knees on him, let him know you're there,' Janette warns. 'All bulls are dangerous, no matter how quiet they appear to be. You know you're going to get hurt; it's not a matter of *if*—it's *when* and *how bad*.'

301

The bull moves slightly underneath her, and she feels her muscles tighten.

'You still want to go through with this?'

Bonnie grins at Janette. 'Cheeky bitch. What do you think I am, a girl?'

George is rock steady, and the onlookers start wagering a bet as to whether he'll buck out or not. Bonnie's heart is pounding, and the rope, sticky with resin, bites into her hand. She's been in a chute before on saddle broncs, and she knows how fast they fly out.

'Remember, chest out, chin down, get up on your rope. Ready?'

She nods assent, sudden fear making her grip the rope even tighter. She lifts her forehand from the rail, and the chute gate swings wide open as his huge head turns in a round sweep.

'Yep, he's gunna buck!'

The power beneath her is awesome, and she hangs on as the bull kicks and bucks wildly, trying to throw this weight off his back. Twenty metres from the chute, Bonnie has had enough and goes for the dismounts—on the wrong side. Janette cringes; she's been off the front of a bull before and knows what it's like to be stood on by more than half a ton of beef.

'Get out of there, Bon!' she thinks. 'Run for it!'

George spins away, and Bonnie realises her hand is still in the rope. She remembers the advice—'Keep on your feet if you get hung up'—as the bull spins and drags her with him over the wet ground. She tightens her grip on the rope and reaches up to loosen the wrap and free her hand. Finally George flicks her away, and she lands face down in the mud before sprinting to the safety of the fence. Her arms and legs are shaking and she waits for her heartbeat to slow.

'God, that was exhilarating!' she laughs. 'That beast has sure got some power!'

302

'How do you feel, girl?' Janette asks.

'My arm is aching from my fingers through to my collarbone and the ends of my ribs are sore, but at least I know I was hanging on with everything I have!'

She walks back to the chute, and Hattie reaches up with a handful of wildflowers she has picked for her.

'Oh, Mummy, dat was so good,' she says. 'You wode dat bugging bull weally well!'

Arthur has promised Bonnie that if they split up, she will face a bitter fight. The promise is proving right. Ahead of her, there is a property and custody battle looming, a battle she dreads. She would have preferred an amicable separation, without the need for lawyers.

Bonnie looks around the donga, at the few material possessions she has. This place is no palace, but it is home, and the children love it. They have accepted that their father no longer lives here, and they see him on a regular basis. They are happy and content.

Bonnie starts to pick up the kids' books, scattered on the lounge room floor. Suddeny she is crying. Let Arthur rattle his sabre. Let him fight for the donga; let him fight her for anything else; but she will fight to keep her children like she has never fought before.

EPILOGUE

Bonnie walks through the drafting yards. They are silent now, apart from the clink of the gate chain as it moves in the breeze The late afternoon sun throws red shafts of light on the steel rails; the dust has long settled and the final mob for the season has headed into the steer paddock. She shuts the last yard gate and looks out to the west. A string of horses plods along toward the watering trough, small puffs of dust swirling from each footfall. They are in no hurry. It is as if they know the watch has wound down; no more trucks to order, helicopters to coordinate. It is all over. The boys who work for her have turned the work horses out, hung the saddles in the shed and headed for a scrub-up in the tub. It's been a good season, helped by fine-tuned team-work. But right now, the only thing the boys are thinking about is hitting the town. Bonnie turns from the yard with a feeling of deep satisfaction for a job well done. This is one round of drinks she doesn't intend to miss.

She leans against her truck, yells out to the fellas. 'Eh! I've got something for you blokes!'

In a triumphant gesture, she punches the air with a bottle of rum. The boys grin, move toward her as she slowly, deliberately unscrews the cap. She throws the cap over her shoulder and it bounces and rolls on the hard earth as she brings the dark liquid to her lips.

'We won't be needing that again,' she laughs, wiping the rum away from her mouth with the back of her hand. She fills her pannikin with rum and the boys pass the bottle amongst themselves. Her back is resting against the truck, her legs drawn up.

'Here's to a good season next year!' she salutes.

The rum bottle is almost empty now, and the boys have drifted away. The sun is dying, bathing the earth in its final golden glow. This is a beautiful time of day, a time to reflect and think and dream. She pours another rum, stares into its depths as she sits alone in the dregs of daylight. Time seems to move so quickly. It seems that only yesterday she was a small girl jumping out of the plane at Bullo River, exploring the country as she held onto old Mary's hand. Mary's dead now, ravaged by one of the myriad diseases which affect her people; but her spirit is alive and kicking in Bonnie. It seems only yesterday that she was standing in the middle of the dining room, reciting Banjo Paterson to guests, basking in the glow of her father's pride; only yesterday that she stood on the airstrip and watched David's plane fly away as she held onto the wriggling puppy, feeling the pain at his leaving that she had to bury so deep. Only yesterday that she held Gus' arm at the Darwin Cathedral before walking up the aisle to marry Arthur. Only yesterday that Georgie hung in the balance between life and death, and Sara told her she shouldn't only call when she needed something. Only yesterday that she stared into the cold,

305

impassive faces of her mother and Marlee as she followed her father's coffin.

The faces of the people she has lost come back to her: Bomma, now reunited with her God; Gill, with her gentle smile; Guido, his eyes exhorting her to push harder; old Dick, swabbing vinegar on her hands to make 'em tough; David Boughen, giving a thumbs-up in encouragement as she passed him before his final flight. And Charles, the ultimate chameleon, who passed the baton to her and made her run with it, spun his dreams like a gossamer web and dared her to share them.

She remembers the last words he said to her, from his hospital bed in Sydney. His voice was frail, but his conviction strong.

'Always buy your round in life. Never walk out when it's your shout.'

She pours the last drop of rum in the pannikin, raises it in a silent salute toward the heavens.